Rethinking Modernity

MW00623961

role of US?
why Europe came to dominate?

Rethinking Modernity

Postcolonialism and the
Sociological Imagination

Gurminder K. Bhambra
University of Warwick, UK

palgrave
macmillan

First published in hardback 2007

First published in paperback 2009 by
PALGRAVE MACMILLAN

Palgrave Macmillan in the UK is an imprint of Macmillan Publishers Limited,
registered in England, company number 785998, of Houndmills, Basingstoke,
Hampshire RG21 6XS.

Palgrave Macmillan in the US is a division of St Martin's Press LLC,
175 Fifth Avenue, New York, NY 10010.

Palgrave Macmillan is the global academic imprint of the above companies
and has companies and representatives throughout the world.

Palgrave® and Macmillan® are registered trademarks in the United States,
the United Kingdom, Europe and other countries.

ISBN-13: 978–0–230–50034–1   hardback
ISBN-10: 0–230–50034–X   hardback
ISBN-13: 978–0–230–22715–6   paperback
ISBN-10: 0–230–22715–5   paperback

This book is printed on paper suitable for recycling and made from fully
managed and sustained forest sources. Logging, pulping and manufacturing
processes are expected to conform to the environmental regulations of
the country of origin.

A catalogue record for this book is available from the British Library.

Library of Congress Cataloging-in-Publication Data

Bhambra, Gurminder K., 1974–
    Rethinking modernity : postcolonialism and the sociological
    imagination / Gurminder K. Bhambra
        p. cm.
    Includes bibliographical references and index.
    ISBN-13: 978–0–230–50034–1 (cloth) 978–0–230–22715–6 (pbk)
    ISBN-10: 0–230–50034–X (cloth) 0–230–22715–5 (pbk)
        1. Sociology. 2. Postcolonialism. I. Title.

HM585.B486 2007
301.09182′1—dc22   2006053293

10 9 8 7 6 5 4 3 2 1
18 17 16 15 14 13 12 11 10 09

Printed and bound in Great Britain by
CPI Antony Rowe, Chippenham and Eastbourne

for my parents, Lakhbir S. and Joginder K. Bhambra,
and my brother, Amritpal S. Bhambra

Contents

Acknowledgements

My intellectual debts in the writing of this book are many and the proper place to start is the beginning, to the University of Sussex where I was first an undergraduate, to LSE, and to the University of Sussex again. John Holmwood has seen this project through from its inception and has read and commented extensively on the revisions made to the manuscript. His interventions have contributed, in large part, to the development of my thought over these last few years and I truly appreciate the generosity of spirit with which he has engaged with my work. I owe thanks also to Mia Rodríguez-Salgado, an inspiration when I was at the LSE, who has given freely of her time and expertise in discussing the arguments made here. For this, and much more, I am grateful. I am also appreciative of the intellectual support from William Outhwaite and for his, and Peter Wagner's, comments on an earlier version, which were invaluable. I would like to thank Libby Assassi, Andrew Chitty, Joan Cocks, Barbara Einhorn, Nisha Jones, Zdenek Kavan, Sam Knafo, Vicky Margree, Gregor McLennan, Mihnea Panu, Raluca Parvu, Robbie Shilliam, Neil Stammers, Jeppe Strandsbjerg, and Paul Yates who have all engaged with the arguments made here at various stages of their development. During the period of writing this book, I have had financial support in the form of postdoctoral research fellowships from the Economic and Social Research Council and the School of Social Sciences and Cultural Studies, University of Sussex for which I would like to record my thanks. I also spent one semester at the Five College Women's Studies Research Centre at Mount Holyoke College during this time and I would like to thank my colleagues there for their hospitality.

Introduction: Postcolonialism, Sociology, and the Politics of Knowledge Production

'Modernity' is the dominant frame for social and political thought, not just in the West, but across the world. The repercussions of the French Revolution and the processes of industrialization stimulated debates about the emergence of a *modern* world and this world was held to require a distinctively *modern* form of explanation. I shall argue that this rests on two fundamental assumptions: *rupture* and *difference* – a temporal rupture that distinguishes a traditional, agrarian past from the modern, industrial present; and a fundamental difference that distinguishes Europe from the rest of the world. These paradigmatic assumptions frame both the standard methodological problems posed by social inquiry and the explanations posited in resolving them. In this book, I call into question the socio-historic evidence for ideas of rupture and difference, and examine how the construction of this evidence itself has led to the development of particular forms of theoretical understandings. Most importantly, the equating of modernity with Europe reinforces a fundamental assumption of much intellectual thought today: that particular structures, emerging first in the West, would become universal.

Some will assert that such claims are no longer novel. The ideas of temporal and spatial disjuncture on which dominant ideas of modernity rest have seemingly been challenged by many postmodern and post-colonial theorists and yet, while there is increasing hesitancy in equating westernization with progress, it is my contention that the West is still seen as the leader or 'signifier' of change. For example, many theorists locate the postmodern turn itself in the advanced capitalist countries of the West and many postcolonial scholars alike continue to use Europe as a reference point, albeit a negative one. I shall argue that there is a need to reconsider the conceptual framework of modernity from a wider spatial

1

and historical context, *one which regards the very concept of modernity itself as problematic.*

By addressing the relationship between modernity, postcolonial theory, and Eurocentrism, I challenge the continued privileging of the West as the 'maker' of *universal history* and seek to develop alternatives from which to begin to deal with the questions that arise once we reject this categorization. This is done in the belief that the ways in which we understand the past are crucial to our understandings of ourselves and the world in which we live today and that if our understandings of the past are inadequate it follows that our grasp of the present will also be inadequate. Although I address dominant conceptions of modernity from the perspective of postcolonial theory, I shall also criticize postcolonial theory itself, arguing that it frequently simply inverts the dualism inherent to the dominant conceptions and, in that way, preserves the very intellectual structure that is being challenged.

I

Modernity, broadly conceived, refers to the social, cultural, political, and economic changes that took place in Western Europe from the mid-sixteenth century onwards. Regardless of the different interpretations put forward by *theorists* of modernity – as to its nature, the timing of its emergence, and its continued character today – ideas of rupture and difference, I contend, underpin all *theories* of modernity. This is highlighted in the work of the French and Scottish writers of the eighteenth century – such as Montesquieu, Ferguson, and Smith – who are largely seen as precursors of the sociological approach as well as in the work of the primary theorists of classical sociology – Durkheim, Weber, and Marx – who all express, in differing ways, the challenges faced by modern European society, a society that they see as distinguished from earlier agrarian societies and as unique within the contemporary world order.

More recent social theorists on modernity, from a variety of traditions, also see it as both distinctive and European in its origins. Wagner, for example, argues that it marks 'a rupture that leads to some specificity of the West in global comparison' (2001b: 6). This is echoed by theorists as diverse as the neo-functionalist Alexander, who suggests that the transition to modernity within Western society provided 'a capacity for transformation unprecedented in the other civilizations of the world' (1995: 1), the structuration theorist Giddens, who states, quite explicitly, that modernity has its 'roots in specific characteristics of European history ... [with] few parallels in prior periods or in other cultural settings' (1990: 174), the Marxist Callinicos (1999), who sees modernity as a particular kind of idea associated with a particular kind of society – one which is exemplified by the modern West, and the postmodernists Smart (1992), who associates the condition of modernity with the development of Western industrial capitalist societies, and Seidman (1997, 1998), who argues for modernity to be understood in terms of the distinctiveness of the culture at the heart of the modern West.

Across a range of theoretical positions, then, modernity can be seen as resting on a basic distinction between the social formations of 'the West' and 'traditional' or 'pre-modern' societies. As Wagner (1994) argues, precisely what these differences are may be difficult to define, but nonetheless they are assumed to establish parameters for defining modernity both spatially and temporally. Moreover, setting out such parameters is defined as both a key task of modern sociology and as a historically objective baseline from which modernity is theorized. Even Wagner's more nuanced analysis of modernity, which emphasizes the importance of differentiating 'between the discourse on the modern project ... and the practices and institutions of modern society' (1994: 4) or, Outhwaite's attempt 'to distinguish images of Europe from real social processes' (2001: 92), continue to locate both the discursive formations and the institutions and processes of modernity in eighteenth- and nineteenth-century societies of the West. Thus, Wagner suggests that while there were hardly any ruptures 'in terms of economic, social and political practices throughout society' there was a discursive rupture that 'instituted new kinds of social and political issues and conflicts' (1994: 4). This discursive rupture is itself located in the West, Europe more specifically, and is believed to have occurred in the late eighteenth, early nineteenth centuries, and, of course, it is associated with the intensification of processes of modernization in Europe in the early nineteenth century and subsequently.

Notwithstanding attempts to distinguish between an historical understanding of modernity and a conceptual, or normative, one, it is my contention that this is not possible. As Blumenberg argues, the modern age 'is not present in advance of its self-interpretation, and while its self-interpretation is not what propelled the emergence of the modern age, it is something that the age has continually needed in order to give itself form' (1983: 468). Our identification of 'modern' society rests on a conception of what it means to be modern – whether the modern is understood in terms of social structures or of discourses – and it is from the Western experience that these definitions are drawn. In fact, this distinction between structure and discourse will be argued to be one of the main ways of maintaining the dominant framing of modernity while seeming to challenge its less palatable aspect of Eurocentrism. As I shall demonstrate, the Western experience has been taken both as the basis for the construction of the concept of modernity and, at the same time, that concept is argued to have a validity that transcends the Western experience. Following Mohanty, I would like to draw attention to the ways in which authors codify others as non-Western and hence themselves as implicitly Western without ever really stating what being Western entails (1991: 51), or, for that matter, what being European entails.[1]

Eurocentrism is a contested and difficult term and there is no clear agreement on its definition; being 'anti-Eurocentric' also, then, has a multiplicity of meanings (Amin 1989; Joseph *et al.* 1990; Wallerstein 1997; McLennan 2003, 2006). Wallerstein (1997) sets out five ways in which it has been argued that social science expresses its Eurocentrism. These are its historiography, the parochiality of its universalism, its assumptions about (Western) civilization, its Orientalism, and its attempts to impose a theory of progress (Wallerstein 1997: 94). In contrast, the critics of Eurocentrism are said to fall into three basic categories. The first, by arguing that other civilizations were also in the process of doing what Europe was doing and could have succeeded if Europe had not impeded them; the second, that Europe was doing nothing that was historically new but was simply (temporarily) at the forefront of a continuation of long-standing trends and developments; and third, that what Europe has done has been incorrectly analyzed and inappropriately interpreted (Wallerstein 1997: 101).

While the first two lines of critique are deemed, by Wallerstein, to fall into 'anti-Eurocentric-Eurocentrism' – whereby the significance, or value, of the European achievement is accepted in its own terms and 'merely asserts that others could have done it too, or were doing it too' (1997: 103) – the third, is believed by many critics to provide a more substantial basis for being against Eurocentrism as it starts 'by questioning the assumption that what Europe did was a positive achievement' (1997: 104). However, it is my contention that by accepting that 'something special was indeed done by Europe in the sixteenth to eighteenth centuries that did transform the world' (Wallerstein 1997: 106-7), and arguing simply for a reorientation in the interpretation of what was done, Wallerstein, too, replicates the Eurocentrism of previous approaches (see also Washbrook 1990). In failing to contest the historical adequacy of the concept of 'Europe' *and* what it was assumed to have done, Wallerstein limits his analysis simply to a question of *significance*. With this, he confirms the point made by many social theorists who suggest that the 'specialness of the West ... becomes simply a factual matter ... [and] it is hard to see many anti-Eurocentrics disagreeing' (McLennan 2000: 281). When being anti-Eurocentric is defined in the terms outlined by Wallerstein one can only agree. However, I would like to offer an alternative definition.

Eurocentrism is the belief, implicit or otherwise, in the world historical significance of events believed to have developed endogenously within the cultural-geographical sphere of Europe. In contesting Eurocentrism, I contest the 'fact' of the 'specialness of Europe' – both in terms of its culture and its events; the 'fact' of the autonomous development of events, concepts, and paradigms; and, ultimately, the 'fact' of Europe itself as a coherent, bounded entity giving form to the above.

II

The implicit 'Eurocentrism' contained within classical theories of modernity is frequently argued to have been superseded in the more recent scholarship on the issue. Delanty (2004), for example, points to the proliferation of theories of alternative modernities, global modernities, hybrid and entangled modernities to suggest that the debates around these issues have moved beyond their initial, limited Eurocentric understandings of the world. Drawing on the work of McLennan, he states that current developments in social theory 'seem to suggest that in fact modernity can be reconciled to a critical and non-Eurocentric social theory and that much of the accusations of Orientalism are unfounded and even confused' (Delanty 2004: 164). This is seen to be indicated by the move away from an idea of the singularity of modernity, based on more traditional, unilinear, historical understandings, to discussions about the multiplicity of *modernities*.

These discourses of multiple modernities have become especially prominent in the fields of anthropology and cultural studies with works by scholars, such as the Comaroffs, who argue against the idea of modernity as the terminus towards which non-Western peoples constantly tend and, instead, put forward an argument for understanding modernity as constitutive of plural global systems that are 'diverse and dynamic, multiple, and multidirectional' (1993: xi, xii). Other academics, such as Peter Van der Veer, argue that instead of speaking of multiple modernities it would be better to speak 'of a multiplicity of histories' thereby retaining 'a sense of the uniqueness and power of European modernity together with a sense of the complexity and variation of its clash with historical processes in many parts of the world' (1998: 285).

While the latter understanding more explicitly reiterates the idea of modernity as tied to notions of modern Europe, the understanding put forward by the Comaroffs can also be seen to be based on unexamined theses of rupture and difference arguing, as it does, for some transformation occurring first in Europe – even if this transformation is not given the evaluative significance it has been given in other interpretations. Delanty (2004), for his part, takes it as read in his analysis that modernity emerged in Europe and argues that, while the subsequent history of modernity is said to bear the impact of its European origins, it has somehow extricated itself from these origins and now can be understood simply as a global phenomenon that is inflected in diverse ways according to local traditions. The *concept* of modernity, abstracted from its inflections or not, nonetheless remains tied to what is generally understood as the European experience.

Delanty is not alone in conflating modernity with Europe and, at the same time, rendering the Eurocentrism of the account invisible to his own self-reflexivity; the majority of social theorists do the same. In a collection of articles on alternative modernities, Gaonkar (2001b) suggests that the emergence of the debate on alternative modernities reinforces the fact that something specifically modern is held to be inescapable. The West is understood as the major clearing house of modernity and in its globalization has travelled from the West to the rest of the world meaning that non-Western peoples must now begin to engage their traditions with modernity in different forms of hybrid 'modernities'. These assertions rest on a number of assumptions, not least that there is an original modernity that was born in and of the West, and that the West is significantly different from the rest of the world such that while it can enjoy an original modernity everybody else has to make do with a hybrid version. Gaonkar concludes his contribution by asserting that a minimal requirement for thinking in terms of alternative modernities is to opt for a 'cultural', as opposed to an 'acultural', theory of modernity such as that articulated by Charles Taylor (1999). I will suggest, however, that this remains bound within the same set of problems as those that Gaonkar has criticized so powerfully.

Taylor believes that modernity is not best understood in terms of being 'a single wave'; but rather, that as cultures 'take on the new practices' they 'turn out to differ in important ways from each other', suggesting that it would be better to speak of alternative modernities than simply 'modernity' (1999: 233). The problem, for Taylor, is that modernity has most commonly been understood in terms of an 'acultural' theory that characterizes the transformations of the modern West in terms of 'a rational or social operation which is culture-neutral' (2001: 172). That is, modernity is understood as a set of transformations which could have occurred anywhere and is not specific to any particular culture. He believes that as long as questions of Western identity in these processes are not examined 'we will fail to see how other cultures differ and how this difference crucially conditions the way in which they integrate the *truly universal* features of modernity' (2001: 180; my emphasis). This, he suggests, could be remedied through a 'cultural' theory of modernity which emphasizes the *particularity* of cultures and the importance of locating the emergence of modernity within specific 'cultural complexes'. He writes that

> they want to do what has already been done in the West. But they see, or sense, that that can not consist in just copying the West's adaptations. ... Just taking over Western modernity couldn't be the answer. (1999: 233)

Thus, what Taylor is implying is that there are 'truly universal features' of modernity, that these come out of the West, and that there is a need to separate these out such that we can see more clearly how non-Western cultures have tropicalized, or domesticated, these features.

Throughout this book I shall be arguing against the idea of separate processes that can be geographically delimited. The ideas of difference and rupture that form debates about modernity should be regarded as 'interpretative categories', whereby the 'unity' and 'integrity' of specific experiences are created by abstraction from wider interconnections. Something of what is involved has been captured by Bruno Latour in his book, *We Have Never Been Modern*. Here, Latour (1993) puts forward an anthropology of science to contest the commonly held idea that, with the rise of science, the modern world was irrevocably brought into being. Latour contests the idea of the temporal rupture posited as integral to the majority of understandings of modernity and reworks our understandings of the emergence of science to develop his arguments. He uses Shapin and Schaffer's work on Boyle and Hobbes to demonstrate how their particular quarrels resulted in the invention of 'a science, a context, and a demarcation between the two' (1993: 16) that is emblematic of the 'Great Divide' represented by modernity. He suggests that the attempts made by Boyle and Hobbes to universalize the 'laws' of science and politics, in terms of them being seen as distinct phenomena, failed to recognize that neither science nor politics were separable from the networks of their practices (1993: 24). The quarrel between Boyle and Hobbes is taken as illustrative of how the Great Divide between 'moderns' and 'others' came to be and how it set about explaining everything by virtue of neglecting, or even actively avoiding, what was in the middle.

Modernism, Latour argues, 'like its anti- and post-modern corollaries – was only the provisional result of a selection made by a small number of agents in the name of all' (1993: 76). By changing the classification principle 'we get a different temporality on the basis of the same events' (1993: 75); thus, we have never really moved forward or backward but have simply been caught up in a process of classification and re-classification – and 'we can still sort ... that is, return to the multiple entities that have always passed in a different way' (1993: 76). According to Latour, we are not radically different to all the 'others' nor they to us and he questions why 'we like to transform small differences in scale among collectives into huge dramas' (1993: 114). He argues, instead, for the existence of 'continuous paths that lead from the local to the global, from the circumstantial to the universal, from the contingent to the necessary' (1993: 117); paths that consist of 'the thread of networks of practices and instruments, of documents and translations' (1993: 121).

During the course of his argument, Latour writes that 'the West may believe that universal gravitation is universal even in the absence of any instrument, any calculation, any decoding, any laboratory, just as the Bimin-Kuskumin of New Guinea may believe that they comprise all of humanity, but these are respectable beliefs that comparative anthropology is no longer obliged to share' (1993: 120). The problem is, however, that while nobody else believes that the Bimin-Kuskumin comprise all of humanity, most of humanity does believe that the moderns are modern, and nowhere in his book does Latour account for this. In arguing for us to recognize that which we have always been, but have failed to see – that is, our constitution as non-modern – Latour is primarily talking to the West about itself. Inasmuch as he is critical of the West's self- conception of itself as separate, and believes it always to have been integrated within networks and associations, he nevertheless appears to suggest that its self-knowledge developed in isolation from those other communities. If everything is relational and interlinked, as he advocates, then was it really possible for Europeans to have thought a science that was so different?

III

The 'politics of knowledge production', implied by my arguments, is frequently associated with a crisis in the humanities and social sciences over their established canons, or over the universality of their categories. However, my starting point is not the 'crises' of various disciplines or their foundational concept-metaphors, but a crisis 'in the histories of the world': a crisis, that is, in the world that such disciplines and concepts assume (Trouillot 1991: 38). The silencing of colonial encounters is only one aspect of a wider narrative of global domination; a narrative that will persist, according to Trouillot, 'as long as the history of the West is not retold in ways that bring forward the perspective of the world' (1995: 107). As I shall argue, much critical theory forged around ideas of social transformation – such as postcolonialism and particularly the theoretical work of the Subaltern Studies groups – proposes the establishment of a standpoint position that precedes social transformation. I shall suggest, however, that a critical standpoint position might best be understood as something recovered *after* transformation rather than something that precedes it.[2] In other words, it derives from positions created by solutions to problems, rather than the positions that constitute the problems (Holmwood and Stewart 1991). I will return to this in subsequent chapters.

The crux of the matter is the relationship between the events under study and their public avowal within particular historical contexts (Trouillot 1995: 147). While it is commonly accepted that any sense of what is known must include an acknowledgement of the present, it is less commonly accepted that historical veracity rests, as Trouillot suggests, 'not in the fidelity to an alleged past, but in an honesty vis-à-vis the present as it re-presents that past' (1995: 148). As Said has also argued, appeals to the past – for example, disagreements about what happened, discussions of whether the past continues in the present albeit in different form, and so on – 'are among the commonest of strategies in interpretations of the present' (1993: 1). Focusing on 'the past' as a fixed reality to be known, and the related concept of knowledge as fixed content, 'diverts us from the present injustices for which previous generations only set the foundation' (Trouillot 1995: 150). It is only in our present relation to the past that we can be true or false to the pasts we acknowledge, for the meaning of history is also in its purpose. Thus, Said argues that 'we should keep before us the prerogatives of the present as signposts and paradigms for the study of the past ... not to level or reduce differences, but rather to convey a more urgent sense of the interdependence between things' (1993: 72).

While the possibilities of the positions we take in this endeavour are limitless, not all are permissible. The historicity of the human condition, whereby we are born into pre-existing conversations regarding our pasts and our presents, necessarily shapes the positions from where we think and argue. This does not mean that any position is permissible, nor that positions need to be eternal in order to justify a legitimate defence, but rather, that the veracity of historical representations requires the establishing of some *relation* to that knowledge. Looking further at our understandings of history it is important to distinguish that, while history may have 'happened' and therefore 'be real', it does not follow that our interpretations of what happened have the same status. Not least because, as Hayden White (1978: 3) argues, it is the historical discourse itself which constitutes what is to be considered as a fact *and* which determines the mode of comprehension by which, then, to understand these facts. As White suggests, 'no given set of casually recorded historical events can in itself constitute a story' or history; the most that is offered the historian are story *elements* that can be '*made*into a story by the suppression or subordination of certain of them and the highlighting of others' (1978: 84). Even chronologies are 'no less constituted as a record of the past by the historian's agency than is the narrative which he [or she] constructs on its basis' (White 1978: 56). History is thus not simply a record of 'what happened', but rather, a record of what it was that we believed happened – conditioned by the standards of the communities in which such claims are made – and, as such, entails necessary inaccuracies and silences.

Accepting that the past is a construction, and that there are plural interpretations of events, should not lead us to the conclusion that any historical narrative is simply one fiction among many. The criterion against which these interpretations are to be judged is not historical objectivity, or a discovery of 'real historical knowledge', but, I shall argue, *plausibility* and a relation to the conditions of the production of history. It is historicity itself, as Trouillot suggests, that makes some narratives more powerful than others (1995: 6). Note that what is *not* being said here is that this makes some narratives more 'true' than others, but rather, more powerful. The basis for their power, further, does not reside in veracity or being a 'better' representation, but in the general acceptance of the *claim* that this is so. While many theorists acknowledge that history involves both the social processes and narratives of that process, few examine in detail the concrete production of specific narratives (Trouillot 1995: 22).

IV

The central assertion of this book rests on the following understanding: that the way in which we understand the past has implications for the social theories we develop to deal with the situations we live in today. Through recognizing the constituted 'other' as always and already present in history and participating in its production, but written out of it, we can begin to reconceptualize forms of theoretical discourse and political practice today. If theory has been largely predicated on an idea of the uniqueness of Europe then calling that into question upends most theory. This, then, provides a clearing from which we can begin to look at the world again and begin to create new forms for the future.

The first section of this book addresses both the general shifts in European traditions of thought during the eighteenth and nineteenth centuries as well as contemporary critiques. It focuses on the emergence of postcolonialism and discusses this in terms of the challenge it poses to standard social theory. The first chapter further addresses the absence of the colonial encounter from the social sciences and the implications of the construction of a specifically 'colonial gaze'. This chapter then turns to a detailed exposition of subaltern historiography and a questioning of its methodology. It ends with a discussion of 'connected histories' (Subrahmanyam 1997) and suggests this approach as a way of dealing with difference in the context of attempting to reconcile general categories and particular experiences. The second chapter focuses on the history of sociology and its subsequent development as a discipline. It addresses French and Scottish thinkers of the Enlightenment who have been regarded as precursors to the development of sociology and then discusses the establishment of the discipline in the post-(French) revolutionary period. This chapter looks, in particular, at the ways in which sociology constructed its understanding of the conditions of its emergence and the implications of such a construction for the ways in which we know the world today. The third chapter in this section looks in more detail at the sociological construction of modernity and traces the development from modernization theory to multiple modernities. It addresses the extent of the challenge posed by multiple modernities to the earlier modernization paradigm as well as identifying continuities between them. This chapter ends with a discussion of the methodology that underpins both approaches – comparative sociology and ideal types – and develops an alternative way of addressing questions of modernity via the idea of 'connected histories' introduced in Chapter 1.

The second section of the book examines the dominant discourses around the key historical events cited in the formation of 'modernity' – the Renaissance, the French Revolution, and the Industrial Revolution – and discusses the extent to which the claims made on their behalf bear up to scrutiny. The fourth chapter challenges the dominant discourses that posit the Renaissance as heralding the emergence and consolidation of the idea of modern Europe and the related claims for Europe emerging as a cohesive, autonomous entity at this time. The fifth, addresses the perceived role of the French Revolution in the emergence of the modern nation-state and the invention of the political project of modernity. The sixth chapter examines the development from commercial to capitalist society and discusses the assumed ruptural aspect of the Industrial Revolution which is seen as heralding the divide between the pre-modern and the modern. Further, it addresses the claims made for these phenomena being regarded solely as internal European phenomena and discusses the implications of a critique of this for subsequent analysis.

The final chapter of the book will then go back to address the question of modernity and sociology, 'after' postcolonial theory and 'connected histories'.

Part 1

Sociology and
Its Historiography

1
Modernity, Colonialism, and the Postcolonial Critique

In this chapter, I shall discuss the emergence of postcolonialism and the nature of the challenge it poses for standard approaches to social theory. I start by addressing the relationship between colonialism and the politics of knowledge production, looking, in particular, at the processes by which particular forms of disciplinary knowledge came to be authorized under colonialism and the concomitant marginalization of 'other' forms of knowledge. This will be followed by a discussion of the emergence of Subaltern Studies as a particular manifestation of postcolonial historiography. The standpoint of the subaltern has been one way in which academics have sought to reclaim the subjectivity of the previously marginalized, but this has not been an unproblematic venture. In questioning standpoint theory, then, I suggest that the attempt to reconcile particular experiences and general categories is best served through an alternative approach, one that builds on the idea of 'connected histories' (Subrahmanyam 1997). This is a precursor to the discussion of the rather different historiographical assumptions built into standard sociological accounts, which will be discussed in the following chapter.

Postcolonialism should not be understood as simply the latest version of a critical engagement in social thought. Kwame Anthony Appiah argues for 'the *post-* in postcolonial' to be understood as 'the *post-* of the space-clearing gesture' (1991: 348). It is a *post-* that must be understood not simply in temporal terms, but also as a marker of a conceptual move going beyond existing theoretical understandings of the world. Postcolonial approaches, then, work to challenge dominant narratives and to reconfigure them to provide more adequate categories of analysis, where adequacy is measured in terms of increasing inclusivity and is oriented 'backwards' as well as 'forwards'. By locating and establishing a voice for the hitherto voiceless within history and society, postcolonial theory seeks to resolve questions of inclusion and exclusion and to make transparent the relationship between knowledge and politics 'in the specific context of ... [a] study, the subject matter, and its historical circumstances' (Said 1978: 15). In the contest for political and social authority, then, postcolonial criticism bears witness not only to contemporary inequalities, but also to their historical conditions (Bhabha 1992).

Nicholas Jardine (2000 [1991]) has argued that the sciences need to be understood as addressing questions and problems that arise in what he calls 'scenes of inquiry': the particular contexts and settings in which the sciences operate and from which they derive their meanings. In this chapter, I will be treating colonial relations as integral to the scenes of inquiry of the social sciences. However, not everything relevant to understanding the production of knowledge takes place visibly as part of the *mise-en-scène*. As I shall argue throughout this book, colonialism is crucial to the scenes of inquiry that are the contemporary social sciences and yet, for the most part, it is largely outside their field of vision.

I

The colonial encounter, which was less an encounter and more a conquest, domination, and enslavement of peoples and forms of life, I shall contend, is constitutive of the very disciplines that express or seek to understand modernity. In a global context, the colonial experience has been one in which contact and communication between human societies and cultures multiplied and intensified. The social interactions that ensued from this process radically transformed the configurations of what was known and how it was known. The British conquest of India, for example, not only opened up a geographical terrain for exploration and occupation, but also enabled the transformation of an epistemological space by, as Nandy argues, 'inducing the colonized ... to accept new social forms and cognitive categories' (1983: 3; see also Cohn 1996). Any critique of colonialism, then, cannot rest only on its record of economic exploitation and human suffering, but must also address the cognitive patterns that became embedded in social actions and representations through the colonial process (Mignolo 1995).

This understanding has been at the heart of scholarly works by those involved in anti-colonial movements, such as Frantz Fanon, Aimé Césaire, and Albert Memmi and has been taken up by subsequent theorists of the postcolonial. Fanon's *Black Skin, White Masks*, for example, addresses the 'arsenal of complexes that has been developed by the colonial environment' and argues that the problem of colonialism rests not only in the interrelations of particular historical conditions but also the (social) psychologies produced by these conditions (1967 [1952]: 30, 84). While accepting the importance of a political economy of colonialism, Nandy (1983) similarly argues for it to be understood in terms of the subjugation of minds as well as bodies. It is in the era of colonialism, he suggests, that the concept of the modern West becomes generalized 'from a geographical and temporal entity to a psychological category' (Nandy 1983: xi). Since colonialism is also a matter of consciousness for Nandy, he argues that it needs to be defeated in the minds of people. Resistance to colonialism, then, only properly begins when people 'become participants in a moral and cognitive venture against oppression' (1983: xiv). Although this liberation necessarily begins with the colonized, it must be a liberation that includes the colonizers. As such, Nandy argues that freedom has to be understood as indivisible, 'not only in the popular sense that the oppressed of the world are one, but also in the unpopular sense that the oppressor, too, is caught in the culture of oppression' (1983: 63).

This understanding was articulated in Gandhi's mission to liberate the British, as much as the Indians, from the yoke of colonialism and has been expressed by other prominent anti-colonial activists and scholars across the world. Césaire (1972 [1955]), for instance, noted the dehumanizing effects of colonization on both the colonized and the colonizers and called for the salvation of Europe alongside the liberation of African nations. Memmi (1965 [1957]) similarly addressed the effects of the colonial situation on both perpetrators and victims and regarded colonization as a specific European pathology in desperate need of remedy. Although using the individualist framework of psychology, neither Fanon nor Memmi believed that the solution to this 'disease' would – or could – be individual, but rather advocated the necessity of social struggle in righting these distorted relationships. Specifically, Fanon wrote that the break up of the colonial world was not about the establishment of *two* zones – the previously colonized and the previous colonizers – but rather, the abolition of one – the colonial world – and the subsequent restructuring of the relations that had sustained it (1968 [1961]: 41; 1967 [1952]: 82).

Fanon's argument in favour of dissolving the epistemological binaries posited in setting up the colonizers' world as radically different from that of the colonized has found contemporary resonance in the cultural critique of Homi Bhabha (1994) and in Edward W. Said's (1978) influential text, *Orientalism*.[1] For Said, 'Orientalism' is 'a discourse of power originating in an era of colonialism' and it is a discourse in which those who are written about do not 'recognize themselves as human beings or their observers as simple scholars' (1995: 345). His trenchant criticism of the concept (and its related practices) rests on the fact that it 'approaches a heterogeneous, dynamic, and complex human reality from an uncritically essentialist standpoint' and, in the process, constructs the 'Orient' and the 'Occident' as ontologically and epistemologically different and distinct (1995: 333).

It is important to recognize the configurations of power and cultural hegemony that enabled the Orient not only to be *discovered* to be Oriental, but also submitted to being *made* Oriental – namely, the relationships of colonization and imperial domination that spanned the vast majority of the world at that time (Said 1978: 6, 7, 41). As Said argues, the concept of Orientalism hides historical events and historical change at the same time as it obscures the *interests* of those involved in its perpetuation. To 'be' an 'Oriental' was/is not simply to inhabit a particular geographical area, but it was/is also an evaluative judgement in that one was/is then also a member of a subject race (1978: 92). As such, Said suggests that the concept of Orientalism is never far from the idea of Europe itself in that defining the 'other' is also an aspect of understanding oneself (1978: 7).

The elaboration of the distinction between East and West has subsequently underpinned theoretical claims, literary works, social analyses, and political endeavours such that without examining Orientalism as a discourse we are in danger of perpetuating its disciplining functions and continuing to reproduce the category of the 'Orient' unthinkingly. In this way, as I shall argue, 'Orientalism', in Said's sense, can be a feature of the categories of social science even when the 'Orient' is not the explicit object of attention. To take a literary example, what is being contested is the common interpretation of East and West as separate and bounded entities as exemplified in Rudyard Kipling's statement 'Oh, East is East and West is West and never the twain shall meet' (quoted in Narayan 1998: 89). As Narayan (1998) has pointed out, Kipling wrote these lines at a historical moment when East and West were engaged in a seriously protracted encounter, namely, colonialism.

II

The colonial relationship, as I have been arguing, constituted one of the fundamental relationships between Europe and its posited 'others' and yet, as Hansen suggests, there has been very little systematic work done on the question of European identity in the context of colonialism (2002: 484). Where this relationship has been considered it is usually in the context of the *effects* of Europe on the colonies – that is, in terms of ideas of 'Western diffusionism and indigenous passivity' (Arnold 2000: 13) – or, colonialism is posited as existing in parallel to events in Europe, but with no obvious relation to them. Pagden, for example, argues for the formation of the European states to be understood in terms of being *accompanied* by 'the creation of Europe's modern overseas empires' (2002: 10), but he does not address the influence of those colonies on the development of the very same modern European states. Kiernan similarly makes but a small concession to colonialism stating at the end of an essay on European identity that, 'whatever Europe is, it owes *in part* to its imperial endeavours' (1980: 60; my emphasis). I would argue more forcefully: that, whatever Europe *is*, cannot be understood *outside* of its imperial relationships. As Said (1986) notes, having 'lost', the colonized are required to take the European conquerors and the period of conquest into account, while, having 'won', Europe can choose to ignore the colonial enterprise as an episode of history to be acknowledged, or not, at will. The asymmetry, as he argues, is striking:

> On the one hand we assume that the whole of history in colonial territories was a function of the imperial intervention; on the other, there is an equally obstinate assumption that colonial undertakings were a phenomenon marginal and perhaps even eccentric to the central activities of the great metropolitan centres. (Said 1986: 58–9)

While the modern idea of history denies 'that the colonizers are at least as much affected by the ideology of colonialism' as the colonized, and implicitly accepts the cultural superiority of the colonizing powers, Nandy argues that what needs to be acknowledged are the ways in which the oppressor and the oppressed are turned into 'co-victims' through their encounters (1983: 30, 99). The issue is not only one about being 'co-victims', however, but also, as During proposes, about a recognition that '(post)colonialist societies have been built by both sides' (1998: 31).[2] It is this complexity that is lost in most observations of colonialism, as the Kipling quote in the previous section attests, or, where it is acknowledged, the direction of impact is primarily from the colonizers to the colonized.

Whereas eighteenth- and nineteenth-century liberal and progressive thinkers justified colonialism in India either in terms of instituting a cultural renaissance in the country, or as hastening the development and spread of modern capitalism en route to the desired stages of liberal self-governance (or, for Marx and subsequent writers, communism), the conservative thinker Edmund Burke refused to accept such justifications of empire. His was one of only very few voices within the metropole to lament simultaneously the impact of colonization on the liberties of the colonized and the distorting impact of colonialism on British political traditions and liberties (see Mehta 1999).[3] It is perhaps not surprising that his was a minority voice at the time, but it should give us some cause for concern that the issues he addressed, namely the relationship between the colonies and the imperial centre, are still so little considered; or, when they are considered, so easily dismissed. As Mehta argues, this 'neglect is evident in both historical political theory and contemporary normative scholarship' (1999: 5).

More recently, while Colley (1992, 2002) and Cannadine (2001) are notable among British historians in addressing the importance of empire to the construction of British identity and vice versa, the view expressed by Runciman (1997) in his three volume treatise on social theory is still more typical. In his case study of British society, Runciman argues that the decline of empire has little significance for understanding Britain in the twentieth century. For him, while the demise of empire was no doubt eventful 'for those whose lives were directly affected by it', that is, those African and Indian societies that were going through processes of decolonization, he argues that it has had no significant impact on British society, 'no qualitative change in England's mode of production, persuasion or coercion was involved in the process' (Runciman 1997: 122). For Runciman, then, decolonization and the condition of postcoloniality are unequivocally the problems of 'others'.[4]

The historian James Joll argues that it is generally accepted that it 'was through imperialism that European ideas became widely disseminated over the non-European world' (1980: 15), yet sociology's central concepts render that imperialism invisible, arguing for the abstract universality of foundational terms to be located outside of particular experiences.[5] As I proposed in the Introduction and will demonstrate in subsequent chapters, colonialism does not enter into the general categories of modernity nor the broad historiography that is modernization theory, but, as shown here, it is even given a marginal role in the sociological histories of particular western countries which had pronounced colonial pasts. Runciman's recognition of the demise of empire as a significant feature of British *history*, for example, does not have any purchase on his analysis of the determinate social structures of British society during the twentieth century. Following on from the earlier sections, then, to understand how knowledge is produced we need to extend our critique to the disciplinary knowledge and procedures authorized under the remit of colonial practices as well as recognize the import of specific colonial practices.

Even where the processes of decolonization and liberation have transferred *political* power to the formerly colonized, the institutional, economic, and cultural contexts of Western hegemony have largely remained in place (Grovogui 1996). As a consequence, we must be aware of finding ourselves in the contradictory predicament of seeking to criticize hegemonic interests while working within 'relationships that are determined by the context of those ... interests' (Fabian 1991: 257). For example, the seemingly universal engagement of postcolonial scholars with 'European' thought rests on the fact that it is this intellectual tradition that 'is the only one alive in the social science departments of most, if not all, modern universities' today (Chakrabarty 2000: 5–6). In much the same way, the entry of feminism into the academy produced an apparent contradiction for some feminists of being in a setting which their analysis defined as patriarchal.

Critical presence within the academy, then, is not sufficient to transform deep-lying conceptions of knowledge and social scientific practice. As Trouillot argues, surface changes in the explicit criteria of what is to be addressed do not necessarily alter the fields of significance within which disciplines operate or then political practice occurs (1991: 18). What is required is a more thoroughgoing analysis of the very constitution of knowledge and a reappraisal of the underlying assumptions upon which discourses and practices come to be premised. As feminist scholars such as Hawkesworth have argued, using a conception of knowledge as something acquired through human practice enables people to examine 'the specific processes by which knowledge has been constituted within determinate traditions and explore the effects of the exclusion of women [and others] from participation in those traditions' (1989: 551). To identify a politics of knowledge, however, is not by that token to free oneself of the consequences of that politics. In the rest of this chapter, I shall be suggesting that as powerful as the postcolonial critique may be, it also often embodies some of the categories or features of knowledge it purports to criticize.

III

Colonialism, as will be argued in this book, was intrinsic to the contemporary scene in which dominant forms of inquiry were formed and yet the colonial is rendered unseen. These forms of inquiry elaborated universal criteria and presumed themselves to be universally relevant and yet, as will be demonstrated, were constructed on the basis of marginalizing and silencing other experiences and voices. Just as feminist scholarship has revealed the masculinist bias of thought presenting itself as universal (see, for example, Hartsock 1984; Bordo 1986), so postcolonial scholarship challenges the universals of modernity and modernization as these are commonly represented.

From Vico to Hegel, written history has been regarded as linked to cultural memory and, in this way, providing 'proof' of the existence of (the ability to) reason (Gates 1985). Without written history, it was often believed that there could be no humanity. This legitimized the disciplining of what was to count as history as well as providing justifications for particular interpretations of the past that would rationalize colonial intervention. It was commonly accepted that Europe had managed to transcend its past by acquiring an historical consciousness based on particular forms and conventions that it was believed were lacking elsewhere despite their universal significance. The refusal to recognize historical consciousness in cultures and societies outside of Europe served a dual purpose: 'other' forms of knowledge were marginalized and the associated societies classified as inferior.

In the nineteenth century, the British Orientalist discourse on India was characterized by the assumption that India did not have the types of materials – for example, documents, dateable records, chronicles – with which the West had constructed its own history, and thus, it was believed that they, themselves, 'were called upon to provide India with a history' (Cohn 1996: 93). For example, the accounts of Indian nationalism that were written by British scholars at that time largely put forward the message that, 'were it not for British mediation, the Indians would have never been acquainted with their own culture or recognized the possibilities of national growth on indigenous foundations' (Viswanathan 1989: 15). Even in recent times, historians such as Joll argue that when the non-European world was reacting against European imperialism it was in European terms – nationalism, proletarian revolution, and so on – that they were expressing their discontent (1980: 15). However, I would argue that it is the claiming of such concepts as essentially European that is Eurocentric, implying, as it does, the endogenous development of such terms within a particular cultural–geographical matrix and simply diffused in a 'benignly osmotic fashion' (Viswanathan 1989: 16) into the minds of the colonized.

Alongside the presumed lack of historical materials, the unquestioned assumptions underpinning such notions were that the native population 'had neither a sense of national history nor a historical consciousness from which a distinct identity could be shaped' (Viswanathan 1989: 15).[6] These assumptions have, of course, been long contested by scholars such as Romila Thapar (1992, 1996) who emphasizes the presence of both historical material and historical consciousness in Indian societies. In a different vein, and following on from the discussion in the Introduction, Nandy questions the very historical enterprise that establishes history with a 'capital H' commenting that, while contemporary scholars have begun to distinguish between 'History' and 'the past', few have yet to 'acknowledge the possibility that [H]istory might only be one way of constructing the past and other cultures might have explored other ways' (1995: 52).

The presumption of historical deficiency was used politically in India to sanction both intervention and the establishment of a period of colonial tutelage (or, in Mill's (1865 [1861]) words, a pure and enlightened despotism) in which time it was posited that the population would be brought to eventual self-governance. Nandy suggests that the new concept of childhood that emerged in Europe in the seventeenth century was paralleled with ideas of primitivism and 'the theory of social progress was telescoped ... into the area of cultural differences in the colonies' (1983: 15).[7] Locke's argument, that a period of tutelage was a necessary stage for children to pass through on the way to acquiring reason, and thus adulthood, was mapped onto colonial relations and the characterization of India as being in the infancy of civilizational progress became a key theme in much liberal discourse, firmly establishing the homology of childhood and the condition of being colonized (see Nandy 1987; Mehta 1999). Political subjugation and the denial of rights and representation to colonial populations – depicted by liberals as children – were thus seen as appropriate measures in liberal terms, not as problematic ones.

The construction of India as a 'child' also had the effect of placing contemporary India in a direct relation to Europe's past. I shall be addressing the emergence of a 'stadial' approach to history in European thought in more detail in the next chapter, but it is readily apparent that if India was the child and Europe the adult, then India was now what Europe had once been and could, it was believed, offer Europeans a glimpse into their own past. The development of the notion of an Indo-European language family, as well as increasing access to the texts of ancient India, led many European scholars to believe that the roots of European civilization were to be found in the 'golden age' of Indian history (see Kaiwar 2003). To resolve the apparent contradiction between the positing of a great civilizational heritage together with the assertion of contemporary political infancy it was necessary to establish a period of decline in the intervening centuries. As Kaiwar argues, this led to the division of Indian history into three periods – the Hindu golden age, the Muslim period of decline, and the British liberation of India from (alien) Muslim rule (2003: 37). With this division, he continues, the territorial boundaries of India were given a consistent unity backwards through time; India was given a 'Hindu' identity at times when no person on the continent would have recognized themselves as such; Muslims were portrayed as interlopers despite the vast majority of India's Muslims being local converts to Islam; interconnections with cultures across the oceans were erased from Indian history; and the Hindu and Muslim periods were followed not by the Christian period, but the British period (2003: 37–9).

Both through the force of military occupation and the appropriation of dominant processes of representation, the British were thus able to subsume the diversity of Indian pasts under 'a homogenizing narrative of transition from a medieval period to modernity' (Chakrabarty 2000: 32). While the terms may have been interchangeable – feudal for medieval, capitalist for modern – the construction of a linear, universal history and the authoritative assertion of where India's place within this schema was to be, enabled the British to assert control over India's past, claim authority over her future, and validate their own presence within the country (see Cohn 1996). The assumption of a social-evolutionary paradigm located India within a known trajectory of history where change was to occur through periods of transition – again, whether from medieval to modern, agricultural to industrial, or feudal to capitalist. The future for India, her transition to 'the modern', was a *known history,* something which has *already happened elsewhere* and was now simply, in the words of Morris, 'to be reproduced, mechanically or otherwise, with a local content' (1990: 10).

IV

I began this chapter with a brief discussion of the politics of knowledge production and the acknowledgement of colonialism as part of the scene of social scientific inquiry. I have illustrated this in detail with examples drawn from India. In the remainder of the chapter, I want to return to more general issues of knowledge production and the parallels between developments in postcolonial and feminist critiques in order to identify problems intrinsic to postcolonial theory. I shall suggest that these derive from being caught up in a simple inversion of the dominant forms of knowing.

One effect of establishing an overarching narrative punctuated by moments of transition is that 'local' histories are then subsumed to the ideological parameters and periodization of the general framework, be it colonial, nationalist, or Marxist. This has the consequence of effacing the particularity of the histories under consideration and silencing the subjects who constitute them. The 'peasant', for example, as Guha (1983) argues, is always seen as constitutive of somebody else's narrative of history, be that as an irrational actor duped or incited into rebellion by local troublemakers (British colonial historiography), as a precursor to the national independence struggle (Indian nationalist historiography), or as constituting part of the revolutionary continuum that would lead to socialism (Marxist historiography). In each, the peasant is regarded as an agent, but is an agent in someone else's story – be that the story, or narrative, of civilizational modernity (life-story of the empire), nationalist modernization, or socialist modernization. The story is never about the peasant. The documents of the British run administration, for example, register insurrectionary events as data in the narrative of Empire, but, as Guha suggests, 'do nothing to illuminate that consciousness which is called insurgency' (1983: 27). While historical works written by those within the British administration narrate the history of 'England's work in India', those written by Indian nationalists and radicals assimilate all resistance 'along the alternative axis of a protracted campaign for freedom and socialism' (Guha 1983: 33). The will of the people themselves, Guha suggests, is lost in the general narratives imposed upon them by historians.

Guha's (1982) formation of the Subaltern Studies collective in the 1980s was premised on the belief that, for too long, the study of Indian history had concentrated on state actors and elites and that it was necessary to restore the actions and the politics of 'the people' to a central position within that history. The primary aim of the collective, as outlined by Guha (1982), was to study and discuss subalternist themes in South Asian history and society and, in particular, to address peasant insurgencies and rebellions during the period of colonialism. While colonialist interpretations had long been contested, it was believed that the recent bourgeois nationalist and Marxist interpretations of the past had similarly failed to address the history of 'the people' as seen from the position of 'the people'. This must prompt the question: who are 'the people'?

In restoring the voice of the subaltern to a central position within Indian history, however, the members of the Subaltern Studies collective had to contend with two immediate methodological problems: that the peasants in India, like elsewhere, had not left written documents of their own and that the documents that did exist, were not neutral in their attitudes to the events being witnessed and inscribed. In addressing these issues, Guha (1982, 1983) starts from the historiographical position of investigating the structure of the disciplines that have contributed to the exclusion of the subaltern and by examining the components of the discourse that have combined to produce 'biased' histories.

The nineteenth-century historiographical turn from narrative chronicle to documentary record had established the archive, and the documents that constituted it, as the repository of truth. As Foucault suggests, the document had come to be seen 'as the language of a voice since reduced to silence' and history was 'the work expended on material documentation' to render vocal that silence (2002 [1969]: 7). The suggestion that the historian's task is simply one of lending speech to the traces of the past, however, fails to recognize the extent to which history does not just happen, but is produced (Foucault 2002 [1969]; Spivak 1985a). As Trouillot (1995) argues, archives do not simply exist as spaces from which historical truth can be discerned, they are part of the very constitution of knowledge that determines how truth is to be known. The archives – 'the institutions that organize facts and sources ... [such that they then] condition the possibility of existence of historical statements' – are themselves premised on particular understandings of what is deemed to be worth being organized in the first place (Trouillot 1995: 52). And, as Trouillot argues, this happens at various sites:

> the moment of fact creation (the making of sources); the moment of fact assembly (the making of archives); the moment of retrieval (the making of narratives); and the moment of retrospective significance (the making of history in the final instance). (1995: 26–7)

Following on from this, Guha suggests that the fundamental problem with the archive is the extent to which the texts that constitute it are shorn of contemporaneity, 'recovered as ... element[s] of the past and classified as history' (1983: 7). By removing these texts from their context, and treating them in isolation of the conditions of their emergence, they are ascribed a neutrality that they do not possess. The bias of these texts, for our purposes, does not reside simply in the bias of their authors, but in the refusal of historians to *demonstrate* what appears to be obvious in them; the bias is in the failure to acknowledge the contestability of the archive and to regard it simply as a neutral repository of facts which can be pieced together to construct History without sustained examination.

As Guha argues, documents are not neutral and in submitting these documents before the court of history we cannot expect them to testify with impartiality (1983: 14). In this context, he argues that the only way to reconstruct their historical presence is by reading official documents – documents produced for administrative use – *against the grain*, and to do so in the name of the subaltern.

Within the Subaltern Studies projects, then, the subaltern was studied and theorized in the context of subaltern groups being engaged in struggles with the law, with bureaucracy, the police and so forth (Das 1989). By making moments of peasant defiance and insurrection central to understanding the subaltern as subjects of their own history, they are no longer seen simply as objects of such domination, 'but are rather shown at the moment in which they try to defy this alienating power' (Das 1989: 314). With this, Guha simultaneously constructs the subaltern as a political subject and, in the process, restores to them their historical being, that is, their agency as historical actors.[8] As well as restoring the subaltern to history, a related aim of the Subaltern Studies project, as suggested by Spivak, was to disrupt the great modes-of-production narrative – in particular, that of the transition from feudalism to capitalism – and, instead, to pluralize and plot moments of change in terms of confrontation (and communication) as opposed to transition (1985b: 205).

V

Guha uses 'the people' and 'the subaltern classes' synonymously to represent *'the demographic difference between the total Indian population and all those … described as the "elite"'*, where 'the elite' signifies both foreign and indigenous dominant groups (Guha 1982: 8).[9] The term 'subaltern' is taken from the writings of Gramsci and, as Prakash (1994) argues, is extended to refer to subordination in terms of caste, gender, race, language, and culture, as well as class. It is further used to indicate the centrality of the dominated/dominant relationships within history and, as such, builds upon notions of 'the standpoint of the proletariat' first developed by Marx, as explicated by Lukács (1999 [1968]: 149–222), and subsequently utilized by feminists in their development of standpoint theory.

Das's (1989) 'subaltern as perspective' and Prakash's (1994) 'subaltern as vantage point of critique' are both modes of attributing epistemic privilege to socially marginalized subjects. Just as earlier forms of feminist engagement came to be criticized as 'feminist empiricism', with arguments for scholarship to go beyond the 'recovery' of women's voices to develop a specifically feminist epistemology (see Harding 1986), so Subaltern Studies 'has shifted from its original goal of recovering the subaltern autonomy ... [to emerge] as a *position* from which the discipline of history can be rethought' (Prakash 1994: 1489; emphasis added). This shift comes, in part, as a result of Spivak's trenchant critique of the original project as positivistic in that it assumed that, if properly executed, it would lead to firm ground, to some *thing* that could be disclosed (1985b: 211). In each case, the earlier position with its emphasis on bias and neglect of particular experiences, be those of women or of peasants, was argued to reinforce dominant epistemologies in the way that it implied that biases could be removed and objectivity achieved.

Hartsock's (1984) translation of a 'Marxist' standpoint of the proletariat into feminist terms is an early argument for standpoint epistemology as a 'subaltern' epistemology, albeit conducted from a feminist, rather than a postcolonial perspective.[10] Domination and subordination, she argues, provide different perspectives from which social relationships can be understood, with subordination providing a particularly privileged vantage point because it necessarily carries an interest in the transcendence of relations of domination and subordination. Thus, Hartsock (1984) argues that it is women's particular disadvantaged and oppressed position within society, or within the sexual division of labour more precisely, that facilitates their ability to see the truth about the society in which they live. These insights, she argues, are not obvious or immediate – that is, they do not emerge simply out of the experience of being a woman – but rather, are mediated and achieved, coming about through an active engagement with the real structures of women's subordination.

Where established disciplines have typically claimed 'transcendence' in terms of the objectivity or universality of their positions, standpoint epistemology claims that this purported 'view from nowhere' is, in fact, a view from 'somewhere', the somewhere of privilege and domination. In this sense, a feminist standpoint is taken as the position with purchase on 'critical truth' and from which it is possible to interrogate the (patriarchal) structures of social life and the disciplines associated with them. As already suggested, standpoint epistemology does not apply only to women's position, but to any position of subordination. The position of the 'subaltern', then, can be seen as the generalized form of standpoint epistemology and the appropriate standpoint for critical inquiry in any domain of social relations structured around inequality (see Holmwood 1995).

A number of commentators, however, have pointed to the problems inherent within a standpoint approach. The idea that subordination provides a privileged vantage point on oppression suggests that the privileged point of view is that of the subjective experience of oppression. Yet, as Holmwood (1995) argues, once the idea of subordination is both generalized and differentiated to suggest that there are different mechanisms and kinds of subordination – associated with gender, race, sexuality, and so forth – subjectivities of oppression become diverse and potentially cross-cutting. In these circumstances, the question of the representation of the point of view of the oppressed (as distinct from that of the critically engaged observer) becomes complex and, for some, impossibly complex. Among postcolonial theorists, this conundrum has been most powerfully expressed by Spivak's (1988) question: can the subaltern speak?

As Holmwood (1995) suggests, standpoint epistemology seems to require the representation of the point of view of the oppressed independently of the particularity of experiences and therefore reintroduces a proto-universalistic claim not so different to that it attributes to conventional epistemology. It claims an understanding of the mechanisms of subordination beyond that which is available to those who are subordinated, and thus it is not the position of those who are oppressed that is being privileged, but the belief in the nature of oppression and its real causes as held by standpoint theorists. This is evident in Marx's initial formulation that the standpoint of the proletariat is not what any individual proletarian believes, but what the proletariat *must become* – which is, of course, nothing more than their convergence with Marx's own position.

This understanding is reiterated in Spivak's explication of Marx and her insistence on the need to distinguish between the two forms of representation – *vertreten* and *darstellen* – that, in English, are conflated in the use of the one word, 'representation' (1988: 276–7). This distinction between representation as 'proxy' and representation as 'portrait' is used to illustrate the argument that, while people living under particular socioeconomic conditions may be members of a class, to the extent that 'the identity of their interests fails to produce a feeling of community ... *they do not form a class*' (Spivak 1988: 277, quoting from Marx). Recognition of oneself as constituting a class, for Spivak then, 'is not an ideological transformation of consciousness on ground level' – that is, it is not simply the subjective experience of oppression – but rather, comes about as a consequence of the appropriation and replacement of the economic conditions of existence (1988: 277–8). In the absence of the latter, Spivak suggests that 'it is the slippage from rendering visible the mechanism to rendering vocal the individual that is consistently troublesome' (1988: 285).

In this form of analysis, then, the importance given to the subjective experience of oppression gives way to a recognition of the different mechanisms and *structures* of domination. With relations of domination and subordination not restricted to any one domain, however, practical circumstances are subject to cross-cutting processes and identity claims such that there is no necessary tendency for the convergence of the two forms of representation. Any claim for unity among the oppressed is perceived as potentially an essentialist position. Yet, standpoint epistemologies are defined not merely by their concern to document or explain relations of oppression, but also to transcend them. Where Moya (2000) argues that, when structures of inequality overlap with categories of identity, a politics based on those identities is both libera-tory and necessary, the problem that confronts standpoint approaches is the apparent necessity to regard politics as the means of *creating* this overlap between structures of inequality and identity. In this way, subaltern scholars are caught between the Scylla of privileging difference and valorizing different identities, and the Charybdis of needing to provide an account of systematic relations of domination to legitimize political projects aimed at the amelioration of disadvantage.

While essentialism is eschewed in theory, then, it is retrieved as a necessary condition for political practice – and so, despite her own critique of essentialism, Spivak, in the end, advocates a '*strategic* use of positivist essentialism in a scrupulously visible political interest' (1985b: 214). What is also visible, however, is the role of the 'elite' investigator who must now 'represent' the subaltern, at the same time as 'misrepresenting' them, in that, she argues, 'the arena of the subaltern's persistent emergence into hegemony must always and by definition remain heterogeneous to the efforts of the disciplinary historian' (1985b: 217). Whether this is an adequate solution to a necessary problem will be discussed in the next and final section of this chapter.

VI

The perceived 'gap' between general categories and particular experiences, I shall argue, can be overcome by addressing difference in the context of what the historian Sanjay Subrahmanyam (1997, 2005a,b) calls '*connected histories*'. 'Connected histories' are histories that do not derive from a singular standpoint, be that a universal standpoint – which postcolonial theorists have demonstrated as being a particular standpoint linked to colonialism – or a standpoint of the generalized subaltern. To give up such positions, however, is neither to lapse into relativism, nor into political impasse. Rather, it is to recognize that politics and intellectual engagement is always a 'conjunctural' phenomenon, and that conjunctures are open to systematic and rigorous reflection in terms of the connections they reveal. Further, as conjunctures, they are occasions where there will be different voices and dialogues, none of which need be privileged as a pre-condition of understanding or 'progressive' politics (see Holmwood 2000a). This is something to which I will return at different points in this book. For the moment, I wish to address the issue of 'connected histories' in more depth.

Said asks: 'What is the meaning of "difference" when the preposition "from" has been dropped from sight altogether?' (1978: 106). It is the 'from' that indicates the relationship and maintains an acknowledgement of the complexity and interconnectedness of the world we inhabit. Dropping the 'from' enables us then to think the fiction of separate and distinct cultures, societies, and peoples. Said argues that his 'principal aim is not to separate, but to connect' and that his interest in this is 'for the main philosophical and methodological reason that cultural forms are hybrid, mixed, impure, and the time has come in cultural analysis to reconnect their analysis with their actuality' (1993: 15). What is needed, he continues, 'is to look at these matters as a network of interdependent histories that it would be inaccurate and senseless to repress, useful and interesting to understand' (1993: 20). Said suggests that we need to look back at the historical archive *contrapuntally*, that is, 'with a simultaneous awareness both of the metropolitan history that is narrated and of those other histories against which (and together with which) the dominating discourse acts' (1993: 59).

Said's *Orientalism* was based on rethinking the largely accepted division between East and West and beginning to reformulate understandings of 'historical experiences which had once been based on the geographical separation of peoples and cultures' (1995: 351). In this, he has been followed by scholars such as Paul Gilroy (1993), who has used the idea of the 'Black Atlantic' to signify a network between the local and the global that provides a more adequate context within which to understand the traffic in human beings than simply trying to understand the phenomenon from one particular place, be that America or then Africa. Using the metaphor of the 'ship', Gilroy further emphasizes the mobility *between* places that was an integral aspect of the condition of slavery (1993: 16). Just as we need to be aware of cross-cutting histories narrated from different perspectives, then, so we need to be aware of the problems associated with the 'conventional geographical units of analysis', whether 'nation-states' or the geographically bounded regions that appear in 'area studies' (Subrahmanyam 1997).

Subrahmanyam, for his part, suggests that the ubiquity of nationalism, and the consequent histories focused on national and state boundaries, has diverted attention away from the possibilities of connections across these boundaries (1997: 761). He borrows Duara's phrase in making a plea for 'rescuing history from the nation' and develops upon this by suggesting that historians need to focus, not only on the local and the regional, but also to move beyond national boundaries in their understanding of historical processes as well as to question those boundaries (Subrahmanyam 2005b: 11).[11] The historical ethnographies of the early modern period that fixed identities and cultures to particular places came about as a result of social and political changes taking place in the countries from which the travellers embarked upon their journeys as well as the very intensification of travel and the associated desire to classify the differences encountered within coherent schema (Subrahmanyam 1997: 761). The establishment of the stadial theory of history that came out of the Scottish Enlightenment was one such example, and will be discussed further in the following chapter. As Subrahmanyam makes clear, however, despite the weight of empirical evidence, the 'urge to define, describe and classify' was not a peculiarly European one (1997: 761). He suggests that 'almost any process of early modern empire building was also a process of classifying'; either identifying difference in order to preserve it, as in the Ottoman *millet* system, or then to assimilate it by virtue of a civilizing mission (1997: 761).

Processes of classification necessarily entail an emphasis on difference and separation over connections and, even today, given that our access to knowledge can only ever be partial and provisional, we have to locate our intellectual endeavours within particular boundaries. But our boundaries need not be reified and nor the peoples, practices, and cultures located within them. It is important to recognize that the general vision of the world, as made up of distinct and separate entities that exist 'independent of our projects of distinguishing between them' (Narayan 1998: 92), is increasingly untenable. Equally untenable is the idea that there are peoples and cultures confined to, and by, the places they inhabit, unsullied by contact with the world beyond their boundaries (Appadurai 1988: 39). While, as Subrahmanyam suggests, it is important 'not to deny voice to those who were somehow "fixed" by physical, social and cultural coordinates', it is even more important to recognize that if we know about 'them' 'the chances are that it is because they are already plugged into some network, some process of circulation' (1997: 762).

The positing of spatial boundaries for the purposes of historical analysis has to be recognized as provisional and not the marker of fixity or local rootedness.[12] Examining the spheres of circulation of commodities and ideological constructs demonstrates that these flows 'often transcended the boundaries defined for us retrospectively by nation-states or Area Studies' (Subrahmanyam 1997: 759). As such, Subrahmanyam argues, we should 'not only compare from within our boxes, but spend some time and effort to transcend them, not by comparison alone, but by seeking out the at times fragile threads that connected the globe, even as the globe came to be defined as such' (1997: 761–2). In making an argument for 'connected histories', Subrahmanyam provides an innovative and productive way out of the bind that sees much global history caught between an evolutionary universal scheme on the one hand, where differences are placed within particular hierarchies depending on the model being used; or a culturally relative exoticism, on the other, which reifies and privileges difference. By allowing ourselves to rethink boundaries, both spatial and temporal, we can then 'redraw maps that emerge from the problematics we wish to study rather than invent problematics to fit our pre-existent cartographies' (Subrahmanyam 2005b: 4).

If the dominant cartographies of Western historiography have been effectively criticized by postcolonial theorists, as I have suggested in this chapter that they have, postcolonial historiography has nonetheless reproduced some equivalent hierarchies in its own representation of history from the point of view of the subaltern. 'Connected histories' allow the deconstruction of dominant narratives at the same time as they are open to different perspectives and seek to reconcile them systematically both in terms of the reconstruction of theoretical categories and in the incorporation of new data and evidence. In the next two chapters, I shall examine the dominant constructions of modernity in Western social science, and sociology in particular, before turning to a reconsideration of the evidence that challenges the idea of modernity as an endogenous 'European' project.

2
European Modernity and the Sociological Imagination

The eighteenth and nineteenth centuries, as I shall elaborate in this chapter, saw the consolidation of a particular mode of thought that would provide the theoretical basis from which Western civilization viewed its relationships to other societies and peoples. The fundamental characteristics of the emerging theoretical paradigm were twofold: first, the assumption of a ruptural break from the past that made the modern world discontinuous from, and 'after', that which had preceded it, and, second, an assumption of the uniqueness of 'the West' in its initiation of a distinctive form of society. As Hayden White argues, this way of thinking involved the West's 'relationship not only to cultures and civilizations preceding it, but also to those contemporary with it in time and contiguous with it in space' (1980: 2). This chapter delineates the shifts in social thought that were central to the development of this way of thinking and, in doing so, discusses how these shifts became integral to sociology as a discipline.

Whatever their other differences, Durkheim, Weber, and earlier theorists such as Saint-Simon and Comte, believed themselves to be living through a great transformation in history and were concerned with understanding how it had begun, and influencing how it would be brought to the completion inherent to it. Although they had differing interpretations of 'modernity', these interpretations, as Wagner comments, were 'always marked by a clear conceptual distinction between a before and after' (2001b: 84). History was understood as proceeding in stages, with each new stage a progression over the previous one. Even Weber's attempt, to move beyond a unilinear, directional interpretation of historical progression, did not escape the evaluative bias of the West being understood as being at the highest point of development, as will be discussed later in the chapter.

Sociology's explanation of modernity (and of processes of modernization, which I will examine in more detail in the following chapter), then, came to be located in the context of an identification of a distinct social domain and an historical understanding of its forms, whereby each form of social organization was deemed to be superseded by a progressively higher one. On this construction, sociology's primary object of study was to discern underlying social structures in their historical diversity, giving rise to a comparative 'science' of societies. The initial turn to the 'social' has been primarily associated with the work of the theorists of the Scottish Enlightenment, such as Ferguson and Smith, and with French theorists, such as Montesquieu and Turgot. With the emergence of this 'proto-sociological' understanding, the concern with the historical emergence of the particularities of different types of human society came to replace what, previously, had been largely a philosophical concern with discovering the timeless, immutable characteristics of human life and its natural laws. I shall begin my treatment, then, with a discussion of the idea of stages of society in the work of French and Scottish thinkers.

I

The development of a distinctive 'social' understanding was a continuation of the wider eighteenth-century intellectual movement known as the Enlightenment and most usually associated with the writings of Hobbes, Locke, and Bacon. While many scholars have argued that the Enlightenment should not be regarded as a unitary, coherent phenomenon, there is general agreement that its importance, in part at least, rests upon the establishment of a scientific framework within which to locate intellectual endeavours (see Gay 1969; Hawthorn 1976). The successes of figures such as Newton and Boyle in the natural sciences in the seventeenth century led to the promotion of the idea that the political and social realm should also be investigated through rational, scientific methods. In particular, Newton's achievement in illustrating the existence of 'natural' and 'universal' principles was taken up both as a challenge and a model for social and political inquiries to emulate (Heilbron 1995; Berry 1997).[1] In this way, the previous scholarly focus on religion was gradually replaced by an emphasis on reason and science, or natural philosophy as it was known at the time. With this, the movement of the Enlightenment challenged the Church's claim to knowledge and contributed to the undermining of the authority of theology as the primary source of explanation.

Science, as it developed in this period, assumed nature to be transparent, something which could be 'read' and translated. As Pagden writes, the feats of astronomy and navigation in the fifteenth and sixteenth centuries had resulted in the reduction of a part of the cosmos to cartography, and science came to be seen as 'the plotting of relationships, of a set of universal contexts ... to which everything, ultimately even man, belongs' (1993: 48). Montesquieu, for example, writing in the 1740s, remarked that the compass had opened up the universe with the discovery of America and this, in turn, enabled Asia and Africa to be connected to Europe (1965 [1748]: 366, 369). This understanding of being able to discover 'cosmos in chaos' was facilitated by science's orientation to systematic experimentation and the eliciting of general rules and principles governing nature and human behaviour (Berry 1997: 56). The belief that nature and, more importantly, that human nature was uniformly the same, made it possible for the thinkers of the Enlightenment to attempt to compare human behaviour across time and space with particular emphasis on differences in context (Berry 1997: 68). The commitment to uniformity in human nature provided the basis for the establishment of a universal framework within which 'the overwhelming diversity evident in the accounts of travellers and the chronicles of historians' (Heilbron 1995: 55) could be located and accounted for.

With knowledge coming to be seen as something that was acquired over time through empirical research and the accumulation of data, the more data that was acquired, the more complete knowledge would be. It was this imperative for completeness, and then systematization, that turned the focus of the *philosophes* towards establishing a taxonomy of the variety of human societies that were known to exist (Jacques 1997). The new forms of ordering and classification that began to be developed focused on ideas of causal regularity and the existence of universal standards applicable across different societies and social modes of organization. While human nature was typically understood as existing independent of, and prior to, social relations, it was, at the same time, believed to be subject to improvement and development through changes in the structures of social relations. It was in this period, then, that the realm of the social, as distinct from the state, came to be seen as a proper site of investigation, and the philosophical focus on human emancipation from superstition was grounded within what was to become a sociological concern with society and social progress.

The stadial (or stages) theory of history, developed primarily by the thinkers of the Scottish Enlightenment, was one solution to the problem of accommodating difference within a universal framework. Although these thinkers were not the only ones to consider the diversity of social practices and institutions present in the world they have been seen as among the first to attempt 'to place this diversity in some sort of order' (Berry 1997: 88). The essential idea of the stages theory of history, and one that was picked up and developed subsequently by sociology, was that 'societies undergo *development* through successive *stages* based on different *modes of subsistence*' (Meek 1976: 6). These stages were generally understood as being from hunting and gathering, to pastoral, to settled agriculture, and to commerce. While the stages are seen as progressive, with each stage marking an advance over the previous ones, the ultimate stage of commercial society was seen as both a distinct stage and as existing contemporaneously with other modes of subsistence. What was paramount for the thinkers of the Enlightenment was to establish the local nature of the effects of particular social arrangements and attempt to understand how these could be altered to produce 'better' effects. Montesquieu (1965 [1748]), for example, in his classic work *The Spirit of the Laws*, sought to demonstrate that individuals were products of their society and that societies varied across time and space. He was not concerned with the condition of humanity in a state of abstraction, but rather, focused on the particularity of nations and cultures as constituted through their geography, climate, traditions, and practices.

Montesquieu's identification of societies as integral and self-sustaining, with diverse social practices that were to be explained by factors such as climate or the nature of the soil, was not deemed adequate by Hume or other thinkers of the Scottish Enlightenment, such as Ferguson or Smith. For them, differences among peoples were to be accounted for by examining the differences between the various modes of subsistence and the particular notions of property that existed. While colonial encounters were not specifically addressed by them, it is not difficult to see that such encounters provided them with their data in many cases.[2] As Meek suggests, it was the increasing availability of literature on the nature and society of the Amerindians (itself a consequence of European conquest) that was fundamental to the emergence of the idea of historical stages of social development. In this, he suggests that, the writers of the Scottish Enlightenment followed Locke's postulation that, 'in the beginning all the World was America' (1764 [1689]: 236), and then sought to determine the subsequent stages through which humanity was to pass before arriving at the current condition of commercial society and civility.

Ferguson (1966 [1767]), for example, argues that it is only by studying contemporary savage and barbarian societies that it is possible to draw conclusions about the influence of different situations on 'our' ancestors.

space/time

'[T]he inhabitants of Britain, at the time of the first Roman invasion', he writes, 'resembled, in many things, the present natives of North America' (1966 [1767]: 75). It is in their present condition, then, 'that we are to behold, as in a mirrour [sic], the features of our own progenitors; and from thence we are to draw our conclusions with respect to the influence of situations, in which, we have reason to believe, our fathers were placed' (Ferguson 1966 [1767]: 80). Even while dismissing the possibility of knowing the exact origins of the inhabitants of the Americas, Robertson also calls for them to be studied in order to complete the history of the human mind (1818 [1777]: 49). This, he suggests, was only possible by studying people as they exist in all the different stages of society, and the inhabitants of the Americas were to be regarded as 'the rudest form in which we can conceive him [people] to exist' (1818 [1777]: 50). With this, both Ferguson and Robertson contributed to the growing belief that 'travelling in space also meant travelling in time; [where] the Others they encountered were earlier versions of themselves' (Fox 1995: 16).

It was with Ferguson's (1966 [1767]) *An Essay on the History of Civil Society* that the *progress* of a people came to be attributed to the subdivision of tasks distributed within it and historical stages regarded as consecutive, evolutionary, and culminating in 'modern' society. While Ferguson, like Montesquieu, believed that physical factors played a part in enabling distinctions to be made between societies, the variables that he took to be fundamental were social ones, namely, the nature of economic activities and the character of social relations. In particular, he considered issues of 'national defence, the distribution of justice, [and] the preservation and internal prosperity of the state' as key measures distinguishing between societies (1966 [1767]: 135). Even the physical factors under discussion were addressed according to the meeting of human needs and the possibilities for social progress that this entailed. When discussing the climate or the existence of fertile land, for example, Ferguson's remarks are directed to what these conditions would enable people to do and produce. Land that required the investment of labour and skill was seen to condition a people to 'retain their frugality, increase their industry, and improve their arts' (Ferguson 1966 [1767]: 142). This, in turn, would have the potential consequence of transforming the mode of subsistence from agriculture to commerce through the accumulation of wealth generated through increased industry and consolidated in the institution of private property.

The association of the increase in wealth with the progress of a society is most apparent in the work of Smith (1863 [1776]) and Turgot (1973 [1766]). Both these thinkers point to the division of labour as

fundamental in the 'turning of land to account' and the subsequent growth of commodity exchange and accumulation of 'movable wealth', that is, money and, for Turgot, also slaves (Turgot 1973 [1766]: 134, 145). Once it was possible to generate a surplus of 'movable wealth', and so establish a reserve or 'a capital', Turgot suggests that that reserve could be safeguarded as insurance against an uncertain future, or it could be used in the advance of manufacturing and industrial enterprises (1973 [1766]: 150, 151). Turgot and Smith differ in terms of the emphasis they place on land and labour, respectively, as being generative of wealth, but in both cases the primary explanation is an endogenous one. The implication is that the utilization of labour applied to land arises initially in the form of serfdom (justified in the case of Turgot by the ownership of land as a productive asset) which then may be transmuted to waged labour. The rise of commerce, then, was generally attributed to the way in which, after the institution of agriculture, a surplus was realized and the division of labour extended.

As such, the emergence of a society based on commerce was not seen to be 'the product of external forces like the pressure of population on resources' (Berry 1997: 97), but rather, was regarded to emerge through an internal reorganization of productive social relations and the accumulation of movable wealth. As the wealth of (some) nations increased and countries began to develop economically, it was suggested that this occurred 'because *within the framework of these changing modes of subsistence* there was a gradual increase over time in the division of labour, commodity exchange, and the accumulation of capital' (Meek 1976: 222). 'Commercial society', then, while indicating a distinctive form of society, was not really regarded as truly distinctive in the way that later writers would suggest was the case with modernity and modern societies. The very expansiveness made possible by commercial activities, brought in its wake more fundamental transformations than were initially identified with the theory of stages and which were intimately connected with the treatment of colonial relations within theories of modernity. While colonial relations receive some recognition within initial discussions of commercial society, they become attenuated to the point of disappearance as the idea of commercial society transmutes into that of 'industrial capitalism'.

II

While it is tacitly accepted that the definition of 'movable wealth' and capital included both money and slaves, discussion of the latter is limited both in the work of the theorists of the time and subsequent commentators.[3] Turgot (1973 [1766]) does refer briefly to the aspect of owning slaves as one element of wealth generation, but this is not expanded upon, nor its implications for subsequent analysis drawn out. For the most part, when writers in this period discuss slavery, they do so as a feature of militaristic societies based on settled agriculture and they take their cases from the Greeks and classical antiquity, not from the active enslavement that they might have witnessed in the emergence of the new form of commercial society that they believed would supersede that based on settled agriculture. While scholars recognized the condition of slavery, then, they did so primarily in the context of it having existed as a practice in the ancient world or, then, as an analogy for contemporary forms of practices (as in Marx's later references to free labour as having the form of 'wage slavery').

By the middle of the eighteenth century, however, a substantial proportion of the European bourgeoisie, in its leading economic powers, generated and accumulated their wealth on the basis of commercial activities connected to the slave trade and other trades of 'dispossession', such as the fur trade.[4] It was not uncommon for people to invest in such commercial activities even as they argued for the abolition of slavery. Locke is one such example who put money into commercial ventures that depended on slavery to generate a return on that investment while, at the same time, being opposed to slavery.[5] Glausser (1990) suggests that despite arguing against the condition of slavery, Locke's language is more figurative than literal; that is, he suggests that Locke is opposed to slavery as a general, abstract condition rather than being opposed to its particular practice in contemporary society. This attitude is largely replicated in the later thinkers discussed here.

Montesquieu is regarded as among the first to bring slavery into the discussion of the Enlightenment and, in doing so, uses satire and irony in presenting a case for its abolition.[6] Turgot, more straightforwardly, writes of the 'abominable custom of slavery' and notes that this 'banditry and this trade still prevail in all their horror on the coasts of Guinea, where they are fomented by the Europeans who go there to buy Negroes for the cultivation of the American colonies' (1973 [1766]: 130). This comment is notable to the extent that Turgot addresses contemporary practices of slavery. For his part, Ferguson's discussion of slavery occurs primarily in the context of corruption and political slavery where he talks about the freedoms afforded the savage and the barbarian in contrast to civilized people (1966 [1767]: 261–72). Elsewhere, slavery is located as an aspect of ancient Greek culture or then in terms of the practices of domestic enslavement (1966 [1767]: 184–8, 115). In *The Theory of Moral*

Sentiments, Smith refers to slavery but once, in the context of its practice within Greek culture in ancient times (1982 [1759]: 281–2). In his *Wealth of Nations*, the chapter on 'the discouragement of agriculture' incorporates a discussion of serfdom and bonded labour, and then there is a relatively substantial engagement with the concerns of slavery and the colonies in the Americas (1863 [1776]: 170–6, 249–89). Both discussions, however, are framed in terms of slavery in ancient times.

The Enlightenment concern with liberty, of necessity, generates a concern with its opposite, slavery. This is especially the case in light of the problem of reconciling practices of slavery in ancient society, where ancient societies and their philosophical self-understandings had been such an important resource for thinking about contemporary problems of social organization and government. This is resolved, in part, by the very development of the stadial theory of history where slavery is made an aspect of settled agricultural societies to be abolished in the civilizing process brought about by the emergence of commercial society (Berry 1997: 129).[7] This focus on slavery in the ancient world, then, serves two related purposes. It locates slavery as a practice of the ancient world, associated with the settled agricultural mode of production in extended household forms – the *oikos*. This, in turn, enables slavery in contemporary society to be seen as a residual form associated with the agricultural mode – and associated forms of unfree labour, such as serfdom and bonded labour – and elides the abolition of slavery in the 'old world' with its emergence in the new. With this, contemporary forms of slavery are not required to be addressed in the context of the *emergence of commercial society*, but simply as a practice left over from previous societies that will be diminished as commerce extends its domain, a tendency further reinforced once commercial society comes to be understood as industrial capitalist society.

None of the thinkers addressed here saw slavery as generative of commercial society, or integral to its functioning, and thus in need of explanation and incorporation into the explanations of commercial society itself despite, as I have already commented, the economic significance of the trades associated with slavery and other forms of dispossession. Any contradiction between thought and behaviour – that is, the co-existence of thinking themselves civilized at the same time as living within societies that perpetrated the horror that was slavery – could be placed outside the scheme that was being established and did not require resolution within it. To the extent that the mode of subsistence was taken as a heuristic device, these thinkers were able to acknowledge the existence of differences between their scheme and the observable phenomena of slavery and dispossession, but these differences did not call into question the integrity of the framework or their self-conception as civilized and polite.

III

While the different thinkers of the Scottish Enlightenment developed their understandings of progress in relation to different ideas of what the stages were – for example, Ferguson grouped societies into savage, barbarian, and polished, while Smith characterized them as hunting, pastoral, agriculture, and commercial – they all, nonetheless, pictured them as successive stages in an historical development. Further, each stage was believed to generate particular ways of being, of behaving, and to establish distinct personalities and character traits. The superiority of commercial society, for example, was believed to be demonstrated by its association with concepts of civility, manners, polish, cultivation of the arts, and so forth.

The vindication of commercial society, then, rested in the accumulation and distribution of wealth across classes such that all members of society were able to enjoy a better standard of living than had previously been possible (Smith 1863 [1776]: 181–7). Alongside wealth, freedom was the other key characteristic ascribed to commercial society. Smith believed that members of commercial society enjoyed a liberty that was denied to the subjects living within societies characterized by other modes of subsistence as the surplus generated by commerce 'bought' the freedom of the individuals within it. As such, freedom consisted, in part, in the ability to choose, and then to change, one's occupation and to be able to better one's own condition through the accumulation of wealth.

A civilized society, according to Hume (1875 [1752]), was one in which property was secure, industry encouraged, and in which the arts were able to flourish. The dissipation of kinship ties and those of ascriptive and exclusive loyalty were further believed to open up space for the development of natural sympathies, sociability, and friendship (see Silver 1990). Civilization was seen to require commerce, and commerce, as it rested on a set of expectations and beliefs, was deemed to require stability and security for, as Berry notes, exchange entails specialization and necessitates giving up a self-sufficient life in favour of one which is interdependent (1997: 125). This interdependence, then, rests on forms of organization and the establishment of rules and regulations to protect individuals from the unpredictability inherent in freely constituted social relations. The development of cities was seen as fundamental to the loosening of individual ties of economic dependence and social subservience. Even though people were still subject to the economic system in general, the introduction of industry was believed to generate degrees of social freedom that had previously not been possible. As Hume writes on the relationship between the refinement of the arts and the impetus to sociability:

> They flock into the cities; love to receive and communicate knowledge; to shew their wit or their breeding; their taste in conversation or living, in clothes or furniture. Curiosity allures the wise; vanity the foolish; and pleasure both. Particular clubs and societies are everywhere formed: both sexes meet in an easy and sociable manner; and the tempers of men, as well as their behaviour, refine apace. So that ... it is impossible but they must feel an increase of humanity, from the very habit of conversing together, and contributing to each other's pleasure and entertainment. Thus *industry, knowledge* and *humanity* are linked together by an indissoluble chain, and are found, from experience as well as reason, to be peculiar to the more polished, and, ... the more luxurious ages. (1875 [1752] 'Of Refinement in the Arts': 301–2)

There were also, however, fears about the negative character traits generated by this new mode of subsistence. The move away from personal dealings and relations in commercial transactions to impersonal ones regulated not by benevolence and kindness, but a concern for one's own advantage and self-interest, was believed to increase the distance between individuals and loosen ties of mutual dependence. For some, and for Ferguson in particular, the rise of commercial society was deemed to entail a loss in spirit, solidarity, and courage and signify the end of virtue itself 'as formerly free arms-bearing citizens had become content to pay mercenaries to defend them' (Pocock 1977: 292). It was believed that the turn away from public militias to private ones would lead to tyranny, military despotism, and the loss of liberty. Liberty, and thus virtue, was commonly regarded as resting on arms and agriculture and, in determining its extent, comparisons with the ancient world were usually invoked. It was believed that liberty in ancient times had entailed a greater participation of individuals in public affairs and politics, but that it failed to provide any protection against the arbitrary use of power in the private realm. Conversely, modern liberty was seen to favour individual independence, but was arrived at via a cost of a relative disengagement from public life as private interest came to predominate (Fontana 1985).

The different authors addressed above, for the most part, established a theory of stages which was used, as Meek suggests, 'not only as the framework of a theory of socio-economic development, but also as the basis of an *evaluation* both of the savage state and of the modern commercial society' (1976: 154). Progress from one to the other was both a normative as well as descriptive concept. It was not, however, as has been discussed, an unambiguous one. This ambiguity, as I shall argue, is deeply rooted in sociology as well. But it is not an ambiguity that challenges either the stadial account or its intrinsic Eurocentrism, since in the one version progress is valorized and in the other there is a looking back nostalgically to a world of particularity and ascriptive bonds that has been lost.

The quarrel between those opposed to the rise of commerce and those who believed it had been worth the loss of virtue entailed, then, had the consequence of ensuring that 'the virtue of commercial and cultivated man was never complete' (Pocock 1977: 292). Further, all theories of human progress now had to take into consideration the idea that, as Pocock writes, 'progress was at the same time decay, that culture entailed some loss of freedom and virtue, that what multiplied human capacities also fractured the unity of human personality' (1977: 293). The Romantic reaction to the stages theory of history sought to reclaim the distinctiveness of societies and cultures outside of any universal framework. Herder (1969), in particular, looked to reconcile universal understandings of humanity with the particular claims of nations and cultures and to disentangle these considerations from a process of evaluating nations according to some rank order. This tension between the universal and the particular can be seen also to exist at the heart of what was to become the subsequent sociological project with the concern to establish general laws existing alongside the attention to the particular. It also constituted a division in sociology between what Gouldner (1973) has called its 'classical' and 'romantic' modalities, evident most recently as modernist and postmodernist orientations.

The Scottish reaction to earlier thinkers of the Enlightenment centred upon their opposition to developing models of human society based on hypothetical notions of human beings. Instead, they can be seen to advocate a 'proto-sociological' investigation into what was seen as the natural evolution of social forms of organization which, as discussed above, were generally considered to be hunting, pastoral, agricultural, and then commercial societies (Swingewood 1970). The existence of a rational order underpinning the social realm and a common humanity were the two assumptions which provided the basis for their belief that all nations were 'destined to pass through the same successive stages of development' (Carrithers 1995: 246).

Meek cautions against seeing the stages theory of history as a conjectural substitute for actual historical research arguing that the establishment of the conceptual framework was 'a kind of generalized summing-up of such historical facts about the development of society as were then available' (1976: 239). He does accept, however, that the chronological (and evaluative) relationship established between different types of culture emerged out of a hierarchical ranking of contemporary cultures that had no evidential foundation. Despite this weakness, Meek believes that the scheme has value 'as the first great theoretical embodiment ... of a set of wider notions ... [namely,] the idea of a social *science*' (1976: 242). The generalized historical narrative, then, becomes a background assumption of the social sciences and is unquestioningly reproduced in subsequent theoretical and substantive initiatives. I shall argue that this, precisely, is the problem; *the evidential basis for the idea of historical stages remains weak just because the idea becomes embedded in the conceptual frameworks of social science.* What is needed is to bring this historical framework to the foreground in order to assess its adequacy; this is the task of the second section of this book.

IV

Heilbron (1995) marks the shift between the *philosophes* and Scottish writers of the eighteenth century and those who followed in the nineteenth century, such as Saint-Simon and Comte (who is usually taken as the first self-conscious sociologist), as a shift from *social theory* to *social science.* However, it was through an engagement with ideas of historical stages that the social scientists of the nineteenth century understood the relationship between history and the social sciences. Once the general pattern of historical development was known, it was believed that the trajectory of development for other societies could be ascertained without direct research as all human societies were deemed to follow the same pattern – that which had been established by Europe (Iggers 1982: 48).

As Baker puts it, while Condorcet had seen 'historical progress as an essentially unilinear, incremental process ... Saint-Simon came to see it as a succession of organic social systems each based on its own organising principles' (1989: 333). In other words, the different 'stages' represented distinct, integrated social structures with both common and differentiating features. This inquiry was organized by the task of understanding the specific features of modernity that had yet to come fully into being. A belief in the existence of basic laws governing society provided the impetus for looking to discover these laws and this, then, became the central focus of social investigation. Where the turn to the nineteenth century has often been seen as bringing to an 'end the speculative or conjectural histories of the Enlightenment' (Wokler 1987: 326), it could be said that, instead of coming to an end, conjectural history was inherited by sociology and built into its self-understanding of its own project.

In part, the self-evident appropriateness of the approach was reinforced by subsequent developments in 'commercial society' and the accelerated pace of social change within Europe. It became increasingly evident that commercial society was developing as capitalist industrial society together with attendant social unrest. At the same time, the process of the re-evaluation of values that had begun with the collapse of the *ancien regime* continued in the aftermath of the French revolution indicating pressures towards increased political inclusion. While the developing industrial society was believed to provide a solution to the political problems of the post-revolutionary period in France it simultaneously came to be seen as the site of emerging problems in need of resolution. As Heilbron suggests, 'Comte and his peers wrote their works fully aware that the Revolution was over: a new era had commenced, industrialization went on' (1995: 8).

This emphasis on industrial society and its social problems, I shall suggest, reinforced the tendency already evident within ideas of commercial society that modern society could be understood as an endogenous development of Europe. Moreover, the idea of industrial society further displaced slavery and other forms of unfree labour from consideration as central issues of modernity. Despite the consolidation of these forms of labour in the new world and Imperial dominions of European powers at this time, theoretical reflection turned inward on the problems of social order evident within Europe.

It was hoped that by directing the elaboration of a rational constitution on the basis of the principles of social science it would be possible to secure the political achievements of 1789 and bring the Revolution to a close under the guidance of an enlightened elite (Baker 1989: 325). Greene argues that, similar to Saint-Simon, Comte believed that 'little more could be done to restore social harmony and political stability until a new system of positive beliefs was erected on scientific foundations' (1981: 62). As natural science was deemed to have 'succeeded in establishing the lawfulness of natural phenomena' it was now put to the task of 'a similar endeavour in the study of society' (Coser 1971: 3). Whereas in the eighteenth century science was seen simply as another, albeit increasingly superior, way of understanding the realities of the world, with Comte, the relations between the sciences were placed in historical progression culminating in the science of society – sociology (Hawthorn 1976: 74). Modern sociology, then, has been seen to be as much an invention of the French Revolution as was the modern state whose excesses that science was devised to combat (Wokler 2002: 70). It both emerged out of the conditions of modern society as well as being a distinctively modern form of explanation of that society.

Sociology's critique of existing conditions rested on an understanding that better social arrangements were not only desirable, but historically emergent. The problems that persisted in the aftermath of the French Revolution were seen to be a result of the persistence of outdated metaphysical principles, such as ideas of natural law and the rights of man. What was needed, according to Comte (1903 [1844]), was the introduction of a system of beliefs based on 'positive', scientific knowledge that would resolve the controversies damaging society and rebuild social harmony. Whereas previously, consensus and unanimity had been based on religion and religious institutions, they were now to be based on science. Comte believed that history was governed by the progressive shifts from one type of knowledge system to another – the theological, the metaphysical, the scientific – with each developing out of that which preceded it. Heilbron suggests that Comte's approach to 'the formation of knowledge as a historical phenomenon' rested on him relinquishing 'the idea that the validity of knowledge could be ascertained with the help of a non-historical and universally valid principle' (1995: 201). As a result of this, he believes that Comte can be seen as the very first to have developed 'a *historical* and *differential theory of science*' (1995: 200).

Sociology, according to Comte (1903 [1844]), was to become the science of society and, in the study of human social life, was to take the natural sciences as its template as the use of scientific methodology was deemed necessary for discovering, or uncovering, the patterns (or laws) of historical development. As Comte believed that the 'sciences differed in their subjects and methods' he suggested that 'social science also ought to be based upon the specific features of its object' (Heilbron 1995: 225). The main features differentiating humans from the rest of the natural world rested in 'our intelligence and our sociability' and, most importantly for Comte, the establishment of an ideal which 'we must be always approximating though we shall never be able actually to attain it' (1903 [1844]: 95–6). Further, our ability to learn from the past suggested that if 'social science was to be a true science, it ought to be based upon a historical law' (Heilbron 1995: 226). This one law was seen to govern the development of the whole of humanity and the different historical epochs were taken to be representative of 'the same fundamental evolution; each phase resulting from that which preceded, and preparing for that which follows it' (Comte 1903 [1844]: 97). Different societies, then, were variations of a general pattern and it was this notion of historical progress – of modernization or then progressive rationalization – which informed the work of the social scientists of the nineteenth century (Iggers 1997). If contemporary sociologists have largely forgotten Comte – or regard his sociologically infused 'religion of humanity' something of an embarrassment – his legacy continues to define the default modernist sensibility of the sociological tradition.

The Enlightenment had virtually abolished the legitimating role of tradition, and social administration and regulation came increasingly to be seen as a process directed from above by knowledgeable people. The idea of development was linked first to the progress of science and then to the progressive application of science to industry and society in general. The *image* of the industrial revolution, then only in its incipient forms in France, was transformed into a *model* through the endeavours of Saint-Simon and Comte (Kumar 1978: 46). It was not simply a description of an already existing reality, but was more a 'guide for political action and social reform' (Badham 1984: 7). These moves set up understandings of society as an internally ordered entity neglecting external relations in its constitution. Industrial society was understood in endogenous terms with the market delimited by the state; and the imperial and colonial relations, that constituted it as part of the global market, were ignored in favour of parochial analyses.

In the transition from a philosophical to a sociological theory of knowledge the individual person was gradually replaced by human society as the 'subject' of knowledge and the relation between the individual and society was emphasized (Elias 1978: 38). This then posed the problem of defining that society, of establishing its parameters such that it was distinguishable from other societies. Insofar as earlier scholars had reflected upon the social this was more often than not tied to their understandings of the state. As Heilbron suggests, 'the idea that human beings can be understood from the social arrangements they form' means that modern societies are not 'the same sort of units as "states"' (1995: 19). However, the extent to which this is the case in practice is open to question, as most social theorists continued to delineate their conceptions of society in terms of national boundaries. After 1789 social theory, as a whole, began to acquire a more national emphasis with the cosmopolitan ideals of the Enlightenment giving way to more 'national' sentiments (Heilbron 1995: 111). This can be seen in the way that the questions they took up for resolution were framed within the context of the relationship between the state and civil society.[8] This process further established the social as an internally coherent, bounded phenomenon that could be understood without any reference to external relations such as the colonial or imperial misadventures that were being undertaken at that time. The implications of these understandings will be developed further in subsequent chapters.[9]

The focus of classical sociology on the institutions of the nation-state, and its conflation of society with the boundaries of that state, is less surprising when we consider that the period of its emergence coincided with the formation of 'the institutional structures of the nation-state ... in the process of territorial consolidation, as in Italy and Germany, or reshaped with the advent of a republic which was born out of deep political crisis in France' (Wagner 2001a: 18). During the early nineteenth century, theories of social contract and popular sovereignty became central to understandings of political legitimacy and the establishment of states. A nation was no longer seen as 'a legally defined unit of orders and corporations with an absolute monarch at the top'; instead it was increasingly understood to consist 'of various sectors that joined to form a rather complex whole. ... This kind of differentiated unit was not so much a "state" as a "society"' (Heilbron 1995: 92). The identification of the person of the sovereign with the state gave way to the state being identified with the people, who were then considered a nation; and the problem of politics became that of discovering 'the true general interest among the mass of particular interests' (Bartelson 1995: 211). Popular sovereignty was seen to have undermined the distinction between the state and community, but, in conflating the two, it also accentuated the differences between them by making the community, or society as it came to be more generally known, the site of responsibility of the state. With the attention of the state turned onto the society for which it was responsible, social theory turned its attention to the state in the name of that society. Sociology thus became a central part of the modernizing project of the state.

V

It is, perhaps, in Durkheim's (1964 [1893], 1992 [1937]) work that this association of society and state became particularly marked. He established society as the domain of 'social facts' appropriate for empirical research in sociology and believed it to have a definite organization and structure that more or less corresponded to state boundaries. Society, for him, did not exist as an abstracted hypothetical domain, but was very much associated with a particular place and time. Durkheim argued that the increasing concentration of populations through the growth of cities and the developing means of communication and transport that diminished the spaces between social segments were the primary factors contributing to the process of social differentiation leading to the emergence of modern societies (1964 [1893]: 256–63). Social harmony was then seen to arise from the division of labour and was characterized, for Durkheim, by the regulation of 'relations between different social functions' (1964 [1893]: 205). Society was seen as a complex, concrete entity that had a reality *sui generis* through 'the association of individuals in a system of social relationships' (Parsons 1937: 353).

In determining the nature of social solidarity in modern societies, traditional or pre-industrial societies were put forward as the objects of comparison and, as Lukes argues, the problem was posed in terms 'of accounting for the historical transition from the latter to the former' (1973: 139). Durkheim argues that in 'elementary' societies, the individual was seen to be bound 'directly to society without any intermediary', and that, in modern societies, individuals depended on society because they depended 'upon the parts of which it [wa]s composed' (1964 [1893]: 129). While he believed that both 'solidarities' could be 'two aspects of one and the same reality', he nevertheless thought that they must be distinguished, and the manner by which mechanical solidarity gave way to organic solidarity identified, together with identifying the 'abnormal causes [that] have prevented it from attaining the degree of development which our social order now demands' (Durkheim 1964 [1893]: 129, 190). The problem with contemporary society, for Durkheim, was that it was not yet fully 'modern'; it was seen to be in a transitional phase in which, as Bryan Turner remarks, the old gods were dead, but the new ones were yet to be born (1992: xxii). It was neither mechanical nor organic, but rather, was constituted by the strains inherent in the transition from one to the other. The task of sociology was to facilitate the realization of the institutions that would overcome the *anomie* produced by transition and secure a modern form of solidarity.

The idea that society changes through a process of institutional specialization, or structural differentiation, began with Durkheim (and with Herbert Spencer, a primary focus of Durkheim's criticism). It was influenced by the development of biology and, in particular, Darwinian

Parsons – modernication theory

evolution (see Holmwood and O'Malley 2003). It became firmly established in the sociological approaches in the post Second World War period with the rise of structural-functional theories of modernization and the development of the 'system of modern societies' associated with Talcott Parsons (1966, 1971). I shall be discussing modernization theory in detail in the following chapter. For present purposes, it is sufficient simply to state that, in the construction of developmental sequences, comparative studies of modernization were deemed necessarily to rely on the Western experience. The presumption of internal integrity was further reinforced by taking whole societies as the basic units of analysis (Bendix 1967: 312; Calhoun 1996: 74).[10] Societies that were seen to consist of differentiated parts were distinguished from other differentiated wholes with different configurations of institutional specialization.

Parsons (1966), for example, understood modernity as developing within Europe and, in particular, as emerging out of the cultural and institutional heritage of Christianity and the Roman Empire. Although the Renaissance and Reformation were fundamental to his understanding of the transition to modernity, he believed that it was only after the evolution of nation-states, and the emergence of industrialization, that the main social institutions of modernity were properly established. These included democratically elected representative bodies, a universalistic legal system, a secularizing culture, and the extension of the market system. This common origin and shared heritage allowed for the evolution of a 'European system' of modern societies that could be understood in its entirety as differentiated from the rest of the world (Parsons 1966: 40–9). Latterly, the United States had become the 'new lead society'. Like Durkheim, Parsons's interest in the future was shaped by the possibilities of intervention to ameliorate the associated negative consequences of modernity (see Nielsen 1991).

The modern epoch within sociological thought, then, has always been seen as the great transition within history: a transition that had begun, but was also in need of completion (Badham 1984). Although Weber was more sceptical of the construction of a unilinear or directional timescale, as Hindess argues, he does operate 'with a hierarchical principle of ranking in terms of which other societies or cultures may be analysed according to the extent to which they realize or depart from the rationalization said to be characteristic of the modern West' (1987: 144).[11] By understanding modernity as that 'era in which several lines of rationalization have met' (Roth 1987: 88), Weber puts the idea of rupture, and a distinctive modernity, at the heart of sociological analysis. In common with

Weber

the other writers discussed here, the history of the West is seen as a precursor of the history of the non-West. Weber further believed that the distinctiveness of the West could only be understood in relation to other historically specific civilizations, be they in the past, or geographically elsewhere. His analysis of the great world religions, including the charting of a transition from the unified world view offered by religion to its dissolution in modern secularized culture, is an attempt to assess the perceived distinctiveness of Western modernity by means of systematic comparison (Whimster and Lash 1987). Indeed, just because his historical and sociological method rested on comparison, it required 'a terminology and typology that would be applicable to all these different civilizations over two and a half millennia' (Roth 1987: 87). Weber's primary concern was with establishing the nature of the 'specific and peculiar rationalism' that characterized the modern West and explaining the absence of those characteristics in other civilizations. In determining absences, however, it is necessary to posit something as the norm from which the other deviates.

I shall discuss these arguments, and their limitations, in more detail in the next chapter as they arise in the context of arguments about the idea of 'multiple modernities' as an alternative to standard accounts of modernization. What should be clear is that, in the attempt to understand contemporary circumstances, two underlying assumptions come to be deeply embedded within sociology. The first is that they should be understood as transitional circumstances, occurring in Bendix's words in terms of 'declining tradition and rising modernity' (1967: 308) and the second is, 'that social change consists of a process that is internal to the society changing' (1967: 308). In the remainder of this chapter, I shall show how these assumptions also create a 'critical ambivalence' within sociology which is frequently associated with the critique of 'modernist' ideas in sociology, but which remains intrinsically tied to them.

VI

Nisbet's (1966) understanding of sociology emerging as a response to the problem of order created by the conditions of modernity – as exemplified by the twin revolutions of industrialism and revolutionary democracy – has been generally accepted within the discipline. At the same time as setting out the themes of sociology – community, authority, status, the sacred, and alienation – Nisbet also highlighted the paradox at the heart of its project, namely, 'that although it falls, in its objectives and in the political and scientific values of its principal figures, in the mainstream of modernism, its essential concepts and its implicit perspectives place it much closer, generally speaking, to philosophical conservatism' (1966: 17). This is because sociology was conceived of as a project attempting to understand 'modern' society in the context of perceiving it also to be the displacement of a 'lost' community – thus, in its very conceptualization, sociology set up understanding modern society not on its own terms, but as the loss of something other, something authentic. While purporting to look ahead, then, sociology's gaze was always also oriented towards the past, seeking to recapture that moment of authenticity before 'it all went wrong'.

Gouldner (1973) develops this distinction in his essay 'Romanticism and Classicism: Deep Structures in Social Science' where he argues that both Romantic and Classical syndromes underlie theories of sociology, and the social sciences in general. He suggests that where the Classical aspect 'stresses the *universality* of the governing standards', the Romantic tendency emphasizes 'the relativity, the uniqueness, or historical character' of them (1973: 359). In this way, sociology, while seeking to understand the events and changes brought about by modernity – and to do so in the name of modernity – has also always mediated its understanding of them through a moral evaluation based on an acceptance of the existence of a diversity of evaluative criteria represented by other cultures (Nisbet 1966; Gouldner 1973). All attempts to conceptualize the modern era could, then, also be understood as *critiques* of it.[12]

Instead of questioning the initial parameters of the debate, romanticism simply displaces this sense of 'lost' community onto the project of sociology and modernist thought itself – not realizing that it is in the positing of a 'loss' that the problems it seeks to resolve themselves reside. What modernist and anti-modernist understandings fail to consider is the idea that the very definition of the conditions of modernity only emerged with the establishment of sociology as a discipline. While histories of sociology unquestioningly delineate its formation 'in the nineteenth century struggle to understand the combined upheavals of the great political revolutions and the industrial revolution', they rarely consider the impact of the East–West construct in this endeavour (Calhoun 1996: 70).[13] As Calhoun argues, the propensity of European thinkers to approach 'human diversity with a vision of differences among types, not [as] a ubiquity of cross-cutting differentiations' (1996: 71) is part of the problem. The extent to which 'otherness' was seen by sociologists 'as a problem of the universality of interpretation across lines of difference', feeds directly into the construction of sociology as a project 'formed in the challenge of *confronting* difference' (Calhoun 1996: 74, 84; my emphasis). The apparent solution is to render that difference to 'tradition' and, therefore, to create the space for its 'deeper' values to be an implicit critique of the inauthenticity of modernity.

The 'problem' of difference, for many, has become accentuated with the 'speeding up' of modernity and the pace of globalization bringing different cultures into 'contact'. This has led some to argue that whereas social theory had presupposed the unity and coherence of the social, today the social is increasingly seen as in crisis, if not at an end (Delanty 1999). It is further suggested that the fundamental socio-historic changes which have brought into being a postmodern world now require the development of new theories and concepts to illuminate those changes (Best and Kellner 1991: 30). While the modernist stance had been to struggle against the diversity of particular traditions and attempt to subject them to conformity and uniformity, scholars of postmodernity, such as Bauman (1987), have argued for the relativity of knowledge as a lasting feature of the world.[14]

The problem with this particular emphasis on difference is that it says little more than that, previously, things were otherwise. If the failure adequately to address issues of 'difference' is one of the fundamental flaws of modernism, it has to be recognized that postmodernism deals with 'difference' simply by purporting to accept its existence as given. While modernism deals with 'difference' by urging 'them' to be more like 'us' (modernization theory), postmodernism, although claiming to deconstruct the (meta)framework, implicitly places 'difference' within the same framework in the belief that 'they' are 'they' and that 'they' should remain as 'them'. It is this that distinguishes postmodern from postcolonial theory despite their mutual antagonism to modernist theory. The former remains part of the reactive, 'romantic' trope of modernism, while postcolonial theory seeks a more thorough deconstruction of the dominant paradigm. Thus, despite attempts to understand the 'slot' of the 'other', albeit reflexively, postmodern-ly, Trouillot argues that there is still little address of 'the thematic field (and thus the larger world) that made (makes) this slot possible, morosely preserving the empty slot itself' (2003: 28). Although he accepts that postmodernism did identify the failure of grand narratives, Trouillot suggests that

> to the extent that it refuses to acknowledge that its own nostalgic mood and negative affect takes for granted the narratives that it mourns, postmodernism itself can be read as one of the latest ruses of a modernity entrapped in its own production. (2003: 70)

In refusing to confront the primacy ascribed to the West's 'geography of imagination', where the 'other' is recognized but is generally recognized as irreconcilably and incommensurably 'other', Trouillot (2003) asserts that postmodernism is an inadequate solution. Further, in accepting the category of the 'other', postmodernism makes 'difference' a primary criterion of comparison and commits itself to the dichotomy between 'us' and 'them' that fails to recognize the heterogeneity of cross-cutting social spheres and social identities.[15] The universal frame of reference for locating 'difference' remains the same and encountering 'difference' makes no difference to what was initially thought. At the same time, the 'other' is excluded from participation in the construction of a world in common by being rendered part of a past in the process of being overcome by mechanisms of modernity initiated independently of that participation.

How this antinomy between modernist and postmodernist thought (together with associated distinctions between the Classical and Romantic, the modern and the traditional, the West and its others, and so forth) operates across a range of debates in sociological theory, its historical development, and its examples will occupy much of the rest of this book. I shall be pointing towards the resolution of problems of understanding and explanation that I identify throughout these treatments before returning to an explicit address of these antinomies and the proposal of an alternative in the conclusion.

3
From Modernization to Multiple Modernities: Eurocentrism *Redux*

[handwritten: unfinished project, observation of the future]

This chapter continues my treatment of the relationship between the idea of modernity and the form of sociological argument, a relationship that arises with the very emergence of sociology as I argued in the previous chapter. With the development of this paradigmatic concern with modernity, the future was no longer seen as being about the reproduction of the present, but was considered to be a space for the further development of projects and trends (Burke 1992). These trends and projects were to be the trends and projects of modernity itself where modernity could also be understood, in Habermas's (1996) words, as an *unfinished project* – one that was not yet realized, but could be used as a normative framework to address global processes. The 'unfinished project' in general terms, however, is the bringing to fruition of what is already predicated in the Western experience. Ideas of evolution and progress are central to the concern with the future and, for most writers, as I have argued, the history of the West is seen as a precursor of the future of the non-West. In this chapter, I will address theories of modernization and the recent idea of multiple modernities, which is argued by its proponents to escape the Eurocentrism that is finally allowed to be a characteristic of modernization theory.

The professionalization of sociology in the post Second World War period coincided both with the dominance of structural–functional modernization theory and a world environment characterized by movements of decolonization and independence. The cold war competition for influence in the third world between capitalist and communist political systems and the associated emergence of a strong non-aligned movement meant that, at least in the immediate post-war period, sociologists were attuned to developments outside of Europe and North America. If, as argued in earlier chapters, colonialism had not had an impact on the development of sociological understandings and analytical categories, as I shall be arguing in this chapter, movements for liberation and decolonization did. In this period, academics who had previously been concerned with interrogating their own past in the West began to turn their scholarly focus to the present conditions of what was seen as the 'underdeveloped' world (Portes 1973: 248). The nature of the relationship between developed and lesser developed countries became one of the primary questions to emerge within sociological research and the problem was largely posed in terms of whether these countries would evolve in a common direction.

Following in the classical tradition of sociology, modernization theory took as its idea of change the standard notion of a linear movement from a traditional past to a modernized future. As discussed previously, explanations of the processes of modernization were primarily located in the context of a historical understanding of societies where each form was deemed to be superseded by a progressively higher one. Traditional, or pre-modern, societies were put forward as objects of comparison with societies already deemed to be modern and the problem was set up in terms of accounting for the historical transition from one to the other. The debate on convergence around modern institutions and the economy, however, also occurred in the context of counterclaims arguing for *divergence* around issues of culture and political organization. This was, after all, the period of the Cold War and the heyday of decolonization. Re-defining the modern and, increasingly, *contesting the modern*, became an integral aspect of determining the nature of the relationship between the developed and less developed worlds.

Decolonization in the 1960s was followed by the fall of communism in Europe in the late 1980s and 1990s. The perceived seismic shift in the global order – in particular, globalization being seen as the creation of a world market after the break up of the Soviet dominated economic bloc – renewed sociological debates about the nature of the modern world leading to the development of a new paradigm, that of multiple modernities. While for some, such as Fukuyama (1992), these events confirmed the convergence claims of modernization theory and the role of the United States as 'lead society'; for theorists of multiple modernities, the removal of 'cold war' constraints instead allowed for greater divergence. The increasingly vocal claims of scholars from the Third World – be they theorists of underdevelopment or then postcolonial theorists – also required engagement and address (see Escobar 1995; Sylvester 1999; Biccum 2002).

Theorists of multiple modernities situate themselves critically in relation to the earlier debates on modernization, contesting the assumptions of linearity and convergence they associate with this earlier approach, and ostensibly taking into account cultural diversity in the expression of modern institutions. In developing this approach to the question of modernity, and its global instantiations, theorists of multiple modernities believe that two fallacies are to be avoided. The first, associated with earlier modernization theories, is that there is only one modernity. The second is that of Eurocentrism, or: 'that looking from the West to the East legitimates the concept of "Orientalism"' (Eisenstadt and Schluchter 1998: 2). Here the argument is that, while the idea of one modernity, especially one that has already been achieved in Europe, would be Eurocentric, theories of multiple modernities must, nonetheless, take Europe as the reference point in their examination of alternative modernities (Eisenstadt and Schluchter 1998: 2). Thus, while theorists of multiple modernities such as Eisenstadt and Schluchter point to the problem of Eurocentrism, they do so at the same time as asserting the necessary priority to be given to the West in the construction of a comparative sociology of multiple modernities.

In this chapter, I take issue with their claim that this can avoid a charge of Eurocentrism as well as the view that multiple modernities offers a paradigm shift from earlier work on modernization. In each position, I shall argue, globalization is understood in terms of the world *becoming* global through the process of *incorporating* other parts of the world into a system whose defining features drive expansion forward, but are essentially *defined independently of interconnections that are argued to come in the wake of globalization*. In this way, modernity is frequently identified as a feature of the West that is exported and has an impact on other societies, which then incorporate the institutional forms while adapting them within local conditions and cultures. It is this way of thinking about modernity that I will be challenging in this chapter.

As will be shown, part of the problem with both modernization theory and theories of multiple modernities is their reliance on ideal types as the means of conducting comparative analysis. Ideal types, I shall argue, reify particular interactions and interconnections, abstracting them from the wider interconnections in which they are also embedded. A way out of this bind is the use of 'connected histories' as discussed in Chapter 1. Where the problem with the concept of modernity has been defined in terms of its failure to address the experiences of peoples and societies outside of Europe and the West, this failure can only be remedied by taking them into account *and* by rethinking the previous structures of knowledge which are bound up with their omission.

I

Parsons (1966, 1971), as I argued in the previous chapter, was particularly interested in understanding the implications of the transition to modernity and looking at why the breakthrough to modernization had not occurred elsewhere than in Europe. In common with most other theorists at the time, he believed that modern society had emerged in the West, and that this provided the base from which the *system* of modern societies then developed (Parsons 1971). Modernization scholars such as Rostow (1960) and Lerner (1958) also believed that Western modernization should be used as a model of global applicability and other societies classified in terms of their relative modernization in comparison with this model; that is, other societies were to be studied in terms of the extent to which they approximated the characteristics of Western industrial societies.[1] Almond and Coleman (1960), for example, in their classic study addressing the political systems of developing countries, sought to understand the phenomena of non-Western political systems in comparison to Western ones. They co-ordinated their studies around a common set of categories derived from the Western experience and used these to establish the comparative framework within which the developing countries could be ordered.[2] It should be noted that while becoming modern in the first instance might derive from peculiar circumstances, which were historically contingent and even perhaps unlikely (e.g., as set out by Weber in his study of the Protestant Ethic), once Europe had become modern it was deemed to be able to show the way to the rest of the world as a model to be imitated. The birth of modernity, it was believed, could be induced.

The two general categories on which modernization theory differentiated between the modern and the non-modern were 'changes in individual subjective orientations and changes in the structure of social [and economic] relationships' (Portes 1973: 249). Research around the former focused on determining the extent to which there was an empirically identifiable modern 'man' and what the characteristics of such an individual would be. This occurred in conjunction with seeking to determine the influences that would make 'men' modern. Such research took the form of investigating 'the impact on the individual of his [sic] participation in the process of modernization' (Inkeles 1969: 208) and the value of possessing such modern traits for social and economic growth more generally. Early theorists of modernity, then, were primarily interested in determining what 'modern man' was like and what the practical implications of being modern might entail in terms of the advancement of non-, or under-, developed countries.[3] In this way, modernity was understood both as a psychosocial syndrome as well as being recognized as a process of national development. At a higher level of abstraction, Portes (1973) argued that psychosocial modernity could be identified with the set of action-orientations defined by Parsons's pattern variables which allowed the specification both of motivational complexes (e.g., achievement versus ascription) and the associated norms and role definitions embodied in institutions (e.g., universalism versus particularism).

The emphasis on institutional regularities was the second dimension through which scholars distinguished modern from traditional societies. It was believed that the patterns – or structures – of modernization had a universal tendency to extend into all social contexts and to institute major changes in social and political structures (Levy 1965). These changes included the emergence and development of the market economy, industrial society, the nation-state, and bureaucratic rationality – modern forms of organization that were seen as impersonal, interdependent, specialized, and formal (Moore 1963: 522). As Portes (1973) argues, modernization was a synthetic term covering a series of societal processes that were seen to converge into a stable whole, that is, modern society. These processes, which were often taken as the principal indices along which countries were measured and then ranked in studies of modernization, included, urbanization and ecological relocation, literacy, social mobility, democratic participation, mass media production and consumption, education, and industrialization and a factory system of production (Lerner 1958; Feldman and Moore 1962; Portes 1973).

Bendix usefully summarizes modernization theory as resting on three related assumptions: first, an understanding of 'tradition' and 'modernity' as mutually exclusive; second, social change occurring as a consequence of phenomena internal to the society changing; and third, a belief that modernity would eventually replace tradition and, in doing so, would have the same effects across the globe (1967: 324–5). In this sense, modernization theory rests on a notion of *convergence* whereby the difference of other societies – as constituted through their traditions – would be erased through the process of the global diffusion of Western institutions. Once the structures of modernization extended to other areas, it was believed that the previous indigenous patterns, or structures, would change and that change would be in the direction of the relatively modernized societies (Levy 1965: 30). Even where theorists of modernization recognized

convergence

the diversity of origins and the 'disequilibrating' processes of industrialization, they still maintained faith 'in a society's historical trajectory towards industrialism' and the common destination of modernization (Feldman and Moore 1962: 167). Parsons's (1964) theory of 'evolutionary universals' similarly outlined the belief that processes of development in the world would be in the direction of greater comparability with Western social systems and their differentiated sub-systems of polity, economy, 'societal community' or civil society, and the 'pattern-maintenance' sub-system of cultural reproduction.

The principle assumptions of modernization theory, then, relate to it being understood as a total social process constituting a universal, and universalizing, pattern. While modernity in its first instance is seen to emerge primarily as a consequence of the internal dynamics of Western societies, modern traits in other parts of the world, Portes suggests, did not 'arise naturally from internal processes of structural change, but artificially from the impact of Western cultural diffusion' (1973: 271), and, therefore, may be resisted. The processes of modernization, then, were taken to be 'the impingement of Western European institutions on new countries in the Americas, in Eastern and Southern Europe, and in Asia and Africa' (Eisenstadt 1968: 256). As a consequence, much analysis of modernization processes rests on an implicit (and often explicit) assumption that 'the highest of modern institutions must inevitably be those that have been devised in the West' (Mazrui 1968: 72), and thus, evolution towards modernity was to be evolution towards Western ways. This evolutionary framework of modernization theory was underpinned by the belief that what had happened in Europe amounted to nothing less than 'the crossing of a threshold between two distinct stages in the history of mankind ... [and] that, though Europe was first ... it is only a matter of time before the less advanced areas also find themselves at the crossing point' (Portes 1973: 248–9).[4] Even where major theorists of modernization – such as Kerr *et al.* (1960), Feldman and Moore (1962) and Apter (1965) – admitted the possibility of different routes to modernity there was nevertheless believed to be only one destination. Any *deviation* from the point to be arrived at was regarded as *deviant* with Rostow (1960), for example, arguing that communism was an outcome of a 'disease of transition'.

II

Although current, critical commentaries on modernization theory tend to represent the earlier position as both dominant and uniform, the distinction between tradition and modernity that formed the basis of much modernization theory was, however, a key point of contestation. Critics at the time believed that using notions of a stagnant past, where the differences among societies were not regarded as relevant to the issue of modernization, and a dynamic heterogeneous present, both distorted the character of traditional societies and obscured understandings of 'the manifold variations in the relation between traditional forms and new institutions' (Gusfield 1967: 351). The presumption of a singular problematic of traditional societies, then, was strongly challenged, with scholars suggesting that traditional orientations varied significantly, both in terms of their general organization as well as in their receptivity to change and in providing legitimizing principles for social transformation (see Apter 1965; Gusfield 1967; Portes 1973). By looking at tradition simply as an *obstacle* to such transformation, one missed the fact that 'certain traditional values form[ed] important ingredients *for* structural change' (Portes 1973: 264). Further, Gusfield argued that what were regarded as traditional societies had actually been open to change, and had instituted purposeful, planned change, long before their present encounters with the West (1967: 353). The idea of a stagnant past (or a stagnant traditional present), then, was called into question by many scholars, particularly from within the discipline of anthropology, but also by dissident voices from within sociology and development studies.

As well as contesting assumptions of traditional societies, many scholars were also concerned to repudiate the notion that modernity would replace tradition in a homogenous way across the globe. With regard to the latter, scholars such as Gusfield argued for the outcome of modernizing processes to be understood as being constituted by 'an admixture [of tradition and modernity] in which each derives a degree of support from the other, rather than [being seen as] a clash of opposites' (1967: 355). This established not only the importance of understanding that different traditional orientations had a different relationship to modernizing processes, but also that this initial difference would then lead to a difference in outcomes. Eisenstadt, for his part, argued that while accepting a certain universality to modernity and modernizing processes it had to be recognized that 'different societies necessarily develop different institutional patterns' (1968: 257). Even within western and central European countries, he suggests, 'the course of modernization was neither entirely continuous nor everywhere the same' (1968: 274). Moore, similarly, stated that the challenge to conventional models of modernization arose from a recognition that 'the destination of modernization is neither uniform nor stable and [that] ... the trajectory of transformation differs in space and time' (1963: 524). This was confirmed through increasing empirical research on contemporary societies which highlighted the wide variety of outcomes of modernization processes leading to a situation in which what was regarded as important was to determine and examine the forces that brought forth the set of orientations typical of modernity in different cultural contexts (see Eisenstadt 1965; Gusfield 1967; Portes 1973).

Scholars critical of dominant sociological explanations of social change were also concerned with the value asymmetry inherent in modernization theory whereby the end stage of modernization was deemed to be preferable to its initial stages (Portes 1973: 251). This value asymmetry was reinforced by the practice of treating developing countries as infant or deviant examples of the West, to be studied in terms of the extent to which they approximated Western experiences (Nettl 1967). In this way, Portes suggests, modernization theory represented 'a more or less subtle return to the Western ethnocentrism characterizing early descriptions of social evolution' (1973: 251). The question of Eurocentrism, or ethnocentrism as it was known then, becomes central, Bernstein argues, 'when it is asked from which historical source the paradigm of modernization is abstracted and universalized' (1971: 147). The methodological problems associated with this will be followed up later in the chapter in the section on ideal types and the comparative method. For now, it is sufficient to note that many scholars at the time were critical of the abstract nature of modernization theory and called for a specific and contextual study of change informed by empirical research on the societies being studied. Scholars such as Moore (1963) and Bendix (1967), in particular, 'advocated alternative strategies of theory-formation and research based on a conceptually more flexible and empirically more sensitive comparative method' (Bernstein 1971: 150).[5]

After its dominance in the 1960s and early 1970s, modernization theory within studies of development was gradually replaced by dependency theory and world-systems theory which contested the linearity of its early explanatory models and argued for more complex understandings of global economic systems (see Cooper and Packard 1997).[6] More importantly, the demise of modernization theory was also related to the explicit move away from structural functional explanations in sociology. The latter was associated with the rise of more radical approaches, particularly those influenced by Marxism, and the related decline of Parsons. The fall of communism in Europe in the 1990s, however, reversed these sensibilities. For a number of commentators, the convergence thesis which had been discarded had turned out to be confirmed, with Fukuyama (1992) most famously proclaiming a new 'end of history'. This is the context in which some writers, most notably Shmuel Eisenstadt, have returned to modernization theory seeking to challenge this triumphant liberalism, while also acknowledging the force of events (see also Tiryakian 1991). At the same time, the processes of decolonization, which had been the initial context for modernization theory, had themselves given rise to post-colonial critiques of the Eurocentrism of dominant understandings of modernity. The new paradigm of multiple modernities, then, was articulated in relation to these varying concerns.

As I shall demonstrate in the following section, the paradigm of multiple modernities does not go very far in transforming the previous debate over modernization. One reason why this is so is that the theorists of multiple modernities use a rather crude version of the modernization thesis, as set out by Kerr, Rostow, and Lerner among others, without adequately acknowledging the considerable modifications that had been introduced by its critics at the time. This is evidenced in the work of Shmuel Eisenstadt who was involved in the modernization theory debates in the 1960s and whose work has been integral to the identification of the new paradigm of multiple modernities more recently. From his early writings on social systems and modernization theory to more recent work on civilizations and modernity, Eisenstadt (1965, 1987, 1998, 2001) has been concerned with identifying the form of modernity uniquely associated with the West and then examining the cultural dynamics of other civilizations in comparison to it. His early criticisms of modernization theory were primarily directed at those theorists like Kerr *et al* (1960) and Almond and Coleman (1960) who sought to evaluate the extent to which other societies approximated the model of Western industrial society. In repudiating the claim that the kernels of modernity were to be found in most cultures and societies, Eisenstadt contested the 'convergence' thesis central to much modernization theory that the development of modernity constituted the apogee of the evolutionary potential of humanity. Instead, he sought to reclaim the *specificity* of cultures that he believed was being denied by the premises of modernization theory; in particular, the specificity of European civilization and European modernity (1987: 3). His argument, following Parsons, was that modernity, as it had emerged in the context of Western Europe, had 'largely developed from within, "indigenously", through the fruition of the inherent potential of some of its groups and through the continuous interaction between them' (1987: 8) and that this potential was not to be found globally.

III

As I have argued, over the last decade, theorists have begun to move from a conceptual language of *modernization* to that of *multiple modernities* with this shift reflecting an unease with the idea of a singular, uniform trajectory applied to the current diversity of contemporary societies within the global world. Eisenstadt and Schluchter (1998) suggest that, with the hegemonic and homogenizing tendencies attributed to the project of modernization not having borne out convergence, not even in the West itself, so the idea of linear historical progress associated with modernization should give way to pluralized understandings of multiple modernities. Similarly, Delanty (1999) has argued that the historical model of transition from traditional society to modern society is no longer viable and social theory ought, instead, to focus on the dissolution of the modern from a single pattern into various trajectories.

In developing the multiple modernities paradigm, and in guarding against the fallacies mentioned earlier, Eisenstadt and Schluchter suggest that the global expansion of modernity ought not to be viewed 'as a process of repetition, but as the crystallization of new civilizations'; albeit, new civilizations that take as their reference point, 'the original Western crystallization of modernity' (1998: 2, 3). This reference point is not believed to be a singular uniform trajectory around which there is convergence, as in modernization theory, but one from which others are understood to deviate or diverge. Thus, the reference point establishes a multiplicity of modernities and this multiplicity, in their view, is sufficient to avoid the other fallacy of Eurocentrism (or Orientalism, as they put it). I would argue, however, that to the extent that these multiple modernities continue to be understood as derived from the creative appropriation, by those that followed, of the institutional frameworks of modernity that are seen to originate in Europe, the problem of Eurocentrism remains integral to the new paradigm.

The literature on multiple modernities, in a similar fashion to that of modernization theory more generally, identifies modernity with 'the momentous transformations of Western societies during the processes of industrialization, urbanization, and political change in the late eighteenth and early nineteenth centuries' (Wittrock 1998: 19). As such, modernity is understood simultaneously in terms of its *institutional constellations*, that is, its tendency 'towards universal structural, institutional, and cultural frameworks' (Eisenstadt and Schluchter 1998: 3), as well as a *cultural programme* 'beset by internal antinomies and contradictions, giving rise to continual critical discourse and political contestations' (Eisenstadt 2000: 7). Understanding modernity in this way allows scholars to situate European modernity – seen in terms of a primary combination of the institutional and the cultural forms – as the originary modernity and, at the same time, allows for different cultural encodings that result in *multiple* modernities. The idea of multiple modernities, then, is consistent with the idea of a common framework of modern institutions – for example, the market economy, the modern nation-state, and bureaucratic rationality – which originated in Europe and was subsequently exported to the rest of the world.[7] This explains the apparent paradox that Eisenstadt and Schluchter can dissociate themselves from Eurocentrism at the same time as apparently embracing its core assumptions, namely, 'the Enlightenment assumptions of the centrality of a Eurocentred type of modernity' (1998: 5).

The focus on different non-European civilizational trajectories is based on the assumption that, even if these trajectories did not lead to an originary modernity as in Europe, they did, nevertheless, lead to complexity in institutional patterns and cultural codes. As Wittrock (1998) argues, repeating the earlier internal critique of modernization theory, these societies were not stagnant, traditional societies, but were developing and transforming their own institutional and cultural contexts prior to the advent of Western modernity. However, it was not until the institutional patterns associated with Western modernity were exported to these other societies that multiple modernities emerged within them. Thus, it is believed to be the conjunction between the institutional patterns of the Western civilizational complex with the different cultural codes of other societies that creates various distinct modernities. Theorists of multiple modernities, then, address modernity in terms of two aspects, its institutional framework and its cultural codes. This separation of the institutional and the cultural allows the former to be understood as that which is common to the different varieties of modernity – and thus allows all types of modernity to be understood as such – while the latter, being the location of crucial antinomies, provides the basis for variability, and thus the divergence that results in *multiple* modernities.

Eisenstadt argues that central to the cultural programme of modernity, as it originated in Europe, 'was an emphasis on the autonomy of man', on emancipation from traditional forms of authority, and a focus on 'reflexivity and exploration', and the 'active construction and mastery of nature, including human nature' (1998: 5). The conjunctions of these developments, he continues, highlighted the openness of the modern political arena and the possibility of contestation within it, with the fundamental tension existing 'between an emphasis on human autonomy and the restrictive controls inherent in the institutional realization of modern life' (2000: 6); that is, a continual tension between a move towards totality on the one hand as contrasted with more pluralistic tendencies on the other. The internal antinomies and contradictions of modernity are thus focused on the relations and tensions between the premises of modernity and 'between these premises and the institutional developments in modern societies' (Eisenstadt 2001: 325). These antinomies are understood to lead to political contestations around issues such as the relations between state and society and the patterns of collective identity resulting in the variations of modernity that are seen subsequently to come into being.

Eisenstadt argues that the first radical transformation of 'modernity', of European cultural premises, takes place 'with the expansion of modernity in the Americas' (2000: 13). In fact, it is the first instance of a *multiple* modernity! Other distinct alternative models of modernity are the communist Soviet types and the fascist, national-socialist types.[8] Even within Europe, then, there was no *one* modernity, but, rather, as Wittrock argues, 'an empirically undeniable and easily observable *variety* of institutional and cultural forms' (2000: 58, my emphasis; see also Therborn 1995). These differences, these multiple modernities, are thus seen to have developed first in Europe and to have continued with modernity's expansion into the Americas, Asia, and Africa. Not only modernity, then, but multiple modernities, too, have their origin in Europe or, following Eisenstadt (2000), in the Western civilizational framework at large. Indeed, he believes it to be significant that multiple modernities developed first, not in Asia 'or in Muslim societies where they might have been attributed to the existence of distinct non-European traditions, but within the broad framework of Western civilizations' (2000: 13). Multiple modernities are, thus, seen to emerge from the encounters 'between Western modernity and the cultural traditions and historical experiences' of other societies: a conjunction whose first occurrence was in Europe itself (Eisenstadt 2000: 23). This avowedly non-Eurocentric point of view of the West now establishes the West as both the *origin of modernity* and as the *origin of multiple modernities*.[9]

IV

What, then, is the contribution of non-European civilizations within this new approach? Among the different multiple modernities originating in the West, as discussed above, are those associated with totalitarian forms – communism (in a line stretching back to Jacobinism) and fascism, with both connecting to forms of ethnic nationalism. Despite their other differences, Eisenstadt (2000, 2001) suggests that communist and fundamentalist movements share, at the very least, a preoccupation with modernity and an engagement with its central ideological problem, that of pluralism versus non-pluralism. These tendencies are seen as movements away from the fragile master Enlightenment code of modernity understood in terms of the autonomy of man and mastery over nature. As such, the space given to codes that develop in other civilizations is in contrast, or even opposition, to the precepts of autonomy, freedom, pluralism, and participation associated with the central form of European modernity. The emergence within multiple modernities of fundamentalist and communal religious tropes, often ostensibly in opposition to modernity and, particularly, European modernity, are thus seen to 'evince distinct characteristics of modern Jacobinism ... and share with communist movements the promulgation of totalistic visions' (Eisenstadt 2000: 19).

The only space given to the codes of other civilizations, then, is to be aligned with the deeply problematic codes of totalitarian modernity, that is, communism and fascism and while the Enlightenment master code is associated with the forms of colonial subjugation alongside which it emerged, these forms of subjugation have no part in the discussion of European modernity. In line with their Weberian heritage, theorists of multiple modernities present an implicitly pessimistic view of the possibilities confronting global societies where totalitarian forms are simply to be regarded as among the multiple forms that modernity brings into being (see Arnason 2000, 2003). This is in contrast to the earlier 'optimistic' view of modernization theory which regarded totalitarian forms as abnormal or aberrant versions of modernity. Therborn, for example, notes that even though modernization theory ignored the effects of colonial and imperial history it nonetheless 'struck a more optimistic liberal note of programmatic change' (2003: 297), one that is missing in the more recent incarnation of multiple modernities.

What is also clear from this discussion is that analyses within the multiple modernities paradigm provide no reason for being optimistic about what might be *learnt* from other civilizations, or how that learning could make a positive difference. These other modernities are seen simply to proliferate and all that is of interest is the extent to which these later versions approximate, or not, to the 'original European' version (to understand multiple modernities in terms of their divergence *from* is implicitly to make an approximation *to*). This valorization of multiplicity, or then difference for its own sake, is closer to the postmodern radicalism of the 'alternative' modernities discussed by Gaonkar (2001a) and others than the proponents of the multiple modernities paradigm might otherwise feel comfortable with. As such, it can be seen as part of the classic–romantic cycle of theorizing about modernity discussed towards the end of the previous chapter.

That this cycle is taking yet another turn can be seen from the incipient popularity of the concepts of 'liquid modernity' and 'reflexive modernization'. Multiple modernities, in this version, are now seen 'to represent non-Western/ Third World expressions of postcolonial social growth' which, according to Lee, 'do not necessarily identify with the reconstructive programme of reflexive modernization or the image of fluidity in liquid modernity, *both of which are associated with developments in the West*' (2006: 366; my emphasis). The rest of the world is simply to be examined in terms of the 'fit' it provides with these particular concepts of modernity – as Lee concludes his article, 'empirical research would give us a chance to assess their applicability [the applicability of the predetermined concepts] in different parts of the world' (2006: 367) – there is no awareness that the rest of the world might provide the basis of generating adequate concepts for thinking about the world.[10]

While theorists such as Wittrock (1998, 2000) and Arnason (2003) point to the importance of interconnections, global conjunctions, and connected and entangled histories in understanding the development of modernity, rarely do they incorporate what is *learnt* from a reading of these histories into their conceptual analyses. Wittrock, for example, argues that during the 'long period of early modern societies in Eurasia, there was a constant flow of cultural, political, and commercial contacts and interactions between different civilizations' (1998: 38). However, nowhere in the rest of his article does he develop this point, but rather, repeatedly iterates the *differences* between early modern societies and their *separate* trajectories, not the consequences of their interconnections. When Wittrock does discuss interconnections in more depth these interconnections are related to processes that are all located *within* Europe (1998: 23, 2000: 40). Explicitly following a Weberian tradition, he suggests that it is possible to see 'the formation of modernity in Europe as the result of a series of basically continuous processes where political, economic, and intellectual transformations mutually reinforced and conditioned each other' (Wittrock 2000: 40). Further, only the trajectory of early modern European society is regarded as being able to develop to modernity without interaction with other societies. All other societies are believed to have 'gained' their modernity only after the impact of, what Wittrock calls, the momentous transformations within Western societies. There is no substantive discussion or engagement with the question of how the multiplicity of early societies may have shaped the development of modernity.

In discussing the importance of widening the perspective 'to include the experiences of civilizations outside of Europe' (Wittrock 1998: 27), then, it is clear that what is meant is to lay the experiences of the civilizations outside of Europe in parallel to Europe, not to discuss the connections between them. Indeed, as Wittrock goes on to argue, these other experiences are 'comparable to, yet radically different from, those of Europe' (1998: 28). Arnason similarly draws attention to the '*parallel* (even if more partial) developments in other regions' which he suggests can be acknowledged while still making 'due allowance for distinctive versions of patterns first invented, but not unilaterally imposed by the West' (2000: 63; my emphasis). Where the commonplace meaning of parallel implies no relation, interconnection, or influence it is clear that Arnason follows Wittrock in asserting the importance of developments in 'other' places without taking their importance into account in the conceptual schemes that are then developed except insofar as they are seen to constitute variations of the 'original' European ideal type. Developments *outside of Europe* are seen as emerging, developing, and existing in isolation to developments *in Europe* – the only point of connection that is allowed is subsequent to Europe achieving modernity and is the unidirectional impact of Europe upon other societies.

The recognition of 'difference', as argued earlier, is an important corrective to dominant universalizing tendencies within social science. However, simply recognizing difference is not sufficient. 'Difference' also has to *make a difference* to the assumptions that informed the initial enquiry; in this case, the endogenous origins and initial development of modernity in Europe. The trail laid by Weber in seeking to determine the causes of the 'Rise of West' and 'the European miracle' has been followed by subsequent theorists attempting to account for the miracle *in* Europe, that is, the presumed initial emergence of modernity there (see the special issues of *Daedalus* 1998, 2000). While the explicit interpretive bias linking the emergence of the miracle/modernity in Europe to an innate sense of superiority may be rejected by contemporary theorists, the specialness of the West as a 'factual' matter – that is, as something that happened that needs explanation – remains firmly in place (see McLennan 2000, 2006). Further, insofar as the civilization of modernity is seen to entail the modernity of civilizations, and however differently other civilizations may then express 'their' modernity, there is a clear understanding of Western modernity as the original form and a form that achieved expression *without relation to others*.

Similarities or affinities between cultures are determined on the basis of whether other cultures are similar, or then different, to those of the West. The image is very much of a bicycle wheel with Europe at the centre and other cultures represented as the spokes on the wheel – all with a relation to Europe and no consideration of the relationships other places may have had with each other. Taking the analogy further, each spoke (culture) is also assumed to have an integrity of its own and to have existed independent of each other until, that is, European modernity diffused out from the centre changing cultures on its way. The difficulty with this model is twofold. First, in setting up the problem in terms of a comparison with Europe the modernity of other situations is not recognized. Second, assumptions of cultural integrity and internal dynamics both homogenize traditions and cultures as well as efface interconnections (see Yu 2006).

The challenge posed to modernization theory by the approach of multiple modernities, then, may have some significance in its own terms, but it is much less fundamental than its advocates suppose. Particularly welcome is its deconstruction of the simple dichotomy, favoured by some modernization theorists, between the traditional and the modern, where the former has generally been understood in terms of stagnation and backwardness and the latter as dynamic and progressive. With their parallel focus on developments in other parts of the world and an acknowledgement of existing cultural dynamics within those societies, theorists of multiple modernities provide a necessary corrective to analyses based on ideas of a stagnant, stultifying East which only awoke from its slumber *after* encounters with the West. It must be acknowledged, however, that such a critique was also present at the time that modernization theory was hegemonic, as discussed earlier in the chapter, and so it is not entirely novel. The basic premise of multiple modernities theorists, of questioning the dominant assumption of convergence and its corollary idea of one trajectory to modernity, is also an important qualification to modernization theory. What is significant in its omission, however, is the failure to address adequately the way in which the West remains the point of reference.

With the multiple modernities approach predicated on the idea that accounting for the internal dynamics of other cultures is sufficient to overcome the charge of Eurocentrism and the belief that maintaining the gaze from the West to the East is a necessary aspect of the comparative method, it is necessary to examine the methodology of comparison and its associated counterpart, ideal types. In maintaining its focus on the internal dynamics of *separate* civilizations and the inability to take a point of view *other* than from the West, I argue that the comparative approach exacerbates the problem of Eurocentrism by ignoring (and even actively excluding through its use of ideal types) the connected and entangled histories that constitute the basis of an adequate understanding of the global context of socio-historic processes.

V

Theorists of multiple modernities, by accepting the emergence of modernity in Europe as an incontestable, value-neutral proposition, closely follow Weber's thinking, and methodology, on modernity (or modernization) in that they believe that to understand the process of modernity it is first necessary to explore the causes of its emergence in Europe and then to assess other cases in relation to this one. This comparative approach is advanced through a methodology of 'ideal types' where different civilizational trajectories are examined in relation with each other or, more usually, with Europe, or the West. It is argued by theorists of multiple modernities that the advantage of using 'ideal types' over the evolutionary approach associated with modernization theory is that it allows differences to be understood as deviances: 'deviances not from a norm but from an ideal type used only for heuristic purposes' (Eisenstadt and Schluchter 1998: 7). Further, they argue that the ideal type of Western modernity serves as *a common denominator* against which to analyze other civilizations and to ensure that it is possible to say more than simply 'everything is distinct and therefore different' (Eisenstadt and Schluchter 1998: 7). However, it is the very nature of ideal types that the processes they represent are internal and separate from those represented in other ideal types (see Weber 1949; Kalberg 1994). The methodology serves only to reinforce differences between societies and the assumed separateness of their trajectories, rather than facilitating an examination of their interconnections.

In his essay on '"Objectivity" in Social Science' Weber argues for the construction of an 'ideal picture' or 'conceptual pattern' of historical phenomena that would bring 'together certain relationships and events of historical life into a complex, which is conceived as an internally consistent system' (1949: 90). By locating the *generic* concepts that constitute historical analysis it is held that one is then able to construct an 'ideal-type' against which subsequent variations could be compared in a value-neutral way. While Weber accepted that such a model could not 'be found empirically anywhere in reality', and that it abstracts from a more complex reality, he believed that it would be 'indispensable for heuristic as well as expository purposes' in that it provided a useful model against which to assess reality (1949: 90; see also Outhwaite 1983, 1987; Burger 1987). What this understanding fails to acknowledge, however, is that, in its construction, the 'ideal type' refers to the 'real', but is then posited as a conceptual 'truth' that exists abstracted from its particular history and location and is deemed to be applicable as a heuristic in all situations. In using this approach to assess 'other' cultures what is effaced is the cultural situatedness of the construction of the ideal type in the first place.

One of the main problems with accepting such an understanding is highlighted in Weber's argument that, even if someone from another culture – Weber refers to a hypothetical Chinese interlocutor – denies 'the ideal itself and the concrete value-judgements derived from it. Neither of these two latter attitudes can affect the scientific value of the analysis in any way' (1949: 58–9), suggesting that agreement on the conceptual analysis and its consequences is a condition of rational, social scientific debate that can transcend cultural location. As Burger comments, 'the implicit assumption of course, always is that the type has been correctly constructed' (1987: 139). So whereas the ideal type is initially posited as a mental construct drawn from constellations of phenomena of 'empirical reality', when 'empirical reality' contradicts the mental construct it is empirical reality that is seen to be at odds and in need of explanation as 'deviation' accounted for in another, discrete ideal type – as opposed to it necessitating a reconstruction of the mental construct itself (Holmwood and Stewart 1991).

Although I do not wish to reduce historical understandings to the language used to articulate them, it is necessary, nevertheless, to acknowledge the importance of the conceptual categories available without which any attempt at understanding would be inconceivable. As Burger argues, accepting a particular interpretation of 'reality' as objective fact has been seen to require 'intersubjective agreement that a certain content *ought* to be given a particular categorical form' (1987: 65).[11] The questions must be posed, however: 'who is part of the intersubjective agreement?' and 'how does the intersubjective agreement come to be represented as universal?', such that Weber's hypothetical Chinese interlocutor must accept the categories despite not having participated in the intersubjective dialogue that is their foundation. Further, what is to be done when those 'facts' on which there had previously been agreement are now disputed (possibly as a consequence of the engagement with new inter-locutors)? As should be clear, the new interlocutors that I have in mind are those whose experiences have largely been excluded from dominant, Western conceptions of modernity; namely, those subjugated in colonial encounters.[12]

Modernization theory sets up the tradition–modernity divide as an ideal–typical divide located within a general theory of linear, evolutionary development. Western societies are located at the apex of this schema – having believed to have crossed a qualitative threshold into the modern – while other societies are located at various points behind desperately trying to catch up through an imitation of the West. Where the Western experience is taken as the first historical example of the paradigm of modernity this argument rests on 'an "original state" view of underdevelopment and development' where 'what are in fact empirical generalizations or concepts of limited applicability ... have assumed the status of generalizing ideal-types' (Bernstein 1971: 150). In this instance, the ideal types are those of tradition and modernity.[13]

Bernstein objects to the ideal typical dichotomy that is set up between tradition and modernity writing that 'the cluster of traits making up the ideal-type of the traditional ... often simply reflect the ethnocentrism underlying the formulation of modernity' (1971: 146). Differences from any perceived norm are then understood in one of two ways: first, as pathological or deviant (see, e.g., Rostow 1960 on communism); and sec-ond, as transitory (see, e.g., Bendix 1967), or as constituting a 'lag' (or to use Marxist language, as 'uneven development') (Bernstein 1971: 151). Theorists of multiple modernities, in turn, use civilizational ideal types to pluralize the problem of modernization theory's use of the tradition–modernity ideal types and to contest its underpinning of general linear theory without recognizing that what they actually do is pluralize that very linear theory within each ideal type society/civilization they discuss – where each civilization is located in a larger (unacknowledged) framework structured by Europe. While the trajectories of modernity may differ, there is believed to be a point of origin from which the initial trajectory derives, against which all others are then to be measured. This is Europe.

Ideal types, then, abstract from connections where general theory sought to subsume connections in a teleological account which was also Eurocentric. The multiple modernities paradigm is anti-teleological, but de facto Eurocentric where its Eurocentrism is carried into its methodology through the failure to recognize connected histories. Further, any 'abstraction' from more complex empirical circumstances must also imply that the circumstances not included in the type are not themselves significant. When setting out the 'general features' of modernity, then, it is evident that theorists do not include the colonial encounters and Imperial systems associated both with its beginnings and its consolidation and expansion. The continual positing of modernity in ideal-typical form, abstracted from its wider contexts, leads to events that were defining for those subjected to them being regarded simply as 'unfortunate' empirical contingencies to be assigned as problems of transition.[14]

Not regarding events such as the annihilation of peoples (as in Tasmania), dispossession and cultural genocide (as in the Americas, and Australia), enslavement (of Africans) and bonded labour (as in India) as significant in understanding the emergence of modernity, gives credence to Lemert's assertion that 'the West was founded and has endured on the basis of the grand denial of the reality of its own aggression and evil' (1995: 205). This aggression and evil should not, however, be understood in terms of being an essential characteristic of the West, but as a socio-historical aspect in urgent need of consideration. The present situation is one in which such events have been ignored, evaded, suppressed and not even contemplated as a part of the history of the West in the West's self-conceptualization.[15] They require urgent address.

VI

As Dirlik argues, by identifying 'multiplicity' with the cultural aspect, 'the idea of "multiple modernities" seeks to contain challenges to modernity by conceding the possibility of culturally different ways of being modern' (2003: 285). However, it does nothing to address the fundamental problems with the conceptualization of modernity itself. Discussions of modernity being identifiable in other places and peoples continue to locate those others in terms of the general categories already identified, where the other is understood as representing a tradition that has an integrity separate from the traditions of oneself. In this way, the other is left as the other and there is no sense that we might learn from them and reconstruct our categories of understanding as a result of the new knowledge gained (Holmwood and Stewart 1991). Thus, while purporting to offer new ways of understanding the concept of modernity, theories of multiple modernities continue to rest on assumptions of an original modernity of the West which others adapt, domesticate, or tropicalize. *Their experiences make no difference to the pre-existing universals.*

As I have argued, one set of fundamental relationships that is missing from the theorization of modernity is that of colonialism. Bernstein, a seemingly lone voice in the 1970s, argued for a mode of sociological analysis which, by taking the colonial situation into account, would demonstrate how modernization theory could be stood on its head: first, by approaching the study of development by means of a historical method and second, by being informed by questions more relevant to the pressing needs of the present situation (1971: 154). Such a conceptualization, he argued, 'both substantively and as reflecting a different tradition of sociological analysis, stands in direct contrast to that derived from modernization theory which is precluded from identifying the dynamics and contradictions of the colonial situation as *sui generis* by a commitment to analysis in terms of "traditional" and "modern" elements which can only yield a dynamic in the concept of "transition", or movement along a tradition-modernity continuum' (Bernstein 1971: 154). What is required, he continues, is for the nature of the relationships between what are regarded as traditional and modern societies to be examined and theorized. Simply pluralizing the civilizational approach to include the experiences and histories of other civilizations does no more than lay those experiences and histories alongside European ones. In contrast, as Subrahmanyam (1997) argues, what is needed is to understand socio-historic processes in terms of them being global, conjunctural phenomena with different, and connected, sources and roots.

De-linking our understandings of socio-historic processes from a European trajectory and focusing on not only the different sources and roots, but also on the ways these interacted and intersected over time would provide us with a richer understanding of the complexities of the world in which we live and the historical processes that constitute it. I argue that there is an urgent need to address these *interconnections* as opposed to reifying the entities that are supposed to be connected, all the while keeping in mind 'that what we are dealing with are not separate and comparable, but connected histories' (Subrahmanyam 1997: 748). The modernization of Britain, for example, as Washbrook argues, 'is inconceivable except in a broader global context of which India already comprised a vital part' (1997: 410). I take as my starting point for the reconstruction of the comparative frame, which will occupy the next section of the book, the argument made by Prakash where he suggests that the erroneous assumption, perpetuated by many theorists, is that the West 'had forged its characteristic commitment to modernity *before* overseas domination' as opposed to *through* it (1999: 12).

Washbrook (1997), for example, argues that the West, prior to the emergence of modernity, is typically represented as a 'closed', or self-sufficient, system of culture in a world consisting of other such systems. Any alternative to this would cast doubt on the 'authenticity' of modernity's origins in the West. However, to take such a standpoint, he continues, is to treat 'as closed and autonomous, cultures and civilizations between whom there is preponderant evidence of deepening contact and interaction during at least the half-millennium before Modernity made any detectable appearance' (1997: 413). Modernity, then, has to be understood as formed in and through the colonial relationship (see Barlow 1997) – colonization was not simply an outcome of modernity, or shaped by modernity, but rather, modernity itself developed out of colonial encounters, encounters which are hardly captured by the idea of 'diffusion'. These colonial encounters, then, also constituted the circumstances for the emergence of the 'fragile emancipatory codes' of modernity at the same time as modernity has been separated from its origins in the colonial relationship, and has been regarded as a resource for the emancipation of others.[16]

With the sociology of modernity having lost credibility, as Washbrook suggests, so, too, there is a need to rethink the conceptual under-pinnings of modern history (1997: 416). To this end, he argues for the adoption of certain methodological assumptions, the most important of which is that societies do not exist as 'closed' entities, but rather, as part of a much wider global context (1997: 417). The histories of other parts of the world, then, can be used to disrupt the commonly accepted history of the West and to demonstrate that 'the West has no simple origin, despite its claims to uniqueness, and its histories cannot adequately be gathered into the form of a singular narrative' (Mitchell 2000: 24). Bonnett similarly suggests that the attempt to rethink the relationship between the West and modernity, and 'to move away from a myopic focus on "how the West made the modern world"', requires us to give up one of the central 'clichés' of our time – that the story of western civilization is the story of humankind itself – and, instead, to understand that Western civilization is *but one of the stories of humanity* (2005: 508). To this end, Bonnett suggests that Harootunian's (2000) understanding of co-eval, that is, co-evolving and co-existing, modernities goes beyond previous approaches by allowing us to think contemporaneity together with the possibility of difference.

Interrogating the colonial inheritance is not only about arguing for a critical perspective on European forms of knowledge; it is also about problematizing the very assertion of forms of knowledge as European. This must be done through the use of global archives, geographies, and histories that would allow us to see that the theories and ideas we use were not created by a culture diffused from a centre which then impacted on the world, but through the interconnections of processes and paradigms that are themselves continually in negotiation and development (see Pollock *et al.* 2000). The development of modernity in other societies is not deficient in comparison to the emergence of European modernity, nor deviant in comparison to an ideal-typical understanding of it drawn from the European experience: rather, the different processes and developments provide a richer interpretation of the concept of modernity and may also provide new, and more adequate, practices for the present and future. In the meantime, sociologists cling to the universalistic assumptions of their theories of modernity in the fear that to give them up is to cede the field to a debilitating relativism (see, for example, Alexander 1995). In contrast, I argue, nothing is lost except a certain insularity.

In the next section of the book, I shall challenge the 'facts' of European modernity, arguing that understanding Europe in terms of global interconnections will provide a better understanding of how modernity has developed and, at the same time, alter our understanding of what it means to be modern, and alter our understanding of the European 'ownership' of modernity as an originary project. I have chosen three areas for examination, involving the discourse of modernity and its institutional forms of state and market. In each chapter, I will proceed by presenting the strong case for European distinctiveness and originality before deconstructing that case in terms of wider interconnections and extra-European contributions, as well as in terms of contesting the ascribed ruptural disjunction between tradition and modernity.

John Goldthorpe (1991) has criticized historical sociology for its failure to establish principles by which selections are made among the contributions to historical debates which provide the evidence for claims made within historical sociology itself. Rather, he says, the attitude is one of 'pick and mix' in history's sweetshop (1991: 225). Certainly, there are 'facts' and 'interpretations' to support the idea of European modernity and frequently these are cited within historical sociology as veridical, despite the availability of alternative interpretations and contestations of the 'facts'. While, unlike Goldthorpe, I do not believe that it is possible to provide a set of definitive principles, I shall argue that, nonetheless, the weight of such alternative arguments is sufficient to suggest that an alternative to the idea of European modernity is both plausible and likely to be productive of new insights about historical and social processes. The general response among historical sociologists to arguments of this sort is that their 'selections' are systematic and that the 'deviant' accounts of any particular event would not add up to something equally systematic (see Bryant 1994; Mann 1994). Quite apart from the privileging of their selections that this involves, I shall argue that this defence is mistaken; the 'deviant' cases do add up to a different systematic account and a different historiographic understanding, namely that of 'connected histories' as an alternative to Eurocentric histories.[17]

Those who argue for the 'facts' of European distinctiveness do not necessarily present their case in terms of all the three areas I shall examine, although many do, but a claim for distinctiveness does depend on rupture in at least one of the domains. For example, Peter Wagner accepts that institutional transitions were very slow and protracted over several centuries and, in consequence, it would not be difficult for him to accept that there were many exogenous influences on what might otherwise be presented as the endogenous development of European modernity. Nonetheless, as we have seen, he does argue that there is a discursive rupture, that is, a marked and decisive shift in European culture, and that this is a decisive marker of European distinctiveness. It is to this claim that I turn first with a discussion of the idea of the Renaissance as effecting a new and distinctive sensibility from which the master code of European modernity, the discourse of Enlightenment, would emerge.

Part 2

Deconstructing Eurocentrism: Connected Histories

4
Myths of European Cultural Integrity – The Renaissance

The period of the Renaissance is widely acknowledged as heralding the birth of modern Europe, with developments and innovations in the arts and learning contributing both to its self-perception as modern as well as to a retrospective labelling as such. The 'discovery' of the New World, in particular, as well as advances in science and medicine, demonstrated – to themselves as much as to later generations – the superiority of their epoch over earlier historical periods. In building on the wisdom of the ancient world, the scholars of the Renaissance developed branches of study concerned with the secular human condition that were later to be termed 'humanism', and then humanities. This saw the development of 'conceptual realism'[1], which was marked by the rise of theory, and was linked to a pronounced emphasis on analysis and criticism. In this way, cartographical discoveries, secular humanism, and social theory came to be seen not only as part of a European cultural movement, but as synonymous with it. As the prevailing modes of thought were altered so, in the arts, a distinctive image of the times was evoked, and it is the art and architecture of the Renaissance which has most visibly endured through the ages as the cultural embodiment of this period. In this chapter, I examine the dominant discourse of the Renaissance as 'modern' and 'European', and assess the claims made by scholars with regard to its epochal significance, endogenous origins, and cultural integrity.

Wallace Ferguson (1948), in his classic study covering five centuries of interpretation of the Renaissance, argues that the problem of the Renaissance is a double problem concerning not only the *facts* of what occurred, but also the *subjective interpretation* of these facts. In each age, he suggests, the histories of the Renaissance reflect the search for the origins of contemporary beliefs and values as mirrored in 'the actuality of an epoch of crucial importance for the evolution of Western civilization' (1948: 386) and, by implication, for the world at large. Despite differences of interpretation, however, the centrality of the Renaissance to subsequent histories is without question. Nisbet (1973), for example, argues that scholarship on the *Quattrocento* approaches something very close to the routinization of charisma; that is, despite sustained critiques of the Renaissance from numerous angles, there has been little impact 'upon the prestige and prosperity of the Renaissance guild', in particular, its construction of the age of the Renaissance as heralding (or, at the very least, 'tilting' toward) the modern (1973: 474).

Over the last few decades, in part as a consequence of emerging debates on post-modernity, there has been further reconsideration of the relation of the Renaissance to the modern world and the contemporary present (see Trinkhaus 1970; Bouwsma 1979). This reconsideration has involved a shift of focus away from social and political institutions to an examination of the relation of the Renaissance to 'the skeptical, relativistic, and pragmatic strains in contemporary culture' (Bouwsma 1979: 10). As Greenblatt argues, the focus of study has shifted from looking at the history of the arts and learning in isolation to examining the ways in which this period has been formative in 'the shaping of crucial aspects of our sense of self and society and the natural world' (1980: 174–5).

It is in the midst of anxieties as to what those senses of self, society, and the world mean that the Renaissance has been continually 'rediscovered' as the lens through which to attempt to understand the (European) roots of contemporary issues. For example, the tension between creativity and authoritarianism that is taken to define the human condition in modernity, as indicated in the previous chapter, is understood in terms of its roots occurring in the Renaissance idea of 'self-fashioning'; that is, the idea of 'man as creator of himself and the world' (Bouwsma 1979: 13). The autonomy of 'man' that this entails is regarded as having its first expression during this period (see, for example, the works of Montaigne 1993 [1575]), as is the 'de-sacralization' of authority that is taken to be its counterpart.

With questions being raised as to the continuing significance of the Renaissance to our contemporary age, the most commonly agreed upon interpretation has become that of the Renaissance as being the crucible for the emergence of the 'cultural codes' of modernity as well as being the fundamental period of transition to the modern world.[2] As Toulmin argues in his overarching discussion of the emergence and development of the modern era, the 'Renaissance was evidently a transitional phase, in which the seeds of Modernity germinated and grew' (1990: 23). Locating the Renaissance in this way enables scholars both to accommodate every anomaly and retain the specificity of the period by arguing, in comparison to other periods, for it to be one of unusual or accelerated transition (Bouwsma 1979).

In this chapter, then, I seek to challenge the generally accepted construction of it as the origin of the 'cultural unity' of Europe and a period of transition to a distinctively modern world. The first section of this chapter looks at the place of the Renaissance in European historiography, briefly examining how it has been understood through the ages and the general claim as to why it is regarded as the 'birth hour' of modern Europe. The second section will look in more depth at two of the characteristics of the Renaissance that have led to its ascription as the birth of the modern, namely, the rediscovery of ancient texts, and the rise in theoretical and conceptual understandings of the world; it will further address the ways in which Europe was constructed in terms of its civilization (incorporating both the arts and learning) and politically (through its territorial organization and administration). The final section contests the iconic status of the Renaissance in the context of claims of it heralding a ruptural break inaugurating the modern and the supposition of a cultural unity, and implied supremacy, of Europe. This chapter is fundamentally concerned with using the work of historians of the medieval and early modern periods, scholars working on the printing revolution, global art historians, and others to challenge and reconfigure the dominant discourses of the Renaissance, and thus, of the idea of 'modern Europe'.

I

Jacob Burckhardt (1990 [1860]), in the nineteenth century, enduringly associated the Renaissance with modernity and, for many historians, this was part of the self-understanding of the period itself. For example, John Hale argues that it was 'between the mid-fifteenth and the early seventeenth centuries [that] thoughtful men – at different times and in different places and with different reasons – came to see themselves as living in a period which, for all its dovetailing into the previous centuries, felt different' (1994: 592). Peter Burke concurs with this assessment arguing that although 'the Middle Ages never knew they were the Middle Ages ... the Renaissance was quite conscious of the fact that it was the Renaissance' (1964: 2).

The literary renaissance, which is argued to have begun in the fourteenth century with scholars such as Dante, Petrarch, and Boccaccio marking a sharp break with medieval traditions, is integral to the conception and formulation of the idea of the Renaissance being a revival under the influence of classical models (Bradner 1962 [1953]; Panofsky 1960). Consciously turning away from the presumed chaos of the Dark Ages, these scholars are believed to have searched for, and tenaciously perused, the forgotten texts of the classical world to see what could still be usefully learnt from authors such as Plato, Aristotle, and Virgil. With the knowledge gained from these texts scholars hoped to reconstruct the ancient world – a society they believed initially to be superior to their own, but nearer to their concerns than the preceding medieval centuries had been – and thereby usher in a new age, one that was, and would be, labelled 'modern', and would ultimately be understood as superior even to the ancient world.

The position, however, is less unequivocal than Hale and Burke propose. In using the term 'renaissance' or rebirth, scholars and thinkers of the time, such as Petrarch and Vasari, were primarily referring to an idea of *cultural* revival. This narrow definition did not prevail with their heirs and successors. As Panofsky argues, the 'gradual expansion of the humanistic universe from literature to painting, from painting to the other arts, and from the other arts to the natural sciences produced a significant shift in the original interpretation' (1960: 18; see also Gouwens 1998). Further, it was not until Michelet (1967 [1847]) entitled the seventh volume of his *History of France*, 'The Renaissance', that it was 'conceived as a period in the history of European civilization, a period with a distinctive spirit, sharply contrasted with that of the Middle Ages' (Ferguson 1948: 177). In characterizing the period as one of 'the discovery of the world, the discovery of man', Michelet anticipated Burckhardt's subsequently more celebrated association of the Renaissance with the development of the individual and the birth of the modern (Ferguson 1948; Burke 1990). Burckhardt, in turn, saw the Humanists as 'mediators between their own age and a venerated antiquity' (1990 [1860]: 135) who sought to bring the insights of the ancient Greeks to life again in their own time and, then, to surpass them.[3]

Gilmore (1960), among many others, has argued that Burckhardt's *The Civilization of the Renaissance in Italy* is the most important work in the creation of the dominant, modern conception of the Renaissance. The prevailing understanding of the key terms 'Renaissance' and 'Humanism', as well as notions of the 'development of the individual' and 'the discovery of the world and of man' were provided by Burckhardt's magisterial study and there is a keenly felt sense 'that the Renaissance was something created by Burckhardt' (Ferguson 1948: 212; Nauert Jr 1995).

Burckhardt

This claim is supported by the fact that virtually all subsequent histories of that period could not but refer to his work as the key point of reference, whether in agreement or disagreement (see, e.g., Symonds 1897; Ferguson 1948; Burke 1964; Kristeller 1974). One of the more recent histories of the Renaissance, John Hale's (1994) *The Civilization of Europe in the Renaissance*, acknowledges the seminal importance of Burckhardt's study in the adaptation of its title and organizes its chapters around Europe, Renaissance, and Civilization – capturing the themes integral to Burckhardt's earlier study.

Burckhardt's primary thesis was for the Italian Renaissance to be seen as the key turning point in the history of European civilization, an endogenous turning point which he believed was to have 'world-wide significance' (1990 [1860]: 120). Burckhardt argued that the political condition in which Italy had been left after the struggle between the popes and the Hohenstaufen in the fourteenth and fifteenth centuries had allowed the emergence, 'for the first time', of 'the modern political spirit of Europe' which was epitomized by 'the growth of individual character' (1990 [1860]: 20, 100). This spirit was seen to be responsible for the 'most elevated political thought and the most varied forms of human development' and confirmed the 'modernity' of the Italian states (1990 [1860]: 65). Thus, in terms of the Renaissance, it was not the revival of antiquity alone which was of importance for Burckhardt, but also the high stage of individualism that was indicated by the cosmopolitanism of the Italian political situation and the importance of this for European (and global) civilization as a whole (1990 [1860]: 100, 120).

Rüsen suggests that the idea of 'the continuity of the European mind, ... [of] the cultural unity of Western civilization from the ancient past until his own time', was a dominant motif in Burckhardt's work (Rüsen 1985: 239). It was only by integrating 'the breakdown of the cultural continuity in the age of revolution with an historical unity of Western civilization' that, Rüsen suggests, Burckhardt was able to establish the prevailing historical identity of 'modern man' (Rüsen 1985: 239–40). Later scholars, drawing on Burckhardt's analysis, further established the Renaissance as being 'a complete break with the Middle Ages' and hailed it 'as the dawn of the modern world' (Ralph 1973: 5). John Hale's definition of the Renaissance, as the recovery of 'the sounds of classical antiquity after the long medieval winter that closed in with the loss of Rome to the barbarians' (1994: 189), elegantly, if ultimately misleadingly, encapsulates the dominant themes of the Renaissance as modern and as European and it is to the exposition of these themes that the chapter now turns.

II

The characterization of the Renaissance as 'the birth of the modern' has usually rested upon its claim to have rediscovered the ancient texts, deemed to have been lost during the Middle Ages, and its concomitant search for new knowledge. Panofsky, for example, suggests that while '[t]he Middle Ages had left antiquity unburied ... The Renaissance stood weeping at its grave and tried to resurrect its soul' (1960: 113). The humanists of the long sixteenth century looked back to antiquity as the fount of all meaningful knowledge and drew on their meagre resources to augment the study and appreciation of that heritage. In doing so, they were also seen to have developed new modes of thinking and new branches of study that were oriented to enriching life in the present. As Kristeller argues, Renaissance Humanism was 'a scholarly, literary, and educational ideal based on the study of classical antiquity' which, in time, established the humanities as 'a broad area of secular learning and secular thought ... independent of (not contrary to) both theology and the sciences' (1962: 22).[4] The rise in theoretical and conceptual understandings of the world engendered by these shifts, together with an increased emphasis on textual analysis and criticism, have often been cited as demonstrative of the unique mindset of the Renaissance scholars (see Gouwens 1998). Burckhardt, for example, talks often of the 'genius of the Italian people' and reveres the contributions of men such as Petrarch and Boccaccio, whom he believes to be a new class of men in the world maintaining a new cause, Humanism (1990 [1860]: 120, 138). Together with subsequent advances in the sciences and geography, these developments were seen to be responsible for the shift from veneration of the ancient world to a feeling of superiority over it (see Butzer 1992; Headley 2000). As Pagden argues, 'both Copernicanism and the discovery of America ... cast a long and menacing shadow over the authority of the whole of the ancient corpus' (1993: 92) and contributed, in large part, to a sense of decisive epochal change.

Addressing, first, the recovery of ancient texts, we see that whereas the medieval humanists had simply accumulated, the Renaissance humanists were said to have discriminated. As Grafton argues, the revival of the classical heritage was 'not only about the discovery of what was lost but the expunging of what was false' (1991: 162). It was with this 'ability to detect the corrupt and the spurious', that the humanists were said to have 'created a critical art without literary precedent' (Grafton 1991: 162). The rise in historical consciousness is another factor that is used by scholars, such as Gilmore (1952) and Panofsky (1960, 1991), to attest to the birth of modernity in the time of the Renaissance.[5] For Gilmore, 'the ability to place oneself in time with respect to an age as a whole, [and] the awareness of historic distance' came out of the development of a sense of perspective within humanist thought (1952: 201). Panofsky further attributes the development of abstract historical thought to the fact that '[t]he classical past was looked upon, for the first time, as a totality cut off from the present; and, therefore, as an ideal to be longed for' (1960: 113). The capacity to see the past from a fixed distance and the sense of temporal location paralleled the growth of perspective in painting and mirrored the optical effects obtained by Renaissance artists (Eisenstein 1969: 36, 37). In this sense, it is argued, the development of a single and individual viewpoint in art was transposed into historical scholarship and to cartographical advances.

Turning to the art of the Renaissance we see that it has commonly been defined by the conscious break from what were perceived to be the Gothic and Byzantine vulgarities of the recent past and the attempts to recapture and build upon the glories of the traditions of the ancient world. It is generally believed that the attempts to achieve congruence between art and reality, and a reappraisal of the relationship between the two during this period, produced a lasting foundation for the changed appearance of European art and architecture that has endured to the present day (see Vermeule 1964; Muir 1979; Panofsky 1991). The ability of Renaissance artists such as Michelangelo and Raphael to rationalize 'an image of space which had already earlier been unified', and to combine beauty and harmony with correctness, was seen as a repudiation of the ancient authorities and as another sign of the emergence of 'the modern' as distinct and superior to the ancient world (Panofsky 1991: 63, 72; Gombrich 1995 [1950]); this was particularly so, given the application of perspective in contemporary cartography and its implications for the ensuing 'voyages of discovery' (Headley 2000). The achievements in this field, particularly of the Italian artists (who were often also cartographers), supported the increasingly widespread notion of having entered a new period of accomplishment where the 'sense of consistent improvement ... led to the word "modern" to be used with increasing frequency' (Hale 1994: 587).

The radical transformation of scientific ideas within sixteenth- and seventeenth-century Europe was further taken to indicate a fundamental rupture from both preceding modes of thought and other cultural groups (see Boas 1962; Ben-David 1965).[6] Samuel Purchas writing in the early seventeenth century, for example, believed contemporary Europe to be the sole home of the 'Arts and Inventions' and argued that 'Alas,

China yeelds babes and bables in both [printing and gunpowder] compared with us and ours: the rest of the World have them borrowed of us or not at all' (quoted in Hay 1957: 121). The medieval centuries were similarly assumed to have contributed little to the subsequent development of science and technology, and the 'Scientific Revolution' is generally constructed as a singular event without external contributions or influences. The changes that are deemed to have occurred were brought about, or so Butterfield argues, 'by transpositions that were taking place inside the minds of the scientists themselves' (1957: 1). This is echoed by scholars such as Alexandre Koyré who believed that during the period of the Renaissance 'human, or at least European, minds underwent a deep revolution which changed the very framework and patterns of our thinking' (1958: v). Cook further suggests that, for Koyré, 'science emerged from "the mathematization (geometrization) of nature" and from no other source but this shift in pure thought' (Cook 1993: 46).

Advances in science combined with expanding knowledge of the globe to initiate a shift in the way the world itself was conceptualized within European thought. In the context of the various 'voyages of discovery' associated with this period, Headley argues that they 'served to establish the peculiarly universalizing character of geography as a new knowledge that could be exploited for religious, political, economic, and military purposes upon a global stage' (2000: 1130; see also Parry 1963). From an earlier vision of the world, dependent on the accumulated knowledge of the ancients, the Bible, and the Church Fathers, Europeans now had to refigure that world to include a new continent of which no prior mention had been made. This called into question the authority of the ancients and, in doing so, initiated the epistemological search – culminating in Descartes – for a new basis from which authority could be said to derive. As Pagden (1993) suggests, the reconstruction of geographical understandings alongside the unsettling of customary intellectual practices added to the general ferment of the period and contributed in no small part to the sense of being modern, and superior.

As has been discussed, then, the claims made for the 'modernity' of the Renaissance rest in its recovery of ancient texts, the emergence of Humanism and the development of historical consciousness, and the seemingly innovative movements in the arts and science together with the 'discovery' of the New World. These movements and events, as well as being understood as 'modern', also contributed to the establishment of a distinct European identity. The emergence of a network of artists across Europe, for example, who borrowed from each other and had a degree of familiarity with developments across schools and regions, is often regarded as crucial to the development of Renaissance art as well as to subsequent understandings of Europe based on a common cultural identity (see Hale 1994; Gombrich 1995 [1950]). For Pagden (2002), the bringing together of Europe 'as a unity' was further facilitated by the association of science with philosophy and, for Headley (2000), with the conjuncture between Christianity and the universalizing impetus of geographical knowledge (see also Butzer 1992). The perceptions of cultural commonality and superiority that these aspects subsequently engendered were intensified through the establishment of a geographically bounded understanding of Europe that focused on both its sense of difference from those it encountered abroad (or regarded as different as a consequence of religion, for example, the 'othering' of Jews and Muslims within Europe) as well as its internal territorial organization and administration.

The territorial organization of the geographical area known as Europe has frequently been understood as having its own internal dynamic that has both created a sense of unity within it and differentiated it from other areas. Michael Mann, for example, argues that over the course of the second millennium the territory of the western Roman empire fused with the lands of the Germanic peoples into a socio-geographical unity called Europe that 'contained a single set of interrelated dynamics' (1986: 373). These 'dynamics', in Mann's explanation, were all endogenous processes with the dominant ones being Christendom, the development of the early modern state, and economic power and trading networks. While there was no head, or centre, to this entity there were 'a number of small, crosscutting interaction networks' of which he argues Christendom was the most extensive (Mann 1986: 376, 377). This was then believed to have provided the mainstay for a sense of European unity until the collapse of Rome following the schism of Protestantism and the outbreak of religious wars in the seventeenth century.

The Peace of Westphalia in 1648 led to the inception of a new multi-state system which was characterized by the simultaneous centralization and impersonalization of political power, that is, states were now more likely to act independently of papal authority and the Church's role as the arbiter of international affairs was greatly reduced (Pagden 2002).[7] This separation between religion and state, as well as the emergence of theories of sovereignty, has been seen as uniquely European and as constituting a key aspect of European identity. Hay, for example, argues that these developments brought about a practical unity in the European political scene and that, combined with the political idealism of the time, 'contributed to the further self-awareness *sep religion d state*

of Europe' (1957: 118). Pagden further suggests that this, more than any other event, 'distinguished the European states from such non-European sovereign bodies as the Ottoman or Ming empires' (2002: 9) and provided the subsequent lodestar for unity, together with the emergence of capitalism and the development of the national state (Stråth 2002: 392). These latter, more recent endogenous developments (to be discussed in more detail in the following two chapters), have been understood to have laid new tracks, not only for Europe, but also the world (Mann 1986: 412, 446).

Having considered the historiography of the Renaissance and addressed the various aspects that are taken to substantiate the claims made for it heralding the birth of modern Europe, the chapter now turns to a critical examination of these dominant interpretations.

III

For Burckhardt and many subsequent historians, as has been discussed above, 'the significance of the Renaissance was that it was the beginning of the modern world ... *the* great divide' (Burke 1964: 133). It heralded not only the beginning of the modern age for these historians, but the beginning of the tripartite *model* of ages – namely, the ancient, the medieval, and the modern – and the problem of transition between stages. As all periodizations are based on understandings of continuity and change, and the establishment of historical epochs relies on both an agreement on longstanding continuities within that epoch and clearly demarcated moments of transition between them – where old continuities are dissolved and new ones forged (Green 1995: 101) – such conceptual terms can be seen to operate as purifying devices maintaining the coherence of the scheme at the expense of the diversity of human experience encountered. Diversity is typically taken to present an organizational problem for the writing of world history, and even those scholars who, as was argued in previous chapters, 'recognize' difference, continue to constitute it as a problem to be located in a scheme of unifying laws and regularities that are predominantly taken from the Western experience. Past, or 'other', societies are located according to how, and to what extent, they differ from the modern West. Periodization, then, similar to other classificatory schemes, is seen as an expedient approach to a complex situation and one whose intrinsic difficulties will be further discussed at the close of this chapter.[8]

Looking at the Renaissance, then, we see that in the twentieth century there was growing disquiet with the interpretation of it as heralding a qualitative historical break. The claim made for it to be seen as 'a uniquely brilliant epoch of civilization and the point of departure for the modern age' has increasingly been called into question (Ralph 1973: 6). The contrast that had previously been posited between the 'dark' Middle Ages and the 'enlightened' Renaissance dissipated as scholars confirmed the continued presence of medieval traits within the civilization of the Renaissance itself (Kristeller 1974).[9] Kristeller's (1974) work on Renaissance Humanism and culture, for example, has been integral to the re-examination of the place of medieval traditions within what have commonly been understood to be 'new' intellectual movements (see also Trinkaus 1970; Nauert Jr 1995). Further, a substantial body of literature has been established that contests the uniqueness of the Renaissance in light of earlier renascences within Europe, for example, the Carolingian or twelfth century renaissance (see Sanford 1951; Haskins 1957; Brooke 1969; Trompf 1973; Sullivan 1989).

One of the dominant claims for the Renaissance to be seen as unique rests in its 'discovery' of the texts of the ancients. Elisabeth Eisenstein asks, however, why humanists should 'be credited with "discovering" ancient works that were obviously known already to some medieval scholars since they were found in the form of medieval copies?' (1969: 46); and, it could be argued further, were also known to scholars within the Greek and Islamic worlds, both contemporaneously and in the medieval period. Eisenstein suggests, then, that 'finding a text' and making it 'generally available' are two very different things and that this difference, attributable to the invention of the printing press, is what actually differentiates the sixteenth-century renaissance from the Carolingian revival or that of the twelfth century.

> Given a classical revival that was still underway when new preservative powers were brought into play, one might expect that this revival would pose peculiar problems. Since it was initiated under one set of circumstances and perpetuated under wholly different ones, it would probably begin by resembling previous revivals and yet take an increasingly divergent course. (Eisenstein 1969: 27)

Prior to the advent of printing, Eisenstein (1969) suggests there had been no methodological recording of knowledge which would ensure that it would be passed on (with more accuracy than had previously been the case) from one generation to the next. Transcribed books were so few that if they were destroyed or lost there was a danger that the knowledge they contained would be lost forever. Thus, the primary aim of scholars was to ensure the survival of valued texts through laborious copying. Since the availability of scribes capable of reproducing texts was limited, the development of printing meant that texts could be reproduced more efficiently and the range of available books was expanded. This was because the number of available manuscripts had always been limited to human capabilities and the whims of those who patronized the scribes. With the advent of the printing press more neglected texts could be produced 'providing individual readers with access to more works – not necessarily new ones, just more of them' (Eisenstein 1968: 114).

The awareness that, previously, texts had become corrupted and that some had been lost intensified the concern that the 'ancient texts recovered by the humanists were not again "lost", ... destroyed, progressively corrupted, transplanted or mislaid' (Eisenstein 1969: 44). This meant that the texts that were available to the latter renascence 'had been enhanced by an order of richness' (Grafton 1991: 176) in that printing 'arrested textual corruption, fixed texts more permanently, and enabled them to accumulate at an accelerated rate' (Eisenstein 1969: 24). It was primarily this shift in the quantity and quality of texts available to scholars that Grafton suggests constituted the 'new' scholarship attributed to the Renaissance. With 'men of learning' being freed from simply copying old texts, in their attempts to retrieve and preserve fragments of the past, energies could then be turned towards building on the work of their predecessors. They could go beyond copying and memorizing to analyzing, discussing, and exploring what else might still be learnt from the recovered texts. Johns (1998) argues that it is necessary to understand these labours, facilitated by the emergence of print, in order to fully appreciate the significance of the printed book and the transformative consequences associated with it. He suggests that the 'fixity' ascribed to print by some authors, notably Eisenstein, was not an inherent property of print, but was part of the *culture* of print that emerged through varying practices, representations, and conflicts between authors, printers, and the reading public.

The claim to have established a critical art without precedent, then, does not take into account the fact that textual criticism, cross-referencing between one book and another, did not become widely possible until scholars had ready access to a variety of books and had confidence in the integrity of the texts they were consulting.[10] Similarly, with the claim to have developed a unique historical consciousness, Eisenstein suggests that it was not until there was the means to attempt to fix knowledge and to know with more certainty the order in which texts had been composed that the past could be understood in terms of order: 'Records have to be permanently arranged in a uniform sequence before any portion of the past, classical or not, can be seen across definite intervals or from a fixed distance' (Eisenstein 1969: 35, 36). The texts that we now situate chronologically were encountered by earlier scholars in a state of disarray. It is not surprising, therefore, that, with the increased production of books, Humanism, during the later years of the Renaissance, appeared better able 'to survey and to appreciate the totality of the arts and the sciences in a large historical perspective' (Kelley 1988: 261). While it is argued that history writing itself, during this period, 'became more analytical and politically and psychologically more sophisticated than the medieval chronicles had been' (Burke 1964: 50), this is less a quality of mind than circumstance. When, with scribal culture, the main concern had been to preserve knowledge the emphasis was probably more on recording events; as printing made that concern less urgent, it was possible to begin looking at what more could be done with the information available.

The introduction of mass printing techniques further made discussion over distance easier as page numbers and diagrams could be cited from identical copies and scholars were able to correspond with each other with a certainty that they were considering the same issues (Hale 1971: 189). This 'turned intellectual work as a whole into a cooperative instead of a solitary human activity ... [enlarging] the amount of intellectual effort applied to individual problems' (Rice and Grafton 1994 [1970]: 8). The use of Latin as the language of intellectual exchange created a community of scholars which, as Jardine suggests, was largely congruent with the Christian world, helping to create 'an ethos of intellectual *amicitia* – the bond of shared humane preoccupations' (1996a: 18). Even if individual scholars were geographically far apart the increased use of paper facilitated written communication and was thus integral to the establishment of the perception of being culturally united in a common pursuit of knowledge. However, any new 'republic of letters' was more extensive and 'hybrid' than is represented within ideas of it as a singular European phenomenon. The transmission of culture and exchange of ideas that resulted in the development of Renaissance Humanism 'was part of a continuous process of cross-cultural fertilization ... [based on] a shared heritage and a set of academic interests in common, rather than a "movement" with conscious ambitions and intellectual goals' (Jardine 1996b: 59). That this 'cross-cultural fertilization' has been written out of subsequent histories of the Renaissance tells us more about those histories than the histories tell us about the Renaissance.

In their search for origins and the subsequent construction of lines of heritage, scholars constructed a self-definition as European in terms of the sources they acknowledged and those they did not. While most historians of this period locate the Renaissance as primarily, and most importantly, concerned with classical antiquity, its sources and its ideals (Kelley 1991), this retrospective construction fails to acknowledge the admiration felt by the men and women of the Renaissance for Egypt – and the Orient more generally – as culturally older than the Greeks and thus closer to the truth in their terms (Bernal 1987: 157). In searching for the sources of wisdom and the arts, scholars in the Renaissance 'looked behind Christianity to pagan Rome, behind Rome to Greece; but behind Greece there was Egypt' (Bernal 1987: 153).

Scholars such as Kraemer (1984) and Makdisi (1989), further point to the influence and contribution of Islamic scholars, both to the emergence of the humanities and to particular understandings of humanism. As Sabra argues, for example, medieval Islamic scholars had engaged with the works of the ancients – in fact, he writes that 'Aristotle had always been an authority, indeed the foremost authority, for Islamic philosophers' (1984: 138) – and were driven by similar theoretical concerns as those of the later Renaissance and Humanist thinkers. Other scholars have similarly commented on both the intellectual contribution of the Islamic world to learning and scholarship within Europe and more widely, as well as their role in 'preserving' writings of ancient civilizations, Greek, Roman, and Oriental (Kraemer 1984; Bernal 1987; Makdisi 1989; El-Bushra 1992). Joll, for example, notes that 'it was through the intellectuals of the Arab world that much of the teaching of European classical antiquity found its way back into the stream of European cultural development' (1980: 8).

The omission of extra-European influences and historical interactions from virtually all histories of the Renaissance seem to suggest that after the decline of classical Greek and then Roman culture the legacy of the ancients lay untouched, simply awaiting recovery by the men of the Renaissance (Harding 1998: 28; see also Keita 1994). The idea that these texts may have been circulating in Islamic and other cultures is not thought of as significant and contributions made by such scholars are ignored and left out of the retrospective construction of a linear, isolationist heritage of knowledge and learning. Further, the idea that these texts 'found their way *back*' suggests an exclusively European claim to a heritage that did not understand itself in such terms. The ancient Greeks were not 'European' and, as much as Greek learning was influenced by Eastern cultures so they in turn borrowed from Greece in their common engagement in the advancement of knowledge (see Gershevitch 1964; Fakhry 1965; Hourani 1976).

The fundamental, irreducible cultural differences that are posited between 'medieval' and 'modern' and between 'European' and 'other' have been strongly contested throughout this chapter. Eisenstein, interrogating the commonly held understanding of the Renaissance as 'unique', suggests that it was less the experience and more what became of it under the impact of the new preservative powers of the printing press that was unprecedented (1969: 27, 45). Thus, it could be argued that there was no qualitative difference between the Renaissance and the earlier Carolingian revival or that of the twelfth century; and nor was there a qualitative difference between the Renaissance and 'the effort to renew the study of the Confucian classics that grew up in the lower Yangtze region of China during the seventeenth and eighteenth centuries' (Grafton 1991: 44–5). What there was, was a historically contingent process that produced an outcome that was different quantitatively by an order of magnitude and which ultimately had a qualitative effect. The problem has been, however, that the qualitative effect has been seen in isolation, abstracted from wider interconnections and regarded as a process occurring due to internal developments in the mindsets of the Europeans themselves. In contrast, it could be argued that Humanism and the cultural transformation that is commonly known as the Renaissance make no sense unless we see at their core the impact of the preservative qualities of the printing press. It was, in part, the advent of this invention, itself originating in China and being carried to Europe in the Middle Ages by the Arabs (Gilmore 1952: 187) – and the corresponding shift from a scribal to a typographical culture – which facilitated a sustained revival and ultimately produced fundamental changes in the prevailing intellectual models of continuity and change.

Moving on to address the arts, we see that travel was regarded as an integral aspect contributing to the distinctiveness of the Renaissance as it was seen to improve artistic techniques and styles. Yet, the artists were only ever assumed to have travelled within what is now understood as Europe. In discussing where these changes were taking place Hale, for example, cites Italy, France, Germany, the Netherlands, England, Spain, Poland, and Russia (1971: 263). Recent scholarship is, however, beginning to contest this isolationist history: 'editors of a recent collection of reprints maintain that, between 1400 and 1700, there were over 250 descriptions of Egypt by Western travellers' suggesting that travels to Egypt were at least as common as those to Greece (Bernal 1987: 157). Not so recent scholarship, such as that by Frothingham (1895), has similarly pointed to the diffusion and movement of artistic styles and artists in the thirteenth and fourteenth centuries between Italian cities, Egypt, Islamic centres – both in Europe, for example, in Spain, and further afield – and the Byzantine civilization. The Renaissance works of art that are so admired today were, in their time, similarly valued within, what Jardine (1996b) calls, a vigorously developing worldwide market based on multilateral exchange and diffusion in which art was both traded as a commodity and exchanged for, and as, inspiration;[11] thus, contesting the commonly held notion that the emergence and development of Renaissance art was fundamentally an endogenous European phenomenon without influence or inspiration from elsewhere.

Even while the Byzantine and Holy Roman empires collided, learned scholars, artists, and traders from both sides continued to collaborate and exchange goods, ideas, and artefacts. An analysis of sixteenth-century art-based transactions undertaken by Jardine and Brotton 'reveal a pragmatic engagement between East and West in which each fully acknowledged the participation of the other' (2000: 61). This leads the authors to argue that cross-cultural exchange ought to be seen as the norm and not as an exception. Further, they suggest that the dominant understanding of the formation of cultural identity as a purely internal phenomenon ought to be discarded as it was more plausibly 'formed out of direct encounters between artefacts exchanged amongst international communities at distinct geographical locations' (2000: 133). By analyzing the manner in which luxury goods and commodities circulated during the period of the Renaissance they have been able to establish how, instead of being culturally divorced from activities in Europe, places like Istanbul, Persia, China, Japan, and India were actually intricately connected through common political and commercial interests (see also Boxer 1984; Scammell 2000). With these possibilities and their implications, Jardine and Brotton argue, 'comes the inevitable recognition that cultural histories apparently utterly distinct, and traditionally kept entirely separate, are ripe to be rewritten as shared East/West undertakings' (2000: 8).

Alongside goods and commodities, ideas and mental constructs also flowed across political boundaries and '– even if they found specific local expression – enable us to see that what we are dealing with are not separate and comparable, but connected histories' (Subrahmanyam 1997: 748). The introduction of trade in firearms and other commodities between Japan and Portugal in the sixteenth century, for example, was accompanied by discussions on the immortality of the soul (and attempts at conversion to Christianity) between Portuguese Jesuits, such as Francis Xavier, and local religious leaders, such as the Zen-bonze, Ninshitsu (see Laures 1952; Pacheco 1974; Boxer 1984).

Further, Perlin, argues that

> in the medieval centuries there existed a vigorous interchange of Indian, Muslim and European astrological and cosmological ideas, repeated between the 15th and 17th centuries when traffic in Latin and vernacular manuscripts accompanied the chemical and alchemical, astrological and astronomical ferment in intellectual Europe. (1994: 98)

This calls into question the East/West divide that is constantly read back through history and also problematizes the cultural binaries associated with some postcolonial analyses of Orientalist discourse (Jardine and Brotton 2000: 61), a problematization that is developed throughout this book.

The development of 'Western science' was another key factor in the promulgation of the 'divide' between the medieval and the modern. Focusing on one of the commonly cited figures of the Scientific Revolution, however, we see that, as Marie Boas argues, Copernicus was not in fact 'a pioneer, and attempted nothing that others had not tried before, for many astronomers [had] used ancient opinion to refute Ptolemy' (1962: 69). Copernicus himself stated that he was not interested in revolutionizing astronomy, nor in creating 'a new heaven and a new Earth. For him, it was better to explain the nature of the old ones more exactly' (Boas 1962: 89). Thus, his achievements were based less on new observations and more on the ability to consult texts systematically and work with previously disparate bodies of knowledge. These included texts from 'non-European' sources such as works by the Islamic scholars, Nasir ad-Din at-Tusi and Ibn ash Shatir, of whom mention has only recently been begun to be made in studies of Copernicus's mathematical astronomy (Bernal 1987: 156). The failure to acknowledge the contributions made by 'non-European' cultures trivializes the achievements of their scientific and technological traditions and perpetuates the myth of the source 'of the growth of European science and technology as lying entirely within Europe' (Harding 1998: 31, 36).

Further, as opposed to understanding the Scientific Revolution in terms of there having been 'a shift in pure thought', it is perhaps better to think of it in terms of the transformation in the number and quality of texts available for consultation. Due to the advances made in printing, as discussed earlier, Copernicus had ready access to more texts on the same topic than his predecessors could ever have hoped for. Scholars were no longer required to travel to search for remnants of knowledge located in disparate libraries, monasteries, and other repositories of books and manuscripts, but were more likely to have collections themselves, or at least access to collections, that were fuller than they had ever previously been. The bringing together of diverse texts, interpretations, and commentaries allowed contradictions and similarities to be identified more quickly and then begin to be worked through in a systematic fashion. As Eisenstein argues, perhaps 'the most significant contribution made by Copernicus was not so much in hitting on the "right" theory as in producing a fully worked out *alternative* theory and thus confronting the next generation with a problem to be solved rather than a solution to be learned' (Eisenstein 1983: 223). Focusing simply on European mental abilities and talents, in terms of explaining the development of scientific knowledge across the ages, is not the most adequate means of understanding what was going on. Even if looking for the explanation of such phenomena in abilities of particular races was not itself inherently problematic, such talents can only ever be retrospectively determined based as they are on the outcomes of processes as opposed to the nature of the processes themselves.

Having looked at various alternative histories and theoretical challenges to the main presuppositions of what has been deemed to have made the European Renaissance unique within world history, I now turn to examine the construction of the idea of Europe itself. Michael Mann acknowledges that a major difficulty in articulating particular histories is that countries and cultures were rarely autonomous. Islam, for example, had been in contact with many other cultures and had influenced and been influenced by them in turn. Another obstacle in the way of arguing for social change as systemic, he suggests, 'is that the sources of change are geographically and socially "promiscuous" – they do not all emanate from within the social and territorial space of the given "society"' (1986: 503). Having made these arguments, however, Mann then turns on the next page to write 'European dynamism was systemic. ... it characterized Europe as a whole, indeed integrating its diversities into one civilization' (1986: 504). Though there may have been differences between north-western Europe and the Mediterranean region, he continues, 'the same spirit pervaded the continent' (1986: 504). The extent to which this pervasive understanding of the emergence of 'political Europe' is an adequate interpretation of the period will now be discussed.

Latin, as the repository and instrument of the dominant culture, is seen to have marked a clear linguistic frontier between Latin Christendom and its Celtic, Slav, Greek, and Muslim neighbours; it also, however, according to Moore, created a distinction between the elite and the masses (1997: 596). The tensions that manifested themselves across the continental landmass thus could be argued as being less to do with proto-national and proto-ethnic sentiments and more to do with the creation and promulgation of a high culture by elites who overrode local values and solidarities in the process (Moore 1997: 597). Further, that the existence of Latin as a common language across Europe did not preclude cultural exchange with non-Latin countries is highlighted by Subrahmanyam. He asserts that the ability of the Mughal ruler Jalal al-Din Muhammad Akbar to converse with the Portuguese Jesuit Antonio Monserrate in the mid-sixteenth century (year 989 of the Hegiran calendar) on matters pertaining to the coming millennium 'points to the permeability of what are often assumed to be closed "cultural zones", and the existence of vocabularies that cut across local religious traditions' (1997: 746, 748).

Further, while Christendom, and then Christianity, has been seen as the key aspect of cultural unity for much of Europe through the centuries this has occurred in the context of the largely unrecognized historical presence of a substantial number of non-Christian Europeans (Rodríguez-Salgado 2005). Along with significant Jewish populations, it is necessary also to take into account the history of Spain, which had been Muslim for a number of centuries, as well as European Muslims in the Balkans, south-eastern Europe and, perhaps contentiously, Turkey. Like Russia – the other great geopolitical entity that stands in a relation of perpetual inclusion and exclusion with Europe 'proper' – Turkey has been a part of the political system of Europe historically even if it has not been recognized as culturally European (Yapp 1992). This further constitutes an ongoing aspect of European (and Muslim) discussions about the nature and limits of Europe. To the extent that Turkey, as with the Ottoman Empire before it, is constructed as a mirror with which to reflect an understanding of Europe back to itself (Yapp 1992), so Arabs, and others, have used 'Europe' for similar purposes (Al-Azmeh 1992; see also Raychaudhuri 2002 [1988]).

The construction of Islam as 'other' to Europe occurs in the context of a history of Muslim expansion in the fourteenth and fifteenth centuries from Spain and the Balkans in the West to India and Indonesia in the East and across much of Africa to the south (Lewis 1990). As such, Yapp (1992) argues that it was only when Christian fears about Muslim conquest receded that secular markers of a specifically 'European' identity began to emerge. Mann similarly sets up the expulsion of the Viking, Muslim, and Hun marauders from the continent as a key aspect in the construction of Europe (1986: 377), but how can one be sure who were the marauders and who were there by virtue of 'legitimate' conquest?[12] Bartlett in his book, *The Making of Europe*, has documented how expansionary activity was rife in the Middle Ages and that conquest and settlement were seen as formative periods, often becoming mythologized as founding moments, in a society's history (1993: 92). Can a marauder only be defined retrospectively, then, in terms of one who did not succeed in conquering? Gellner writes 'I like to imagine what would have happened had the Arabs won at Poitiers and gone on to conquer and Islamize Europe. No doubt we should all be admiring Ibn Weber's *The Kharejite Ethic and the Spirit of Capitalism*' (quoted in Mann 1986: 503).

Another distinguishing characteristic of Europe has been understood to be its movement towards political and administrative integration of previously localized and fragmented units within a wider, civilizational complex known as Europe. Moore argues, however, that the events and developments that are traditionally seen to have contributed to the formation of Europe as an autonomous civilization 'had an essential Eurasian context' (1997: 599; see also Braudel 1977). Discussing the emergence of urban centres in north-western Europe, for example, Moore argues that this 'was an aspect of the general recovery after the decline of late antiquity ... which was precipitated by the simultaneous expansion and meeting of the Tang and Islamic worlds' (1997: 599). The changes that are seen to have occurred in the sixteenth and seventeenth centuries within Europe were not once-and-for-all changes and were not limited to Europe. The 'circulation of powerful myths and ideological constructs relating to state formation existed in early modern Eurasia, and ... these often transcended the boundaries defined for us retrospectively by nation-states' (Subrahmanyam 1997: 759). This raises the question for Moore of whether, instead of discussing the developments taking place within western Europe as purely local or regional affairs, we should instead regard them as aspects within the reshaping of civilization within Eurasia after the decline of its ancient empires (1997: 600). Moore argues that the long-term changes, which underpin accounts such as those by Michael Mann discussed above, ought to be seen 'as recurring intensifications rather than as the once-for-all changes associated with the categories in which classical social theory has tended to discuss comparative history' (1997: 600). In discussing 'state formation' in the eleventh and twelfth centuries and then in the sixteenth and seventeenth centuries, Moore writes that the differences that are commonly ascribed to these events 'are differences of degree, not of kind' (1997: 600).

IV

It can be seen that the dominant discourse that sets up the period of the Renaissance as the birth of the modern as well as the birth of Europe has been increasingly challenged by medievalists and historians of the early modern, those interested in the printing revolution, global art historians, critics of comparative histories, and others. It has been demonstrated that the dominant understandings of the Renaissance, upon which the majority of social theorists base their theoretical and conceptual understandings of the world are, at best, inadequate, partial representations of the historical period in question. With this, it is not suggested that there is ever a perfect or complete understanding, but rather, that there are more plausible interpretations of what happened than those currently in use. Accepting that there are plural interpretations of events does not necessarily imply that all interpretations are equal, as has been argued both in the Introduction and earlier in this chapter, but that it is necessary to examine the contemporary plausibility of historical accounts within the communities engaged with them. Opening up earlier readings does not 'falsify' what had been thought previously, or replace it with a 'truer' account, but serves to expose the politics by which it came to dominate our understandings today. This then allows us to see how and why particular aspects of that history were illuminated or occluded. Again, as stated earlier, this is not to suggest that there is a 'complete' history which can be known, but that it is in the process of 'knowing' history that we know ourselves: that is, a reflexive approach to history provides greater opportunities for discerning more adequate contemporary understandings where, as was discussed in the Introduction, adequacy is determined in terms of the present as opposed to trying to establish a more accurate reading of the past.

> We have to recognize as best we can the purposes built into and encrusted upon the essences and categories we use, and we have to assess as best we can how well those purposes fit our own. (Carrier 1995: 26)

As Said writes in *Orientalism*, the growth of knowledge is not merely additive or cumulative, it 'is a process of selective accumulation, displacement, deletion, rearrangement and insistence within what has been called a research consensus' (1995 [1978]: 176). Extending Said's criticisms of 'Oriental Studies' to historical inquiry at large provides one way of opening up the possibility of rethinking histories today: in particular,

Said's critique of 'Oriental Studies' as having constructed an image of the Orient that rested on presumptions of it being 'absolutely different' and 'a closed system', impermeable to change regardless of 'empirical' findings or 'the actualities of the modern Orient' (1978: 177), can be usefully drawn into other fields of inquiry. Addressing the Renaissance, we see how a dominant understanding, established in the nineteenth century, set the cultural parameters of what was understood to be modern and European. The establishment of the Renaissance as a temporal period with a defined spatial location further compounded the intellectual boundaries that were drawn upon a particular historical reading. Ascribing the aspect 'modern' to a particular Europe, for example, made the task of subsequent scholarship the demonstration of its absolute difference and internal coherence: further, adapting Said, the very designation of something as 'modern' involved an already pronounced evaluative judgement on oneself and the other about whom one spoke (1978: 207).

Classification on the presumption of a concrete referent makes the 'other' appear to be in need of explanation and diverts attention away from that which is understood to always, already exist. Where Orientalism, the discourse of the West on the Orient, is about understanding the 'other', what it ignores in the process are the assumptions of the self against which the 'other' is distinguished; that is, it fails to consider the assumptions of *Occidentalism* that are also present in its articulations (see Wang 1997; Venn 2000). In terms of the Renaissance, the establishment of a common cultural understanding of 'modern Europe' can be seen to have deflected attention away from the fundamental ambiguities inherent in such a project and the focus was instead on shaping representations on the basis of difference. These differences, however, are not only situated within a common frame, but relative differences are elevated to the status of absolutes. Further, as Carrier notes in the context of anthropology, despite the 'twin and opposing characterizations of the modern West and societies in other times and places' used within the discipline, 'the Western half of this dialectic is [usually] hidden' (1995: 3, 4). The 'occidentalists' of anthropology, and other social science disciplines, unthinkingly accept a particular version of the West as a valid representation of its core (Carrier 1995: 13) – and it is this acceptance that is being challenged here in the rethinking of the Renaissance.

To restate the underlying argument of this chapter: the ways in which we understand the past have implications for the social theories we develop to deal with the situations we live in today. By widening the context of that historical understanding we expand the knowledge available to us in the development of contemporary theoretical models. If most theory today is predicated on the uniqueness of Europe, which in turn derives from an understanding of the Renaissance as an endogenous, epochal event of particular significance, then calling that radically into question upends most theory. This, then, provides a clearing from which we can begin to look at the world again and begin to imagine new forms for the future. Keith Jenkins's view that the failure of historical methodology ought to be celebrated as it is *this* which allows 'radical otherness to come, [and] new imaginations to emerge' (2003: 5) is not accepted. Rather, it is asserted that only through recognizing the constituted 'other' as always and already present in history, but written out of it, can we begin to move towards the development of human communities which provide the space for the full expression of human creativity – however we choose to define that. As Jardine and Brotton state: 'Our shared histories mean that we inhabit a cultural environment rich with possibilities for future fruitful collaborations and contestation' (2000: 185). In looking at East–West understandings today, it is important to remember both, that this is not the first instance of engagement, and that the West does not come to this cultural encounter 'as the inevitable senior partner' (Jardine and Brotton 2000: 184). This particular interpretation arises from a defined historical moment and one which has been called into question in this chapter.

5
Myths of the Modern Nation-State – The French Revolution

The iconic status of the French Revolution does not exempt it from also being one of the most contested events within history; in fact, the latter is probably a pre-requisite for the former.[1] One point of seeming agreement between theorists and historians, however, is the role of the French Revolution in what Furet terms, 'the invention of the political form of modern society' (1988 [1986]: 18), or, more poetically, 'the empirical modality through which the world of free and equal individuals has made its appearance in our history' (1990: 798–9); that is, the invention of the modern nation-state. French revolutionary historiography has been central to the establishment of '1789', or then the period from 1789 to 1815, as the birth-date of a new historical epoch, the modern. As Furet (1981 [1978]) argues, the Revolution was not understood simply as an event within a complex of events, but rather, was seen as constitutive of the *advent* of a new age; one founded upon the idea of equality and expressed through the establishment of modern political institutions. This heightened the sense of the present as unique and unprecedented and, as a consequence, problematized the way in which the relationship between the past and present was theorized (Furet 1981 [1978]; Crossley 1993; see also Foucault 2002 [1969]; Baehr 2002).

For many historians the idea that the past was shaped by already existing institutions and social forces increasingly gave way to the notion of events occurring as a consequence of human action.[2] The general change in the way of representing, and thus legitimating, the past led to ideas of continuity being superseded by accounts of rupture and the need to explain that rupture (see Ford 1963). Guizot (1997 [1846]), for example, sought to explain the progressive nature of European society in comparison with the stagnant forms of civilization believed to exist elsewhere and previously in terms of the institutions established during the French Revolution. Michelet (1967 [1847]), similarly, depicted it as an extraordinary event departing radically from all that had preceded it and foreshadowing the turmoil that was to come. In this way, Furet (1981 [1978]) suggests, the Revolution was understood both as the foundation of the future and as a singular event. Attempts to understand this period of instability were put in the context of generalized reflections on the nature of historical consciousness and the Revolution became a constitutive element of world-historical narratives delineating the emergence of the modern world.

In constructing the history of the French Revolution as a story of the origins of the modern world, this history then also becomes a discourse of European identity as modern (see Woolf 1992). The redefinition of the relationship between the political and the social that was entailed in this endeavour was accompanied by a rethinking of notions of sovereignty and nationalism which, together, established the state as 'an object of empirical inquiry' (Bartelson 1995: 221). The analytical border between nation-states was made co-extensive with the recognition of their territorial separation and conflated with the category of 'a people', whether organized around language, culture, or *ethnie*. With the nation-state being seen as the embodiment of the political project of modernity, a project that became global over time, thinking about the modern or the nation-state, as Chakrabarty argues, 'was to think a history whose theoretical subject was Europe' (2000: 34).

This chapter, then, discusses those aspects of the French Revolution that have led scholars to see it, as Fontana writes, as 'a unique case-study in the history of the progress of modern society' (1985: 12), and as one which was assumed to have world-historical significance. While there are various aspects which could be considered – namely, the emergence of democracy, the idea that the masses could change the world, the assumed triumph of secularism, the legacy of tyranny – this chapter focuses primarily on the instruments of governmentality that were subsequently taken to be constitutive of the emerging nation-state. It analyzes the significance of the emergence of the new institutions and types of social relations that were brought into being by the French Revolution (and by the responses of states to subsequent Napoleonic invasion). The increasing importance of theories of 'nationalism' to questions of state formation will be discussed as will the failure of these theories to address adequately the relationship of colonialism to the same. This chapter, then, contests the dominant understandings of the nation-state that ascribe a particular significance to its emergence in the French Revolution – namely, the setting up of a distinction between the 'original' and the 'copy' – and argues against the conception of cultural progress that locates 'others' within a history whose theoretical framework is predicated on the European experience. It is the association of the political dimensions of modernity with the French revolutionary period that is particularly in question in this chapter.

I

The modern idea of sovereignty has been integral to the formation of the nation-state and, as Cranston argues, it is seen as 'one of the most conspicuous, and lasting, innovations of the French Revolution' (1988: 97). These debates about the nature and limits of political power, however, go back at least as far as the Protestant Reformation (see Elton 1963) and the Peace of Westphalia which followed the Thirty Years War (see Teschke 2003).[3] These events raised fundamental questions about political obligation and obedience challenging, as they did, the hitherto theocratic nature of political authority. The move to identify the monarch with the notion of legitimate governance gave the centralizing states of the seventeenth century latitude in their bid to break away from papal claims to dominion and, in time, established the notion of territorial sovereignty associated with the absolute right of the monarch.[4] This was subsequently transformed, through the work of Rousseau (2004 [1762]) and others, into the absolute sovereignty of the people and was seen to provide inspiration for the events of the French Revolution.[5]

Rousseau's (2004 [1762]) interpretation of the social contract and his assertion that any government that does not guarantee the rights, liberty, and equality of all who live within its jurisdiction deserves to be replaced has been regarded as integral to the form and development of events in France during the revolutionary period. As Cranston argues, it was during this period that 'the republican leaders claimed that the sovereignty of the nation had been conferred on the people while they, the leaders, merely exercised the government' (1988: 103). How far this was an accurate assessment of the situation is not of primary concern here although it would be as well to note that Cranston holds the view that, although the 'Jacobins of the republican phase invoked Rousseau's ideas of *la volonté générale* and popular sovereignty, ... [they] rejected the political structures and procedures which Rousseau held to be necessary to their realization' (1988: 104). Despite this, it cannot be ignored that the abstract theories of the social contract and popular sovereignty, at the very least, inspired the French Revolution and, with the Napoleonic Wars that were to follow, disseminated the practices associated with these concepts more widely throughout Europe and, subsequently, the wider world.[6]

As the identification of the person of the sovereign with the state gradually gave way to the state being identified with the people, who were then considered a nation, the problem of politics centred around discovering, as Bartelson writes, 'the true general interest among the mass of particular interests' (1995: 211). During the nineteenth and twentieth centuries, there were generally two competing interpretations of what the 'true general interest' would, or should, be, with concepts of national self-determination vying with those of workers' solidarity and revolution both in practice and in theory.[7] Both the development of competing theories of nationalism and the growth of socialist theories contributed to the particularity of the emergence of the modern nation-state. For one, the attention of the state was turned onto the society for which it was responsible leading to the emergence of the modern idea of state intervention. Popular sovereignty was seen to have undermined the distinction between the state and community, but in conflating the two it also accentuated the differences between them by making the community, or society as it came to be more generally known, the site of responsibility of the state.

In summary, then, the importance of sovereignty to the discourse of modernity rested in three areas. One, embodying the shift from 'divine right' to 'collective will' that set up discovering the 'true general interest' of the people as the central issue within social thought. Two, establishing the legitimacy of the state's intervention in the 'public sphere' and making this a constitutive element of the workings of the modern state; and three, setting up the state as the object of empirical inquiry with an inside and an outside where the outside (e.g., the colonies) was not seen as having a relation to the inside.[8] The following section will discuss the issue of governance within France at the turn of the nineteenth century and examine the implications of the emergence of state institutions both in France and in other countries. As Eugene Weber argues,

> the political nation of the Ancien Regime functioned side by side with traditional community and social structures. The ideological nation of the Revolution had to compete with these. It was not invented upon their dismantling; its invention implied their dismantling. (1976: 113)

II

The years prior to the Revolution had seen extensive debates and discussions around the question of what was to constitute legitimate governance in France, debates that the crown itself had been involved in. The rapid rise of the bourgeoisie (perhaps more accurately defined as the propertied class) during the eighteenth century had led to the emergence of a socially and economically powerful group that was beginning to look for ways of exercising influence within the political realm – it soon found them.

> The ever-mounting strain of military expenditure on an inefficient financial system, together with the unwillingness of those in charge of the state to undertake any serious or at least sustained effort at structural reforms, made some sort of breakdown [of the *ancien regime*] practically unavoidable. (Doyle 1980: 194)

When the absolutist system did eventually collapse – in the aftermath of the publication of the state budget – the opposition forces, beyond convening the Estates-General, agreed on little else and the next few months were spent debating the ways in which the systems of finance, administration, and justice could be overhauled and fiscal privileges abolished (Doyle 1980: 195).

The immediate consequences of the Revolution left France with a constitution, representative institutions, the Declaration of the Rights of Man and the Citizen, and the decree of 11th August abolishing feudalism. In the following two years 'the victorious moderate bourgeoisie, acting through what had now become the Constituent Assembly, set about the gigantic rationalization and reform of France which was its object' (Hobsbawm 1977: 85). Changes were proposed, and implemented, in the areas of civil law, taxation, and the reorganization of feudal laws. Education and research were made state matters and, perhaps most importantly, the dominant role of the church in these matters was put to an end. Education was secularized and the temporal power of the Church was fundamentally undermined by various ecclesiastical reforms (Woolf 1991: 239–43). Academic institutions began to be regarded as existing for public purposes and the achievements of science were associated with national prestige. In 1794, as a consequence of a deputation from Saint-Domingue addressing the Constituent Assembly in Paris, and reinforced by insurrections across the French Caribbean, a clause abolishing slavery was included in the French Declaration of

Rights – this was overturned in 1802 with the reinstatement of slavery in the colonies (see Dubois 2004; Fischer 2004).

The government was radically changed and centralized through the abolition of regional, sectional, and municipal privileges; venality of offices was also abolished and there was an end to the privilege of birth, with privilege now becoming the reward of ability and property. As Furet argues, as a consequence of the revolution 'bourgeois civil society freed itself from its feudal fetters and achieved the freedom of individuals and of the market' (1988 [1986]: 29). In this it was assisted by the peasantry who, through their resistance, gained more in practice, in terms of abolishing feudalism, than by any of the 'revolutionary' measures instituted by the Assembly. That the achievements of the Revolution lasted was by no means inevitable, what made it more likely that they did so, was the emergence of the figure of Napoleon and the outbreak of the 'Napoleonic Wars'.

The principles of 1789, which had been couched in a universal language, were, under Napoleon, nationalized and put at the service of a specifically French imperial order. Within the countries under Napoleon's direct control, such as Italy, there were attempts to restructure them in the image of France. The administrative systems, military requirements, and taxation procedures were streamlined, principles of centralization implemented, the privileged groups reformed, a uniform code of law imposed, and the power of the state extended over the lives and resources of its citizens (Broers 1996: 137). In the German lands, tiny states were re-organized into a confederation consisting of fewer, amalgamated states and, even in areas where there was resistance to actual French military presence, such as Spain, the ideals of the revolutionary period were accepted and incorporated into the fabric of state life.

The Napoleonic state was seen to be a successful regime and hence it was emulated (see Woolf 1992). Nearly every major European government, Ford (1963) argues, emerged from the revolutionary Napoleonic period with its administrative organization profoundly altered, its conception of warfare (and what was needed to prepare for it) changed, as well as a radical increase in the level of public participation in political matters. As Hobsbawm writes,

> Since it was evident to the intelligent adversaries of France that they had been defeated by the superiority of a new political system, or at any rate by their own failure to adopt equivalent reforms, the wars produced changes not only through French conquest, but in reaction against it. (1977: 115)

ed

The specific construction of the state at this time, and the establishment of the particular institutions mentioned above, were taken by later theorists to signify the turn to modernity. A powerful concept of the state had come to be realized as the consequence of a successful uprising of the masses; one which was understood to be modern as opposed to simply an adaptation of the traditional absolutist state. One of its specifically modern elements was seen to be its 'penchant for intervention in the workings of the society it governed ... [particularly] through attempts at state-controlled public education' (Broers 1989: 492). Education was understood as being of increasing importance, not just in the 'construction' of a national identity as will be discussed below, but also because it served new conditions; conditions that 'were no longer local ones, but national; they were urban, they were modern' (Weber 1976: x). The establishment of the Civil Code was an attempt to regulate the administration of the new state and 'however authoritarian it was, [it still] represented a decisive break with any residual theories of arbitrary absolutism' (Broers 1989: 492). The new duties created by the administrative reforms led to the development of a large bureaucratic class and new standards of efficiency were set, with the state now expected to maintain civil order and protect private property. One of the characteristic features of the modern state was that it was not only capable of monopolizing the legitimate use of violence within a particular territory, but that this came to be seen as one of its constitutive functions. Finally, the development of the institutions of the modern state brought about new types of social relations that were also understood to bring society together in new ways. These institutions, seen initially to have emerged in France and only subsequently developed across the continent, were taken by later theorists as indicative of the turn to modernity. One such aspect was that of nationalism and it is to an examination of this phenomenon that this chapter now turns.

III

The nineteenth century saw the emergence and development of two differing understandings of nationalism. The first, believed the nation to consist in the conscious and voluntary consent of a self-defined population that wished to live under a particular administrative regime; the second, *pace* Herder, considered the nation to be a living organism based on the unconscious 'spirit' of a people. Both forms developed either out of the specificities of the French revolution or in reaction to its Napoleonic aftermath. Although there are theorists who place the emergence of the origins of nations in a more distant past (see, for example, Smith 1986), the majority of scholars would agree with Carr's statement that the *political* ideology of nationalism began to take shape when Rousseau, 'rejecting the embodiment of the nation in the personal sovereign or the ruling class, boldly identified "nation" and "people"' (Carr 1945: 7). Cranston argues that until Rousseau assigned an ontological status to the nation, independent of that of the kingdom, it had been the sovereign who had 'constituted' France, who had united the peoples divided by conflicting loyalties (1988: 101). The emerging ideology of nationalism, then, made this role of the sovereign redundant as the nation was understood as developing out of the general will of the people self-defined and was not limited to the boundaries of the pre-existing state.

For Rousseau (2004 [1762]), the nation preceded the state, but once constituted, the state was seen to have the potential to strengthen nationalist feelings. To this end, education and culture were deemed to be of vital importance, particularly in the rural areas, and the Napoleonic regime was the first to utilize the resources at its disposal to 'make' a people. The unity, and uniformity, of the state was seen as something to strive for and language was understood to be a significant factor in its achievement. As Eugene Weber (1976), in his book, *Peasants into Frenchmen*, suggests, if people could not understand the workings of the Republic they could not participate within it and so, whereas previously linguistic diversity had not been an issue, it was now perceived as a threat to the political and ideological unity of the Republic. To this end, the Convention 'acted to abolish dialects, and to replace them with the speech of the Republic, "the language of the Declaration of Rights"' (Weber 1976: 72). It was believed that by teaching the people French one would 'civilize' them and aid 'their integration into a superior modern world' (Weber 1976: 72–3): a world which was exemplified by the urban metropolis of Paris.

Language was also put forward by Herder (1969) as being the most significant of cultural phenomena in the second variant of nationalism that came to predominate at this time. Here, linguistic differences were not understood in political or ideological terms, but were instead taken as forming the basis for the organic growth of peoples and nations; with each nation seen as representing a truth of its own. As Bartelson suggests, for Herder the variety of languages was a natural corollary of human diversity and 'the incommensurability of languages correspond[ed to] an analogous incommensurability of cultures' (1995: 205–6). Thus, Herder believed that language demonstrated the inadequacy of viewing nations as 'daily plebiscites', as assemblies that one could join and leave at will. Instead, as Anthony Smith argues, Herder advocated the idea of the nation as an organic totality and believed that the natural and sole basis of a territorial state was its unique spirit and society (1996: 187). It was believed to be this unique spirit that people felt compelled to protect in the face of Napoleon's attempts to impose a uniform pattern upon Europe.

The popular resistance that emerged in reaction to invasion by Napoleon's armies had inspired many intellectuals to start thinking about the state in national terms. Old solidarities of language, community, and religion were strengthened and reinforced and in the aftermath of Napoleon's defeat there was an affirmation of loyalty to traditional monarchies and governments. The years after the defeat of Napoleon saw Europe as a whole embroiled in conflict between the ideologies and practices of the forces of reaction, liberalism, nationalism, and socialism. Whereas the initial movements towards national independence were inextricably linked to universal(ist), social(ist) ideologies, by the time of the 1848 revolutions the 'axiomatic assumption of a united front of nations struggling for liberty against a league of monarchs' (Talmon 1967: 192–3) was finally discredited and political unity was achieved through the conscious exclusion of social concerns. The general reaction to Napoleon in the occupied countries, then, transformed the elitist universalism of the Enlightenment into the more popular language of political Romanticism.[9]

Looking at the example of Italy, we see that the ideals of the French revolution – namely that sovereignty of a state resided in its people – and the promise made in the Convention of 'fraternity and assistance to all peoples who wish to re-conquer their liberty', had aroused Italian patriots to act in terms of establishing their own nation-state. 'National' histories began to be published and the idea of Italy was promulgated through books and journals leading to literate Italians becoming increasingly aware of themselves as 'Italian' (Woolf 1979: 330). The question of national independence became particularly acute, however, when France occupied Italy between the years 1796 and 1815. The discordance between French political principle and French foreign policy highlighted the paradoxical situation that, while France was promoting the ideal of an independent united nation, its presence in Italy was an obstacle to the realization of this ideal (although Napoleon did create a Kingdom of Italy, an entity that had not previously existed as a political unit).

Mazzini, one of the leaders of the movement for national self-determination in Italy, proclaimed that although the French Revolution had liberated people from the dominance of kings and priests it had offered no new principle of integration. This, as Talmon argues, was instead 'provided by the idea of the nation, represented by Italy' (1967: 117). Despite an entrenched dislike of French occupation, then, Italian intellectuals did not completely reject French political culture. As Broers suggests, even radicals like Mazzini and Garibaldi 'saw a centralized, unitary republic [modelled on the French state] as the only form of government which could mould a nation-state' (1989: 492). The increasing agitation for self-determination that came in the mid-nineteenth century, then, saw nationalism acting as a centripetal force in the consolidation of the territorial boundaries of the Italian and German states, and as a centrifugal force leading to the eventual disintegration of the Austro-Hungarian empire (Droz 1967: 170). In all cases, the subsequent states, were constituted along the lines of the model bestowed by the French Revolution and the extent of the influence of French occupation can be seen in that 'the unified Italian state which emerged in 1861 virtually patterned its institutions on those perfected in Napoleonic France' (Broers 1989: 489).

During the nineteenth century, the nation, or people, became a social category signifying the arrival of the masses. Regardless of the 'truth' of either ideology of nationalism, both forms have been fundamental in establishing the nation as the constituent unit of social and political life. In this context, as Hobsbawm argues, nationalism came to embody the principle that the political and ethnic unit ought to be congruent and hence the nation becomes that body of citizens whose collective sovereignty constitutes them a state – where the state is seen to be their political expression (1994: 18). Its importance further rests in the accompanying dramatization of the narrative of modernization whereby, as Smith argues, the '"myth of the modern nation" refers back to a pre-modern era which is "nationless", and [thus represents] ... part of the radical break between traditional, agrarian and modern, industrial societies' (1996: 192). The emergence of the nation-state has formed a central aspect of the theory of modernity both in terms of its transitional status located at the cusp of the move from the traditional to the modern and as a signifier of the modern political form.

Concluding this section, we see that the question of legitimate governance, which had dominated political theory in the eighteenth century, was partially realized through the spectacular event of the French Revolution. The shift from royal absolutism to popular sovereignty, together with the doctrine of national self-determination, transformed the political landscape of western Europe and had consequences for much of the rest of the world as well. The birth of the modern political community in the form of the nation-state, which had been heralded by the Revolution, was consolidated through the person of Napoleon who successfully orchestrated one of the greatest projects of organization and rationalization ever attempted. Together with the transmission of the ideology of nationalism, the development of the model of the modern nation-state as 'a territorially coherent and unbroken area with sharply defined frontiers, governed by a single sovereign authority and according to a single fundamental system of administration and law' has been seen as the most important legacy of the French Revolution (Hobsbawm 1977: 113).

This model was not only enforced upon various regimes during the Napoleonic Wars, but the success of its centralized, administrative modernization led to it being emulated and adapted by most of Europe leading to a general rationalization of the European political map and its political communities. The Revolution had fundamentally transformed the social and political structure of France and the subsequent Empire had had an impact upon the countries it waged war on through the advance of its soldiers and the introduction of new ideas and ways of organizing the state. The changes were to remain and were to be fundamental to the perception of a new era having dawned in Europe: the era of the modern, or modernity. Further, the changes that occurred were deemed to be the result of endogenous processes and their interpretations were generally self-contained within the geographical-cultural sphere of Europe. Instances of transition within these self-defined boundaries were predominantly understood as being of a similar character whereas instances of transition outside of these boundaries were often understood in terms of the existence of a cultural 'lag'. It is to these interpretations, and the extent to which they can be justified, that this chapter now turns.

IV

The emergence of political modernity – that is, rule by the modern institutions of the nation-state – has been seen to have emerged in Europe in the aftermath of the French Revolution and then become global over time. This trend towards global ubiquity is most often understood in terms which conflate colonialism with modernizing processes such that the emergence of nation-states in non-European parts of the world are seen to be part of a 'natural' progression of world history. With the assertion of national identity in these areas often being a form of the struggle against colonial exploitation Chatterjee argues that the national question in the non-European world has to be understood as historically fused with colonialism (1986: 30). However, the colonial question needs to be considered as integral to the development of the nation-state not just outside of Europe, but within Europe as well. As the nation-state emerged as a colonial state, the writing out of the colonial relationship from understandings of its emergence impoverishes our analyses of it. The failure to address this complex relationship is key to the continuing misapprehension about the 'singularity of modernity' and its dispersal globally from Europe outwards. This misapprehension does not only rest with 'European' scholars, but is also to be found among scholars of the Third World with Ashis Nandy, for example, arguing that nationalism in India was 'a direct product of the western past and thus an imported category' (1994: 89). The adequacy of positing such categories as 'European' has already been challenged earlier in this book and its specific connotations in the context of the construction of the nation-state and nationalism will now be discussed.

The emergence of 'governmentality', for example, – Foucault's (1991) term for the emergence of a novel form of governance made possible through the development of 'expert knowledges' and aimed at the welfare of society as a whole – has often been linked to the shift in governance from legislation to administration that is seen to have occurred in the aftermath of the French Revolution and changed the nature of the European state.[10] This was, in turn, argued to be linked to the transformation of the social into a medicalized, sanitary entity to be controlled through 'seeing and knowing' (Joyce 2002: 97, 105), or, to use a more resonant term, surveillance. Most analyses of this shift pay little attention to colonialism in outlining their understandings of governmentality, and yet, the colonies have been seen by many as the 'laboratories' of the, often repressive, social policies instituted in the 'home' countries (see Cohn and Dirks 1988; Mitchell 1991). From a different angle, Bayly (1993) suggests that the reign of the Mogul emperor, Akbar, in seventeenth-century India, as well as those by his successors, were underpinned by modes of surveillance that are generally attributed to having first emerged in Europe. Intelligence gathering, report writing, and surveillance of the general population are modes of governance that are not unique to Europe, nor did they only emerge elsewhere after the impact of colonialism, but were used by other empires for their own purposes; purposes that were not unrelated to those of the subsequent European empires (see also Fisher 1993).

Recent literature, particularly in the area of the history of 'colonial' science and medicine (Prakash 1999; Arnold 1993, 2000; Kumar 1995, 2003), has begun to draw attention to the extent to which policies and practices initiated and developed in the colonies were subsequently exported 'back' to the metropoles influencing the development of modes of governance there. Prakash, for example, argues that it was in the colonies that populations were explicitly 'constituted as subordinated subjects, whose health, resources, productivity, and regularities were the objects of governance' (1999: 126). Fingerprinting, for example, 'which has come to be used worldwide as the "scientific" means of identifying an individual, was first utilized for this purpose in India by the colonial government in Bengal' (Cohn and Dirks 1988: 226; see also Visvanathan 1988). In a different, but related, context, Viswanathan states that English literature had appeared as a subject in the curriculum of the colonies long before it was ever institutionalized in the home country and that the passing of the Charter Act in 1813 had 'enjoined upon England to undertake the education of the native subjects, a responsibility which it did not officially bear even towards its own people' at that time (1989: 3, 23).

Colonial expansion, in strengthening the alliance between science and the state, thus also led to the emergence of the concept of 'state science/medicine' (Kumar 2003), which, according to Prakash, 'opened a vast new field of practices connecting it to the population' (1999: 157) and provided governments with a model in terms of dealing with their 'own' populations. As Chakrabarty argues,

> Since the British did not go to India in search of pure knowledge, all these studies were produced in the cause and in the process of governing India, and it is this pervasive marriage between government and measurement that I take as something that belongs to the deep structure of the imagination that is invested in modern political orders. (2002: 84)

Whereas government had been seen within liberal discourse as only harmonizing and securing with law and liberty the autonomous interests in civil–social relations, the colonial regime was forced to violate this liberal conceit as it was '[u]nable to position its knowledge and regulations as disciplines of self-knowledge and self-regulation of its Indian subjects' (Prakash 2002: 88). Thus, the principle of 'intervention in the interests of the public good' can be seen to have developed in justifications of colonial rule at the time that it was also being internalized in governmental discourses within Europe – a relationship, however, that has been ignored by, among others, Foucault himself.

More recently, scholars have begun to recognize the importance of colonialism in the construction of Western states with Kaplan, for example, arguing for 'the history of European nations [to] be read as a product of colonizing relations' (1995: 94). Cohn and Dirks similarly suggest that colonialism is implicated in the very project of the nation-state to the extent that it 'played an active role in the cultural project of legitimation and in the technological development of new forms of state power' (1988: 229). The project of the nation-state, they suggest, is both constituted and represented by the forms of knowledge created and accumulated by the state in its attempt to mark and measure aspects of its citizens' lives (1988: 225). Others, such as Stoler, have reinforced the necessity of examining 'the cultural politics of the communities in which colonizers lived' to appreciate better the different ways in which national identity was constructed and maintained away from 'home' (1989: 136).

Anthony Smith's (1983 [1971], 1986) work on nationalism has, in a different vein, looked to reorient the study of nationalism away from its exclusive concern with Europe as the site of the historical emergence of this phenomenon and seeks to examine whether there are different types of nationalism. In doing this, he deconstructs the work of other theorists of nationalism and argues that their central mistake is taking on board 'a broadly diffusionist outlook, which holds that the original "Western" or "Central European" version of nationalism provides the criterion for subsequent types' (1983: xi). A common interpretation of this process of diffusion locates the origins of nationalism in England and France, sees it spreading out to Germany and Italy, which then, collectively, become the historic examples from which others borrow, imitate, and adapt. This understanding, labelled Eurocentric by Smith, emphasizes the Western origins of the spread of nationalism and 'the "alienity" of its content from the thought and sentiments of the populations and lands to which it was carried' (1983 [1971]: 29). The explication of this model in the work of two prominent theorists of nationalism will be addressed and then Smith's critiques of their Eurocentrism looked at in more detail.

Elie Kedourie (1994 [1960]), for example, sees the doctrine of nationalism as deriving from particular philosophical and political conditions present in Europe in the eighteenth and nineteenth centuries and then subsequently being imported to the rest of the world by the educated elites of those areas through imitation and adaptation of the original model. Nationalism is 'ethnicized' in that it becomes adapted to local social conditions and the traditions of the locality are politicized through the lens of nationalism. This, Kedourie sees as an insidious perversion of indigenous cultures through manipulation by elites – although, when a similar process happened in Europe it was not understood as such.

In this way, Chatterjee argues, that is, 'by designating as deviant all those cases which do not fit the classical form', it is possible to save the purity of one's paradigm (1986: 3).

The establishment of this distinction, between a normal, orthodox type of nationalism and a modified, adapted, or more usually, aberrant type, 'is designed to explain how a profoundly liberal idea [nationalism] could be so distorted as to produce such grossly illiberal movements and regimes' (Chatterjee 1986: 3) as are seen to have characterized the late twentieth century in particular. Distinctions are made by theorists between those movements which were seen to have based themselves on a 'civic' conception of nationalism, concerned primarily with attaining rights for those within a particular territory, while the illiberal type is understood to have distorted this initial intention. This understanding, however, rests on a misconception of the initial project of nationalism which did not ever exist in isolation of the sorts of atrocities that have since been associated with it. The only difference being that, in the first instance, those atrocities were carried out against 'others' who were geographically and culturally at a distance, whereas modern nationalism can be seen to have brought the associated problems closer to 'home'.

Benedict Anderson (1996), in his book *Imagined Communities*, follows a similar line to Kedourie where he suggests that the emergence of printed vernaculars was fundamental to the emergence of nationalism and nations in Europe in the eighteenth and nineteenth centuries. These nationalisms are considered modular nationalisms and later versions, such as those that developed in Africa and Asia, are deemed to have been pirated from, or at least modelled on, these original forms. As Taylor argues in the context of modernity, all 'they' (i.e., non-Europeans) 'want to do [is] what has already been done in the West' (1999: 233). In response to this theoretical construction of the emergence of nation-states and modernity, Chatterjee asks:

> If nationalisms in the rest of the world have to choose their imagined community from certain 'modular' forms already made available to them by Europe and the Americas, what do they have left to imagine? (1996: 216)

He goes on to argue that this being the case, it would appear that those in the postcolonial world are condemned only ever to be the consumers of modernity; never its creators, or authors: 'Even our imaginations must remain forever colonized' (1996: 216).

Smith (1986) sets up his theory on 'the ethnic origin of nations' as a counterpoint to this type of Eurocentrism arguing that as ethnicities exist everywhere each nation has its origin in itself and, as such, is not derivative of any other. Despite this, however, Smith does not really escape putting forward Eurocentric explanations for the emergence and spread of nationalism. Although Smith has an alternative point of *legitimation* for the existence of nation-states, his model for their *formation* follows the traditional pattern set out by historians as described earlier in this chapter (1986: 138–49). In this way, Smith mirrors Wallerstein (1997) in arguing for a reappraisal of the significance ascribed to events without contesting the specific form of their construction.

With the prevailing assumption of a particular version of the nation-state having emerged in eighteenth-century Europe, and then being modelled or copied by others, there is no option but to theorize others in relation to that original model and as being imitations of it. Regardless of Smith's attempts to move beyond seeing nationalism as solely 'European', and attempting to understand it as something that has always and already been present in the world, he does not escape the charge of constructing subsequent nationalisms as imitations of the original ones. In recognizing that these nationalisms express themselves 'differently' to the European ones, they are still theorized in terms of expressing themselves differently from what went before – with what went before being understood as original. Even if '*ethnies*' exist independently and universally, the manner in which they are expressed in the world, and take on significance, according to Smith, is theorized in terms of the 'original ethnic polities of England, France and Castilian Spain' (1986: 139).

This idea of an ethnic core to nations from which a national identity is developed is unsustainable for a number of reasons.[11] Historically, as Rodríguez-Salgado (1998) argues in the context of Spain, the concept of national identities in earlier centuries is problematic to the extent that the national entities with which they are associated simply did not exist. During the sixteenth century, for example, Rodríguez-Salgado argues that Spanish identity 'was a cosmopolitan, collective construct' reflecting the miscellany of Iberian kingdoms which, although they may have been known colloquially as Spain, did not exist as such in any significant way (1998: 251, 233).[12] In fact, as Rodríguez-Salgado argues, it was the 'experience of war abroad', particularly in the Americas, and the camaraderie that this engendered 'that forged the bonds that knit hostile Iberians into "the Spanish"' (1998: 251); and thus, by implication, colonialism itself, not some original *ethnie*. It is this refusal to acknowledge the impact of colonialism as integral to processes otherwise thought of as occurring endogenously within Europe that is under question in this book.

V

While there were particular developments in France in the late eighteenth and early nineteenth centuries that led scholars to interpret it as the point of departure for the emergence of the modern nation-state, this interpretation of it as originary and others as imitation, however, is not the only way of understanding the phenomena. The emergence of the nation-state occurred in the context of the emergence of the colonial state and developments that are generally ascribed to one are done so in the context of abstracting phenomena out of the relationships and interconnections between them. The course of events does not have to be understood as beginning with the French Revolution and then diffusing outwards, but would be better understood as occurring in the context of the wider interconnections of which particular events were a part. This would enrich our understandings of specific events as well as understand the wider contexts in which they occur.

Events, I would argue, are best understood as located in, and constitutive of, particular historical webs where the webs themselves are relational and, in the manner of Said (1975), possible 'beginnings' as opposed to origins of future events. Said argues that whereas the idea of 'origin' presupposes that which develops from it, that of a 'beginning' is developed as a complex of relations which allows for construction and re-construction; thus permitting shifts in perspective and understandings of knowledge (1975: 372). As such, despite its constant and insistent depiction as an event of unique, world-historical proportions, the French Revolution and the emergence of the 'model' of the modern nation-state could instead be seen as *an* event in a world of events which together brought into being our modern world.

Since social and political thought has largely been constructed on the uncritical acceptance of the assumptions challenged here, calling those assumptions into question necessitates a re-evaluation of those theories. This has been demonstrated with reference to contemporary theories of nationalism where setting up a distinction between the 'original' and the 'copy' has implications for the manner in which different histories are understood and analyzed. Following Foucault, in describing the original what is taken as paramount is the history of changes and transformations, the ways in which new forms rose up to produce the landscapes we know today; the copy, however, is understood in terms of inertia, a slow accumulation of the past, a sedimentation of things in which what is looked at is what is held in common as opposed to what is unique (2002 [1969]: 157–8). This then maps onto the way in which things are valued, with the original being more highly regarded than the copy, which is mere imitation. As Bhabha (1994) argues, historical agency is transformed through the process of signification; and the positing of something as a copy, as mimicry, is to articulate presence in terms of its 'otherness'. This makes the question of representation also a problem of authority as the representation of identity in terms of 'presence' and 'semblance' brings the 'other' into being '*as a subject of a difference that is almost the same, but not quite*' (Bhabha 1994: 86, 89).

The difference between being English and being Anglicized, for example, or between being European and being Europeanized, is the difference that produces knowledge as a form of social control 'in which to be Anglicized is *emphatically* not to be English' (Bhabha 1994: 87, 90). Mimicry *repeats* rather than *re-presents* and hence, that which is taken to be a copy can be known, controlled, and guided (Bhabha 1994: 88). It is noted, for example, that 'when nationalism emerged in the other countries of the West, despite the fact that it was the product of a sense of disadvantage with respect to the standards of progress set by the pace makers [Britain and France], there was no feeling that the nation was not culturally equipped to make the effort to reach those standards' (Chatterjee 1986: 1). Yet, when there was a similar take-up of the nationalist ideology in other parts of the world, it was asserted that some 'historical time of development and civilization (colonial rule and education, to be precise) had to elapse before they could be considered prepared for such a task' (Chakrabarty 2000: 8). *This refrain of 'not yet' emanates from a historical conception of cultural progress that justifies colonial intervention in the name of that progress and, in doing so, denies coevalness*[13] *with others.*

As has been discussed in earlier chapters, it was in the aftermath of the French Revolution that theorists began to look for new ways of understanding the world believing that the categories and theoretical constructs of the Enlightenment were no longer sufficient for this end. Not only was it presumed that the French Revolution had fundamentally changed the nature of social and political life, but it was further believed that the processes of industrialization were also irreversibly altering the organization of life and marking a qualitative shift from what had gone before to what was now emerging. The following chapter now turns to address the other key event in the general historiography of modernity that is commonly understood as giving it its claim to uniqueness and its European origin: the Industrial Revolution.

6
Myths of Industrial Capitalism – The Industrial Revolution

Along with the emergence and development of the political institutions of modernity which, as discussed in the previous chapter, are forever associated with the revolution in France in 1789, there is another revolution which it is believed transformed the organization of economic activities in the world, namely, the Industrial Revolution. The traditional century of the industrial revolution, from 1750 to 1850, is seen as producing 'a radical shift in the structure of the economy, in the composition of total output, and in the distribution of employment' thus creating a qualitatively different type of economy (Hartwell 1965: 181). This is not simply one of a number of discontinuities in the historical record, but one which, as Hartwell argues, established '*the* great discontinuity of modern history' (1971: 57), that between tradition and modernity. Industrialization is not only seen to bring about the modern world, but is regarded by many theorists as constitutive of it; as Krishan Kumar writes, for example, '[t]o become modern was to go through the process of industrialization' (1978: 111); and not to go through it was, in some sense, to have failed.

As the 'breakthrough' to industrialization is firmly located within western Europe (or more precisely, for some theorists, England), becoming a key marker in the construction of Europe's identification of itself as modern, then, to become modern is to go through a process of Europeanization (or imitation) that involves the crossing of a qualitative threshold. In this chapter, I examine the dominant discourse of the Industrial Revolution and address the relationship between conceptions of 'the industrial' and theories of commercial and capitalist societies. I am less concerned with the relative merits of any one particular theory regarding industrialization and capitalism as against any other, and more concerned with examining the (Eurocentric) premises underpinning the theories, whatever their other differences. I then assess the claims made by scholars with regard to its English, or European, origins and examine the consequences of abstracting this account from the wider global context; that is, the consequences of effacing colonial relations from the dominant explanations. I conclude this chapter by re-thinking these dominant accounts in the light of an historical sociology of connections.

I

Within economic history, de Vries (1994) argues that the Industrial Revolution, or the British Industrial Revolution, is one of the most important historiographical landmarks lending structure and coherence to historical narratives and defining research questions. Just as the Renaissance marked the beginning of modern history, he suggests, so the Industrial Revolution should be seen as marking the onset of the modern world. Such claims are never uncontested, and de Vries argues that the focus of the debate around the origins, causes, and development of the Industrial Revolution – again, similar to the field of Renaissance Studies – 'has shifted from the details of an established agenda to the agenda itself' (1994: 250).[1] For example, following Kuhn, Cannadine (1984) suggests that as particular paradigms of research are refined, and then undermined by further research, so a new interpretation emerges that not only recasts concerns about data previously used, but, by acknowledging different concerns, calls forth new questions and new organizational frameworks as well. As such, as Flinn notes, 'the conception of the Industrial Revolution has ... undergone some astonishing metamorphoses' (1966: 2); whether from cataclysmic suddenness to gradual evolution or then from being responsible for all the ills (and benefits) of society to being reduced, statistically, to historical irrelevance.

Following Flinn's (1966) earlier discussion of the writings by economic historians on the Industrial Revolution, Cannadine's (1984) survey of the same is also concerned with the 'agenda' of the revolution and the different phases within that historiography. In the hundred years since, as Cannadine suggests, 'Toynbee's *Lectures on the Industrial Revolution* [published in 1884] effectively began modern discussion of the subject' (1984: 132), four distinct phases are identified. These different phases, according to Cannadine, reflect the differing concerns of historians and theorists with the dominant preoccupations and problems of their own

*phases of industrial
historiography*

time, although the consequent 'paradigms' owe less to Kuhn and more to Weber's idea of historical studies organized in terms of (changing) structures of value relevance. In this, Cannadine also concurs with Flinn who suggests that the generations of historians who have studied the Industrial Revolution 'have each reflected, as is the habit of historians, the particular point of view of their ages' (1966: 14).

The first phase, initiated by Toynbee's popularization of the term Industrial Revolution, is associated with the emergence of histories primarily concerned with the social problems generated by the processes of industrialization. While early sociologists, such as Saint-Simon and Comte, had seen in the emergent industrial society an opportunity for progressive emancipation from the feudal system (see Baker 1989), towards the end of the nineteenth century it was the 'crisis of industrial society' itself that came to be of prime concern.[2] The institution of private property and free competition, together with the lack of government regulation of economic conditions, were factors cited by scholars to account for the visible poverty and general decline of living conditions in the nineteenth century. Problems of poverty and alienation were attributed to the breakdown of traditional communities and the dissolution of social bonds that were taken to be a consequence of the new forms of economic organization (Polanyi 2001 [1944]; Hirschman 1977). Academics such as the Hammonds and the Webbs, for example, drew 'explicit links between the bad conditions of the present and the horrors of the Industrial Revolution' (Cannadine 1984: 135; see also Hartwell 1971).

The second phase in the historiography of the Industrial Revolution suggested by Cannadine was similarly pessimistic focusing on the seemingly cyclical nature of economic activity and short-term fluctuations associated with the interwar and immediate post-war periods (see also Flinn 1966). In the 1950s and 1960s, however, with the 'unexpected, unprecedented efflorescence of western capitalism', the Industrial Revolution, instead of providing the historical context for contemporary social problems, suddenly became 'the past guide to present endeavours', that is, successes (Cannadine 1984: 149, 154). Earlier discussions of the trade cycle gave way, in this third phase of interpretation, to economic growth theory and the development of a general model of the processes of economic growth. This is captured in the work of modernization theorists, as discussed in an earlier chapter, with scholars such as Rostow (1960) arguing for the revolution to be recognized as the origin of the economic 'take-off' that was to have world historical significance.

This optimism was not to last, however, with – as Cannadine (1984) suggests, using the titles of Galbraith's publications – 'the affluent society' giving way to the fourth phase characterized as 'the age of uncertainty'. From the 1970s onwards, then, economic historians and sociologists began to focus on issues of 'post-industrial society' (Touraine 1971; Bell 1974), the 'cultural contradictions of capitalism' (Bell 1976), and de-industrialization (Bluestone and Harrison 1982); discussions which emerged in the context of a widespread rethinking of earlier certainties and a questioning of the previously accepted grand narratives of western modernity. With reference to the literature written after Cannadine's original article, it could be argued that there is now a distinct fifth phase. From the 1990s onwards, in response to the collapse of the communist regimes in Europe and the creation of a world market, there has been a re-emergence of the theoretical paradigm of 'growth theory' and the Industrial Revolution has increasingly come to be discussed in the context of issues of globalization and neo-liberalism (see Greasley and Oxley 1997; Petras and Veltmeyer 2001). As a consequence, theorists have sought to 'rehabilitate' the distinctiveness of the revolution as the critical point of departure in the emergence of the modern (global) world, albeit one now inflected as producing 'multiple modernities'.[3]

Despite being critiqued, dismissed, celebrated, and contested in varying degrees, but with relative regularity, over the past hundred years or so, the Industrial Revolution, nonetheless, remains as a fundamental touchstone of both economic historians and those who wish to place Europe at the centre of analyses of global economic change (whatever the normative implications ascribed to the latter). The following section addresses, in more detail, the association of the Industrial Revolution with Europe and discusses the relationship of industrialization with capitalism.

II

While most general histories of the Industrial Revolution place its emergence in Britain in the mid-eighteenth century, a number of historians have argued for its origins to be located further back in time and for the revolution itself to be understood less in terms of being a discontinuous moment of history than as a process of slow, stable, if uneven, growth which did not occur only in Britain. Despite their differences in locating the moment(s) of change within a particular time frame or the disagreements concerning the nature (discontinuous, or gradual) of the process there is still a general working assumption that at some point, at least from the sixteenth century onwards, the growth of the economy in England (or Britain, or at the most, western Europe) visibly accelerated. The explanations for this acceleration are commonly located in the seemingly unique conjunction of the following factors: technological innovations, the mechanization of production, the concentration of factories, the growth of urban centres, a unified land and water transport network, commercial agriculture, the spread of banking and finance, and a rise in population. While many of these phenomena that were not necessarily new, in conjunction they were considered to have an amplitude that influenced the development of society and the economy in unprecedented ways.

It was precisely these concerns that gave rise to debates over 'the Weber question' (see, for example, Marshall 1982; Lehmann and Roth 1993); namely, whether these conditions were sufficient in themselves to generate the 'discontinuity' of capitalist development or needed some transmutation within an autonomous ideational factor – the Protestant ethic – to provide a motivational discontinuity in attitudes to economic action. Although economic historians were not concerned with the 'Eurocentrism' of Weber's account, it is evident that his emphasis on a contingent ideational or cultural factor (however mundane that factor in itself) contributes strongly to the idea of the 'endogenous' European origins of capitalist modernity.

The most commonly cited technological innovations of the time were, as Briggs writes, 'the mechanization of the textile industry, the emergence of a new technology of coal and iron, and the introduction of steam power' (1960: 21); with the latter two then being seen to be instrumental in the transformation of other industries. These innovations, together with the network of businessmen prepared to take risks, Briggs suggests, enabled 'a smooth "take-off" from trade to industry' (1960: 27). This 'take-off', however, occurred in the context of England still being a primarily agricultural country and one in which merchants also continued to play a significant role. Briggs (1960), for example, argues that while the emergence of a credit system, together with the establishment of a systematic rail and canal network, facilitated processes of industrialization, these advances were also regarded as valuable in improving agricultural processes. As Deane and Cole (1962) suggest, even by the end of the eighteenth century more than a third of the working population earned their livelihood in agriculture and thus any understanding of national industrial growth has to take this sector into account.

The specificity of British agriculture – with its efficiency of production leading to rising productivity and the consequent release of labour for other activities – is seen by many historians as fundamental to the shift from a predominantly agricultural-based economy to an industrial one (see O'Brien 1977; Landes 1999). From being seen as an obstacle to industrial growth in earlier histories of the Industrial Revolution, then, O'Brien (1977) argues that questions of agriculture and economic progress are increasingly being regarded as intertwined. He suggests that the long process of institutional change that separated the majority of the rural population from access to, or income from, land – commonly known as 'enclosure' – differentiated British agricultural patterns from those on the continent and facilitated the process whereby, quoting Eric Jones, 'rural labour became wage labour dependent' (O'Brien 1977: 180). This process, as we shall see, is regarded by Marxist scholars such as Robert Brenner (1976, 1977), as integral to any explanation for the rise of a specifically capitalist mode of industrial production. In particular, he argues that economic development within England 'depended upon a nearly unique symbiotic relationship between agriculture and industry' whereby 'an agricultural revolution, based on the emergence of capitalist class relations in the countryside ... made it possible for England to become the first nation to experience industrialization' (1976: 68). The relationship between industrialization and capitalism will be discussed in more detail later in the chapter.

The sustained development of processes mentioned above contributed to changes in the distribution of the population across the country and consolidated the growth of industrial towns, ports, and cities leading to greater urbanization than had existed previously. This steady shift in population from the rural, agricultural areas to the developing urban centres was accompanied by the drawing in of women and children into the remunerative labour force from their previous, generally unpaid, occupations within the household and agricultural economy. According to de Vries (1994), the intensification of work, with all members of a household undertaking paid work, loosened strict kinship ties and opened up the household unit to 'outsiders'. Further, the associated reduction in leisure time, he believed, made self-sufficiency less possible and contributed to an increase in the consumption of commodities. For example, he suggests that as women entered paid employment there was 'a reduction of typically female-supplied home-produced goods and their replacement by commercially produced goods' (1994: 262). The purchasing power of women had the related consequence, as suggested by Hartwell, of commencing 'the social revolution in the status of women' (1971: 96). The extent to which this is so, however, is deeply contested especially with the model of the household economy in which all members worked, soon to be supplanted by the 'male bread-winner' norm in which, once it was economically viable, women were brought back into the home (Bythell 1993; de Vries 1994; Assassi 2007).

As well as population movement and migration, the period of the Industrial Revolution has also been associated with an increase in population size. Despite the difficulty in obtaining accurate or consistent data on this question, or being able to confidently ascertain the extent to which the growth of the towns and cities was due to 'natural increase' as opposed to population movement, Deane and Cole (1962) suggest that in the eighteenth century the rate of natural population increase of different regions within England was closely connected with their pace of economic advance. More specifically, Goldstone has suggested that it was a change in the condition of labour – from self-employment to dependence on waged employment – 'in the context of an industrializing economy that provided increasingly regular employment for wage labour in industry and agriculture that allowed earlier family formation and hence increased fertility' (1986: 29).

These demographic changes, together with the increased number of occupations and specializations requiring new and different skills and functions, were believed to have significant social implications. Membership within groups was seen to have become more fluid as greater social and physical mobility weakened kinship ties and altered the patterns of social relations, structures, and roles (see Kumar 1978; de Vries 1994). The pre-industrial 'mob' became the industrial 'masses', and later, 'proletariat class' and, together with the decline of community, this notion of the 'industrial masses' became, as Kumar argues, 'one of the most commonly remarked and agreed upon features of the emerging industrial society' (1978: 78–9).[4] The generally accepted idea, that community was being lost, required explanation, and solution. This led to the development of various theories of alienation and *anomie* which still have purchase today. The point of convergence for these differing theories is that they all rest on a belief that the turn to industrial society was the defining moment of change. It was at the point of the transformation of the economic system at which community was lost; and in its place had emerged mass society.

The emerging society was not necessarily seen in a negative light, however, as Durkheim's (1964 [1893]) work on the division of labour and mechanical and organic solidarity demonstrates. Durkheim argues for the division of labour within industrial society to be seen as a source of social solidarity in the emergent forms of social organization although he does acknowledge that it can also, on occasion and, in particular, in the moment of transition, present pathological forms resulting in a state of *anomie* (1964 [1893]: 353, 368). As the market extends and industrialization gathers pace the new conditions of industrial society demand the development of new forms of social organization. However, as Durkheim argues, as 'these changes have been accomplished with extreme rapidity, the interests in conflict have not yet had the time to be equilibrated' (1964 [1893]: 370). Thus, he suggests that it is not the division of labour itself that produces the condition of *anomie* associated with industrial society, but rather, that it is the failure to establish the necessary social relations for its regulation that leads to this.

This emphasis on a regulatory political (or, for Durkheim, moral) economy makes the emphasis in theories of industrial society one of *internal* connections and divisions, despite the fact that the 'expansiveness' of industrialism is also noted. The concept of the 'division of labour', within sociological analyses of industrial society, became one of the defining characteristics by which modern society was understood along with the idea of class. The focus on social structure addressed the organization of social life in terms of national institutions and social relations and established the idea of society as an autonomous, organized whole. The structural features of industrial society and, most importantly, the establishment of the worker as a social category became integral to the later constructions of the discourse of modernity; in that, a modern society was an industrial one and modern problems were those generated by an industrial society and would be resolved through the solution to the 'labour problem'.

Of course, aspects of this account are contested within other forms of sociological understanding, such as Marxist interpretations, which suggest that where labour is divided there is always an irreconcilable conflict (or contradiction) between the interests of different groups. The development of industrial production leads to the emergence of two basic classes with irreconcilable interests – the bourgeoisie and the proletariat – and that the 'de-skilling' integral to the increasing scale of capitalist production renders all workers uniform determining their constitution, in Marx's terms, as a 'universal class' (1976 [1867]: 788). However much this may be seen as a radical challenge to more standard historical and sociological accounts of industrial society, it retains those aspects which are at issue here, namely a representation of history in terms of a sequential development of modes of production and endogenous processes of social change within each mode. Indeed, in important respects it reinforces these features by identifying a single factor in the historical development across modes of production, namely that of the struggle between classes with its form in capitalism being the ultimate struggle to produce, finally, a classless society.

Industry, urbanism and the rise of modern cities, and social class all contributed to the idea that a radically new type of society was being consolidated, one that was based on new principles of social organization. These brought about new forms of social relations as well as new social institutions and practices which were, in time, seen to require a new mode of understanding. Not only the present, but the future also was understood as industrial and it was the industrial society that 'came to be identified as the distinctive type of modern society' (Kumar 1978: 55) providing an identifiable marker between societies that were industrializing and those that were deemed to be not yet industrialized.

III

With the evident significance of industrialism as the motor of rapid social change, it became easy for a number of distinctions within the history of social thought to become conflated. For example, in a recent book examining ideas of the market in modern European thought, Muller (2002) moves from a discussion of commercial society in Smith and Burke to civil society in Hegel to capitalism in Marx, suggesting that the different terms are simple synonyms. This fails to recognize the historical and theoretical differences between each form and, in particular, the use of the bridging category of civil society serves to establish the primarily national context in which each has come to be considered. In this section, I examine the historical shift from commercial to industrial capitalist society and the implications of the theoretical move away from the earlier stadial theory of history, which placed commercial society at its moral apex, to a binary division operating within the different stages. This is made to mark a distinction between tradition and modernity, where modernity is represented by the transition to industrial capitalist society, and where the co-existence of forms is no longer viable.

As we have seen, earlier social theorists associated modernity with the rise of commercial society, although it was not clear how the category of commercial relations could fully differentiate their experience of something novel from what had previously existed within any large-scale trading empire (see Polanyi *et al.* 1957). Indeed, to the extent that commercial society was identified as the moral apex of the stadial theory of history, it was understood to exist *alongside* other, 'earlier', forms and was not regarded as being responsible for, or implicated in, their transformation. As Heilbroner (1973) suggests, for Smith, every society under favourable conditions would, and should, pass through the four stages in the prescribed order. What made it likely that they would progress towards commercial society was the human impetus towards improvement and self-betterment; the reasons why they should progress in this way was to alleviate poverty and misery and bring about true liberty which was only possible in a commercial society (Heilbroner 1973: 245). The route to national wealth was now seen to be commerce, not conquest, for it was believed that a nation could increase its wealth by engaging in mutually beneficial trade. As such, in the work of Smith, *moral* progress was understood in terms of a moral imperative, albeit one *imperative* which effaced relations of colonial dominance and slavery from its hegemonic account. In *The Wealth of Nations*, for example, Smith argues that it is not to the establishment of colonies that one should object, but rather, to the prevention of their free intercourse with others: 'A nation that founds a colony in an unoccupied territory, or in a territory occupied only by savages, makes it subservient to the benevolent purposes for which it was destined by Providence, and extends the empire of civilization to, it may be, an indefinite extent' (1863 [1776]: 601).[5]

The identification of the unique characteristics of commercial society, then, was more designed to encourage good governance than to identify an 'unbound Prometheus', to use Landes's (1969) graphic image; that is, an innate characteristic which, in its diffusion outwards, would give rise to its supplanting of other forms of society. With the development of industrialism, the distinction between modern commerce and earlier commercial forms became easier to identify and, at the same time, commercial society was provided with a 'principle' that guaranteed its dominance. The principle, or logic, of transformation was generally taken to be technological development through market competition, and/or, class struggle. In this way, the 'cosmopolitanism' of commercial society gave way to the evolutionary teleology of industrial capitalism and modernization theory.

Ellen Meiksins Wood (2002) argues that, to the extent that capitalism is understood simply as the highest stage of progress of commercial society or as a particular version of commercial society, then the imperatives specific to capitalism (i.e., specific social property relations and modes of exploitation) go unacknowledged and unaddressed. In contrast, drawing on the earlier work of Robert Brenner, she argues for capitalism, or the capitalist market, to be understood as a distinct social form arising out of historical conditions peculiar to England in the sixteenth century. The distinctiveness of these conditions is said to rest in the nature of the English state which was both politically and 'materially' centralized – that is, it is seen to have had 'an impressive network of roads and water transport that unified the nation to a degree unusual for the period' (Wood 2002: 99) – as well as a system of land tenure, or property relations, that saw land being worked by 'tenant-farmers' as opposed to peasant-proprietors. It is this system of property relations, in particular, that Wood cites as significant in the decline of the English peasantry, the polarization of rural society into larger landowners and dispossessed masses, and the emergence of the 'famous triad of landlord, capitalist tenant, and wage labourer' (2002: 103). This latter, in turn, she suggests, contributes to the emergence of a domestic market for which there is no historical precedent and which provides the context in which English industrial capitalism emerges, develops, and then diffuses globally.[6]

The argument that a form of agrarian capitalism specific to England makes industrial capitalism on an international scale possible is not, however, uncontested, with Immanuel Wallerstein's (1974, 1980) world-systems theory offering an alternative Marxist explanation for its development. The commercialization model, associated with Wallerstein, is based on the argument that modern industrial capitalism emerged from technological progress and the expansion of markets – both of which were features of the earlier commercial society – within western Europe. Put simply, Wallerstein's focus is less on productive relations internal to states and more on the network of trading relations between them. His argument rests on a discussion of the relationship between state structures, exchange relations, and the position of owners and producers within the European capitalist world economy. In this model, then, Wallerstein (1974) presents a supranational perspective to the emergence of capitalism, albeit one which traces the origin of the transition from feudalism to capitalism to the expansion of trading relations in western European countries.

The 'transition' to which Wallerstein points covers three key phenomena: 'the initial *transformation* of feudal Europe into a capitalist world-economy', 'the subsequent *incorporations* of outside non-capitalist systems into the ongoing and necessarily expanding capitalist world-economy', and 'the *proletarianization* of labour and the *commercialization* of land within the capitalist world economy' (1979: 141–2). Despite the differences of emphasis and interpretation allowed to the various aspects of 'transition', the overarching singularity of the process described – the expansion outwards from an initial core that is European – is agreed upon in both standard accounts of industrialization as well the different Marxist ones. Wood, for example, argues that an effective challenge to the Eurocentric neglect of Western imperialism requires a consideration of 'the very specific conditions in which traditional forms of colonialism were transformed into capitalist types of imperialism'; conditions, which she suggests, have their basis in particular forms of 'capitalist social property relations' (2002: 33). However, by arguing that '[o]nly a transformation in social property relations ... can explain the dramatic revolutionizing of productive forces uniquely characteristic of modern capitalism' (2002: 144), she locates the change to 'capitalist types of imperialism' outside of the relations that constituted imperialism and as preceding imperialism, and continues to offer a local account of a global phenomenon. It is an account that sees capitalism as emerging in the West, and England more specifically, and then being transmitted to the rest of the world. It is this idea, then, that industrial capitalism is/was something which emerged in western Europe and then diffused outwards, that is contested in this book.

IV

Sidney Pollard has suggested that the Industrial Revolution should not merely be regarded as the repetition of the British model across Europe, but rather, as a process involving 'continuous adaptation to a continent- wide opportunity' (1973: 644). Pollard goes on to mark the difference between the industrialization of Europe and the industrialization of other areas by suggesting that '[s]omewhere near the outer periphery of Europe there is the watershed between societies which on contact with the new industrialism were capable of imitating it and becoming part of it, and areas, which at least for a long period, were transformed away from it, becoming specialized as "colonial" economies' (1973: 644). Although the pace of industrialization was seen to differ between European countries, with England, or Britain, initially ahead, Joll argues that 'it was nevertheless a shared experience ... [contributing] more than anything to tightening the links between the European countries' (1980: 13).[7]

This narrative of industrialization, with a 'lead actor' and other imitators or 'follower' countries, is not unusual. Nor is the hierarchy which distinguishes between those imitators within Europe, who are quickly assimilated to the dominant narrative, and those outside of Europe who are regarded as irreducibly different. As is evident in this construction, the British Industrial Revolution is seen to be integral to developments elsewhere in Europe and imitation within Europe is quickly transformed into the idea of interconnectedness. This is so whether the response is one of de-industrialization in the face of the expansion of British industry into continental Europe – for example, the degradation of the textile and metals industries in Austria and parts of Germany – or then the stimulation of industries complementary to British ones – as in Belgium (see Pollard 1973). As Pollard writes, it would not make much sense to try to understand the history of the Industrial Revolution within any one region in Britain in isolation to developments elsewhere – for 'one of the significant features of the industrial revolution in Britain was its complex regional inter-relationships' (1973: 638) – and so it was on the Continent, he suggests.

In fact, as we shall see in this section, the attempt to find evidence of a special European significance, with Britain perhaps in a lead role, founders. Pomeranz (2000), for example, suggests that there was little to indicate that there was any Western European industrialization prior to the 1800s that would mark any difference to that of non-European economies; there were similar processes of commercialization and, what he calls 'proto-industrialization', occurring in other core centres outside Europe.

These processes outside of Europe, however, are typically seen in terms of a (cultural) inability to imitate and they are not understood as interconnected even where active steps were taken to undermine domestic industries elsewhere and obstruct their competition with European manufacture. The British production of cotton textiles is often commented upon as a leading example of success of the factory mode of production. Yet, what is missing from this narrative is the simultaneous destruction of the cotton textile industry in India (as well as elsewhere) which opened India up as a market for the export of British goods. Morris (1963), for example, the main theoretician against the 'de-industrialization' thesis in India, argues that the failure of the Indian textile industry had less to do with the practices of British colonialism than internal factors including the unpredictability of the monsoon weather patterns.

Despite acknowledging that prior to the First World War India had 'one of the world's five largest cotton textile industries, one of the two largest jute industries, the third largest railway network, and a substantial coal mining industry' (1963: 614–15), Morris still suggests that India in 1800 'was a society which had none of the basic preconditions of an industrial revolution' (1963: 616). He goes on to argue that the advances that had been made in India were all a consequence of the interventions and efforts of the British Raj, namely the 'introduction of a modern, stable political environment' (1963: 616), but the failure to industrialize fully had nothing to do with colonial policies and was attributed, instead, to the general international economic context, the unpredictability of the weather, and population increase.

While there is an ongoing debate regarding the extent to which Britain did, or did not, contribute to the 'de-industrialization' of this sector in India (see Morris 1963; Habib 1980; Simmons 1985; Harnetty 1991), what is significant is that the literature on this debate rarely crosses over into discussions regarding the success of industrialization in Britain. In the main, the impact of de-industrialization in India upon the subsequent success of British industry is rarely discussed, these successes are always seen to be endogenously created, achieved, and maintained.[8] Within these debates, David Washbrook is, however, a notable exception arguing, as he does, that the mechanization of the cotton textiles manufacture in Britain has to be understood as part of 'a much longer "global" history of the fabric itself' (1997: 417).

Cotton, as Washbrook argues, first came to Britain from India, as did the knowledge of how to design, weave, and dye it. To understand its mechanization simply in terms of an evolution from a pre-existing British domestic system of production without recognizing the context of its relationships with other parts of the world is seriously to distort its history. The interchange of ideas and commodities, which was highlighted in the previous chapter on the Renaissance, is largely missing from dominant western accounts of the emergence of industrialization. Indeed, as Pannikar states, 'in the era of the political domination of Asia by Europe from 1860–1948, it was generally forgotten by European writers that Asia had not merely borrowed from Europe but also contributed liberally to the growth of [what came to be seen as] Western civilization' (1959: 301). It could further be argued that the world beyond Europe also contributed substantially in material terms to the commercial growth which stimulated the development of the West. This was largely due to the exploitation of resources in other countries, the institution of slave labour, and the trades of 'dispossession' whereby Europeans gradually took over the trades of the peoples with which they came into contact, for example the dispossession of the fur trade from the Algonkins (see Wolf 1997 [1982]).

The 'triangular trade', in Eric Williams's (1994 [1944]) classic account, between Britain and France, Africa, and colonial America was seen to provide an important stream of capital accumulation which contributed to the financing of the Industrial Revolution (see also Inikori 1987; Solow 1987). The slave ships, he argues, 'sailed from the home country with a cargo of manufactured goods. These were exchanged at a profit on the coast of Africa for Negroes, who were traded on the plantations, at another profit, in exchange for a cargo of colonial produce to be taken back to the home country' (1994 [1944]: 51–2). In this way, he suggests, the triangular trade provided a triple stimulus to British industry (as well as the French). James also argues that in the eighteenth century nearly all the industries which developed in France 'had their origin in goods or commodities destined either for the coast of Guinea or for America' and that even if the French bourgeoisie traded in other things, their success or failure depended on the traffic in slaves (1989 [1938]). Further, Saint Domingue, a French colony up unto the end of the eighteenth century, produced about forty percent of the world's sugar and over half its coffee (Geggus 1981); it was also the largest foreign market for the export of French goods and hence vital to the French economy. The wealth generated by the slaves in the sugar plantations in the West Indies 'mostly returned to Britain; and the products they made were consumed in Britain; and the products made by Britons ... were consumed by slaves who were themselves consumed in the creation of wealth' (Mintz 1986: 43). As Blackburn (1997) notes, then, the sugar colonies contributed to substantial increases in national wealth in three main ways: the profits generated internal to this trade, the expansion of external markets for British goods, and through the supply of cheaper foodstuffs, primarily, sugar.[9]

Following Barbara Solow (1987), this is not to suggest that slavery 'caused' the Industrial Revolution or was the only factor in its emergence or that without slavery the Industrial Revolution would not have occurred; but it is to point to the importance of understanding colonial slavery as integral to the ensuing development of industrializing processes. For example, while Richardson argues that the relationship between the slave trade, plantation agriculture, and British industry is even more complex than that suggested by Williams and others, he does acknowledge that there was, by the end of the eighteenth century, 'both a substantial rise in the level of British slave trading activity and colonial sugar production on the one hand, and a marked acceleration in the rate of growth of British industrial production on the other' (1987: 741). Similarly, Eltis and Engerman (2000) question the causal significance ascribed to the slave trade while accepting its long-term economic implications for processes of industrialization. They also go on to suggest the importance of recognizing the moral implications of slavery to the development of Europe's idea of freedom arguing that Britons could only describe their own social and political institutions as 'free' by studiously avoiding 'the fact that what was happening in the Caribbean was at odds with what was happening at home' (2000: 141).[10]

V

As Jack Goody (2004) writes, and has been discussed above, there is little overall consensus among historians and social scientists with regard to issues of modernization, industrialization, and capitalism. The one issue on which there is seeming agreement, however, is the central contribution of Europe to the emergence and development of these processes and their subsequent diffusion outwards. It is this belief in Eurocentric diffusionism – that is, the belief that Europe eternally advances, progresses, and modernizes while the rest of the world struggles to catch up – that James Blaut (1993) seeks to undermine in his book, *The Colonizer's Model of the World*. He argues that while it is commonly believed 'that the economic and social modernization of Europe is fundamentally a result of Europe's *internal* qualities' what this does not take into consideration is the immense impact, and inter-relation, of these areas on the developments occurring within the geographical territories of Europe (1993: 2). This interpretation, for example, does not take into consideration – or actively downplays – the influx of wealth from the colonies that contributed substantially to the initial 'take-off' period of the industrial revolution; the involuntary contribution of slave- and bonded-labour to this process; nor the manner in which areas, such as Africa, Latin America, and India, were de-industrialized and deliberately underdeveloped in order to ensure market supremacy for British and European commodities.

Theorists, such as Samir Amin (1977) and Andre Gunder Frank (1975, 1998), further contest the notion that capitalism, as distinct from industrialization, was the product of an exclusively European conjuncture of events. Frank, for example, argues that the conditions for 'the rise of the West to hegemony and the transition to capitalism in Europe cannot be found within Europe alone'; they have to be sought in the world as a whole (1992: 390). While scholars such as Blaut, Amin, and Frank may disagree over specific points of analysis regarding the ways in which pre-capitalist societies ought to be understood, there is a common belief that any analysis has to be based on an examination of the global context within which capitalism emerged. If the world-system is a *world*-system then why should we presume that Europe – one part of the world – unproblematically constitutes the centre of that world? The focus on Europe, Perlin (1994) argues, is a consequence of a misreading of historical developments exacerbated by a widespread neglect of the writings on pre-colonial Asia and Africa (see also Grovogui 1996). It is the one-dimensional aspect of most analyses, then – captured by Perlin's question below – that is also under question here:

> Where balance of trade and payments are concerned, the fundamental questions have been seen to be those of why and how precious metals were 'exported' from Europe, with little or no attention to the problem

of why, from the 'other side', there existed a long-term, structurally stable, even increasing demand for them, attracting their movement into Asian regions. (1994: 92–3)

Looking solely at the point of supply and ignoring the question of demand places undue emphasis on the self-conscious activities of the producers and occludes 'the whole train of causative ramifications that take us into the interiors of regions' which few scholars have recognized as contributing to world trade (Perlin 1994: 94).

Wallerstein's (1974, 1980) theory of the 'world-system', for example, places its origins in Europe and its development in the expansion of the European economy which subsequently incorporated much of the world within its ambit. Prior to the eighteenth century, however, as Washbrook (1988) demonstrates, there were a number of different regional networks with the characteristics ascribed by Wallerstein to the European one – such as relations between core and periphery – in which Europe either did not participate or was the peripheral member (see also Perlin 1983; Abu-Lughod 1989; Subrahmanyam 1997). As Washbrook argues, once the commercial centres across various regions are linked up into circuits of trade we see that 'South Asia was the hub of several of these circuits, [and] was responsible for a much larger share of world trade than any comparable zone' with the weight of its economic power reaching, for example, Mexico (1988: 60). As such, explanations for Europe's subsequent dominance that rest on an endogenous account for its rise are inadequate in the longer (and wider) view.

The issue is not simply one of extending and filling in the gaps in the patterns already constructed on the basis of an examination of European economic development, but the bringing forth of other realms of interaction that are equally as complex as the European and continuous with its processes (Amin 1972; Habib 1980; Perlin 1994; Subrahmanyam 1997). Scholarly work on the trade networks that brought together the Atlantic ocean as a distinct region, the Bay of Bengal area, the Western Indian ocean, the African sea – as well as then pointing to the links between these regions and across them – illustrates the long history of complex interconnections and negotiations between peoples across both sea and land (Das Gupta 1985; Subrahmanyam 1988; Perlin 1994; de Silva 1999; Law and Mann 1999; Keita 2002). Pointing to the interactions between these distant places, Alvares writes, for example, that 'iron ore mined in south-eastern Africa, was forged in South-western India, fashioned in Persia and Arabia, to end up as the weapons and chain mail of the Saracens as they faced the Crusaders' (1991: 41).

The issue is not only one of a network of commercial centres and trading posts existing elsewhere, however, but also of a need to recognize developments within agriculture and manufacturing. Perlin (1983), for example, points to the growth of urban manufacturing and the increase in peasant production within India in the seventeenth and eighteenth centuries and situates these developments within the wider international context. Subrahmanyam similarly argues, in his historical account of the growth of rural industry and commercial agriculture in the Krishna-Godavari region in India, that by the end of the seventeenth century, these areas had 'an economy of producing centres, underpinned by a marketing network, wherein imports, exports and locally traded goods all found a place' (1990: 110).

Maintaining the belief in what Blaut (1993) terms, *Eurocentric diffusionism*, that is, a belief in the idea that cultural processes flow *out* of Europe and *towards* the rest of the world, then, is problematic for a number of reasons. First, it establishes a theoretical framework for understanding that has at its core the idea 'that progress in European civilization and expansion of that civilization in space were different dimensions of the same historical force' (Blaut 1993: 26). Theories of modernization, as discussed in a previous chapter, rely on an acceptance of the European pattern of development as being specifically 'European' and 'natural'; and further postulate that this ought to be the future course of all non-European countries. The unpopularity of these propositions, particularly in the context of decolonization, led to the emergence of a critical body of thought that sought to demonstrate the central role of the world beyond Europe in processes of industrialization and modernization (Blaut 1993). Subsequent postcolonial scholarship further presented the theoretical point that making the trope of capitalism foundational to our understanding of the world homogenizes 'the histories that remain heterogeneous within it' (Prakash 1997: 495).

Constructing the discourse of capitalism as a process that became global over time posits 'historical time as a measure of the cultural distance (at least in institutional development) that was assumed to exist between the West and the non-West' (Chakrabarty 2000: 7). This further legitimates the binary of civilization and barbarism and allows an internalist history of Europe whereby Europe is understood as the site of first occurrence. We were all seen to be headed in the same direction and Europe simply provides the model of where it is that the rest of the world would arrive. Chakrabarty argues that if we examine the epistemological assumptions underlying Marx's use of categories like 'bourgeois' and 'prebourgeois', or 'capital' and 'precapital', then we see that the 'prefix *pre* here signifies a relationship that is both chronological and theoretical' (1992: 1493) with 'capital' being posited as a philosophical and universal category by which history, and the rest of the world, is knowable in terms of its differences from it. The narrative of historical transition, then, is reified as *the* narrative of history and Third World histories today are written within the problematics of this narrative – be it development and industrialization, capitalism, or modernity.

In an historical context, Perlin (1994) argues for the question of economic change in South Asia (as in other places) to be taken up as one involving a framework of relevance that escapes political or continental boundaries, and instead, locates traders and producers, commercial centres, manufacturing industries and agricultural sites across the world as part of a complex of processes, developments and changing structures. In particular, he argues against the dominant understanding of such processes as resulting from the influence of *foreign* capitalistic agents entering non-European areas and suggests, instead, that we look to reconstruct the ways in which, for example, 'local merchant capitalisms were disrupted and dismantled in favour of the increasing presence of metropolitan Europe' (1994: 59, 83). This allows us to rethink the construction of boundaries and order within the pre-colonial world and to review

> the eventually dominant role of the European Companies in undermining the bases of Asian merchant activity and institutions, and in subverting the multilateralist inter-Asian trading structures in favour of increasingly bilateral flows and an international division of labour centred in metropolitan western Europe itself. (Perlin 1994: 59)

Contrasting 'indigenous' developments with those initiated from 'outside' perpetuates the reified categories of 'Europe' and, in this case, 'Asia', that previous chapters of this book have worked to dismantle. Both European and Asian actors ought to be understood as operating within 'a general theatre of developments, within which increasing European involvement led to changes in the distribution and character of manufacture and commerce in South Asia' (Perlin 1994: 86–7); as it did, it could be added, in the modes and forms of manufacture and commerce in Europe. Bringing in the 'others', that traditional accounts have left out of their theorizations of capitalism, industrialization, and modernity, forces us to reconsider the theoretical understandings developed upon previous historical interpretations.

The preceding discussion of the processes of industrialization, for example, points to a political economy, but this is not one of liberal economics or its Marxist variants. It is a political economy that has colonialism as central to it and, yet, this is precisely what is effaced in both liberal and Marxist political economy. Any logic of industrialism that can be isolated has been demonstrated to have existed in other places and at other times and so can never be regarded as unique or causal in itself. The question is not one of the efficiency of, for example, Indian manufacture, but the colonial squeeze applied to it in order to privilege British interests. The one aspect that is missing from hegemonic explanations, then, is that of the relationship between any industrializing impulse and the ability to use 'force' both in terms of establishing forms of 'unfree' labour as well as expanding the reach of the market for one's goods. Colonialism was integral to both.

Bringing together the various issues addressed in the chapters in the second section of this book, my argument is that the claim for a specifically modern European identity, or modernity, is no longer sustainable. The dominant discourse of the Renaissance, positing it as the birth-hour of modern Europe, has been effectively challenged as have the discourses putting forward the French and Industrial Revolutions as singular, endogenously European events of world-historical significance. It has further been demonstrated how ideas of the 'modern' naturalize history through their representations of power and domination and how deeply rooted the 'compulsion ... to think and translate the world through the categories of the European imperial-modern is' (Chakrabarty 1994: 87). While Chakrabarty has argued for scholars to make the 'attempt to write difference into the history of our modernity in a mode that resists the assimilation of this history to the political imaginary of the European-derived institutions' (1994: 88), I suggest that writing difference into a history already written is not enough. It is not enough to be critical of modernity, or to recognize flawed institutional practices, or even then, as Chatterjee exhorts, to write other histories which, in contesting singularity, open up for negotiation the very relation between parts and the whole (1994: 48). *In re-writing histories at the heart of understandings of modernity and narratives of historical progress we must also reconstruct the very categories of understanding in the process.*

The emergence of the idea of modernity *as the new* required the assumed temporal break – between the pre-modern and the modern – to be mirrored spatially. This occurred with the colonial space becoming the 'non-place' and the history of modernity, as has been argued, then rested on 'the *writing out* of the colonial and postcolonial moment' (Bhabha 1994: 243, 246, 250). Further, with the spatializing of the time of modernity a particular theory of cultural difference was instituted – one which installed 'cultural homogeneity into the sign of modernity' and ultimately demonstrated the ethnocentric limitations of the concept (Bhabha 1994: 243). Shifting the frame through which we view the events of 'modernity' forces us to consider the question of subaltern agency and ask further: 'what is this "now" of modernity? Who defines this present from which we speak?' (Bhabha 1994: 244).[11] Postcolonial scholarship, as has been demonstrated, has been integral to the exercise of opening out and questioning the implied assumptions of the dominant discourses. It has further provided the basis from which to reclaim 'a series of regulative political concepts, the *supposedly* authoritative narrative of whose production was written elsewhere' (Spivak 1990: 225). The task here, following Spivak, and which will be discussed at greater length in the Conclusion, has been less about the uncovering of philosophical ground, than in 'reversing, displacing, and seizing the apparatus of value-coding' itself (1990: 228); thus accepting the possibility, in times of the postcolonial, of a critical realignment of colonial power and knowledge through a methodology of 'connected histories'.

Conclusion: Sociology and Social Theory After Postcolonialism – Towards a Connected Historiography

A key concern of this book has been sociology and its sense of the past. The conceptual categories of sociology, I have argued, are dependent on a particular historical understanding, but have been argued to be timeless, or universal, in character. I have argued that the categories are not universal, but embody a form of Eurocentrism. It has been my contention that the distinction between the discourse on the modern project and the practices and institutions of modern society is inadequate to address the world we inhabit and the problems we share. In fact, not only is such a separation inadequate, it actively contributes to the perpetuation of inequalities and injustices that are in urgent need of consideration and resolution. The distinction between discourse and structure that permeates sociological understandings – both in its dominant and postmodern forms – permits the perpetuation of inadequate concepts by admitting a multiplicity of forms of inadequacy and turning attention away from the problem of adequacy itself. This can be seen clearly in the way that modernization theory has given way to the theory of multiple modernities, which has, in turn, been supplemented by alternative, plural, and entangled modernities. These, I submit, are variations on a theme where the theme is always the necessary priority of Europe, or the West, in any understanding of the world.

While the privileging of Europe, and the West, in the context of a history of imperialism, colonialism, and slavery that covered almost the entirety of the globe would be understandable, what is less so, is the failure of most theorists who privilege Europe and the West then also to consider the histories of imperialism, colonialism, and slavery that enabled Europe, and the West, to achieve this dominance. As such, 'provincializing Europe' is not only about bringing to the fore other histories and experiences, but also about recognizing and deconstructing – and then reconstructing – the scholarly positions that privilege a part of the world without any recognition of the lives (and deaths and living deaths of slavery) that have contributed to that part of the world becoming privileged. Addressing the construction of 'modern Europe', then, is necessary for an adequate engagement with the history, and present, of the world. It is only by understanding how Europe came to represent the world at large and offering a more adequate explanation of the interconnections that came to constitute it as such, is it possible to think a global history and a global sociology.

Chakrabarty (2000) makes the argument that, we (the postcolonial we) cannot think ourselves outside of the West, outside of categories constructed in the West's engagement with the rest of the world, and that thinking about other contexts will inevitably take us back to the histories of the West. While I do not fully agree with this position, I do recognize the need to engage with Europe and the West and the traditions that have been posited as European or Western. As I argued earlier, the concepts and traditions are not European; what is at issue is the claiming of these concepts and traditions *as European*. It is this move that effaces the histories and lived realities of all those others who thought and acted, and places Europe as the unique home of the innovative, the creative, the thoughtful, and the active. The rest of the world is simply the rest of the world with a negative designation; it is the non-West, the non-European, the Third World in contrast to the First, the underdeveloped in relation to the developed. We will need to engage critically with Europe and the West, until the processes by which these constructions are produced and reproduced are made transparent (see Hall 1992).

Dirlik's (2002) claim that even voices critical of Europe subscribe to a form of Eurocentrism, as a consequence of their focus on Europe, has increasing resonance within scholarly debate. To the extent that criticism of Europe simply inverts the dominant paradigm and offers a particularity in contrast to that universal then his argument has force. In this book, however, I have sought to do something different. I have sought to understand the conceptual framework of sociological discourse on modernity, deconstruct its claims to universalism through a recognition of its own particularity as well as the particularity of others, and then to reconstruct a framework of understanding on the basis of 'connected histories'. This, I argue, provides a more adequate way of addressing the experiences of peoples across the world without reducing their experiences

theory of social action *belief / action*

to 'deviant' particularity; examining wider interconnections permits the construction of a general structure of thinking that is predicated on the provisionality of any claim to adequacy.

Following William James (1904), action comes from belief where belief is nothing other than thought at rest. Acting, however, as Holmwood (2007b) suggests, brings about both an engagement with other interlocutors, and produces unanticipated consequences. These, then, require further thought, thought that comes to rest in new beliefs providing a new context for action. It is difficult to act without believing in the truth of one's actions, but acting changes the circumstances in which the initial thought arose. The changed circumstances need not circumscribe action to a repetition of what was initially believed in order to maintain the integrity of belief, for it is not belief in itself that is of importance, but rather the relation of belief to the circumstances in which we find ourselves. Thinking upon the new circumstances can lead to new, different, or the same actions. My intention is not to privilege change over continuity or vice-versa, but to suggest that the setting up of these two as oppositional is the issue. Once the provisionality of adequacy is accepted, 'connected histories' becomes the most suitable way of addressing issues without lapsing into postmodern relativism or political impasse.

The once standard philosophy of science sought external standards against which the contingent claims of the social could be tested; more recent philosophies, however, have increasingly called this understanding into question. Knowledge has come to be regarded as inherently social – that is, 'communal, interconnected, interdependent, and relative to larger blocks of things known and projects undertaken' – and thus, the legitimacy of knowledge is produced and constrained through these things and through the socially constructed standards of the communities of which we are members (Nelson 1993: 141, 150). Built into any system of representation, then, is the claim for normalcy – the normal, that is, usual standards of a community. Acknowledging that these standards frequently entail resistance to their dominant norms and forms of power and representation is to acknowledge the possibilities of constructing those norms and forms differently. As mentioned, for many, this raises the spectre of relativism, but, as I shall suggest, this is a misunderstanding of the processes under discussion. Relativism is not the necessary outcome of accepting the social construction of knowledge, and calling for a return to the deficient philosophical understandings of the past is certainly no answer.

To argue that knowledge is socially constructed and open to further reconstruction is to highlight the importance of the politics of the present (and the past) in our interpretations. This is not to suggest, however, that knowledge is infinitely susceptible to contemporary invention for, as Appadurai has argued in a slightly different context, there are sets of norms within societies, 'pertaining to authority, continuity and inter-dependence, which govern the terms of the debate' (1981: 217). Such norms, Trouillot suggests (1995), inhere to all societies and thus, while anything *could* be possible, only some things are *permissible*. It is this aspect of permissibility, or *plausibility*, that guards against the lapse into relativism. Thus, relativism is not prevented by invoking universal standards, but by invoking the negotiated standards of relationships within and between communities. Under the earlier philosophy of science, history is judged solely in terms of its *accuracy* (correspondence) – where accuracy relates to endeavours attempting to ascertain how things 'really were' in the past – I argue, however, that such claims to accurate representation only arise in relation to collective standards of adequacy negotiated in a contested present.

For example, it may be correct under a particular set of understandings to represent the emergence of the modern world state system in terms of the 1648 Peace of Westphalia, on the basis of discussions over sovereignty and rights, as a consequence of thinkers such as Hobbes, Locke, Rousseau, and others mulling over the pertinent problems of the day. That it is *rarely* considered as emerging out of the 'long, brutalizing engagement between Europeans and other indigenous populations throughout the world (Persaud and Walker 2001: 375) does not make these earlier interpretations any less accurate in their own terms. It does, however, mark their limitation, that is, the rendering invisible of the experiences and claims of 'others' from the dominant narratives of what occurred. For example, this discourse has been markedly unable to integrate 'the Haitian Revolution, which occurred a mere twenty years after the American Revolution and was the first to abolish slavery', into its dominant narratives (Grovogui 2001: 436). As Grovogui argues, despite having written volumes on human freedom, Western philosophers and theorists have been reluctant to theorize the emergence of the first 'black' state as one of the momentous events that augured modernity (2001: 436–7). After postcolonialism, it is no longer possible to discuss the modern state system without an acknowledgement of colonization.

The events of the Haitian Revolution, even as they occurred, were deemed unthinkable by the most radical writers of the Enlightenment, and the revolution that was thought 'impossible' by those contem-poraneous with it has been further silenced by the historians who have failed to engage with it. As Trouillot says, the revolution that was contemporaneously unthinkable has become, in history, a non-event (1995: 95–6). Buck-Morss (2000) cautions, however, that there is the danger of conflating two silences here, the silence of the past and that of the present. The Haitian Revolution – with the self-emancipation of its slaves, the abolition of slavery, and institution of suffrage across the colour bar – was known about and discussed at the time, whether as inspiration for the subsequent slave revolutions across the Caribbean and the American mainland (Sidbury 1997; Dubois 2004), or condemned in the parlours and salons of the 'civilized' world, or then transmuted into the language of wage-slavery and class struggle in the early writings of Marx (Buck-Morss 2000). More recently, however, as a consequence of 'the disciplinary discourses through which knowledge of the past has been inherited' the Haitian Revolution has become largely invisible (Buck-Morss 2000: 845). It is this latter kind of disciplinary silence with which I have primarily been concerned in this book.

The accumulation of 'other' voices in fields previously dominated by particular voices can only enhance the theories that we then establish on the basis of this knowledge. It has to be recognized, however, that these silences cannot be addressed simply by adding them to pre-existing understandings: as Trouillot states, it is not sufficient to 'add native [/woman], stir and proceed as usual' (1991: 44). New historical understandings cannot be added to pre-existing ones without in some way calling into question the legitimacy and validity of the previously accepted parameters – both historical and ethical. As Keita (2002) argues, the 'regained voices' were not previously lost; they were voices associated with historical activities that were not seen as significant within dominant Western accounts. Thus, what is being argued here is not, simply, that an event like the Haitian Revolution ought to have been considered as one of the constitutive events of modernity and it has not been; nor that to rectify this omission we must now just add it to the previous list. Rather, that the silence that surrounds the Haitian Revolution (and like events) is constitutive of the very idea of modernity and its use in sociological interpretations of the contemporary world.

A proper consideration of such phenomena entails a radical rethinking of the concept of modernity itself that would also, but not only, rethink the canonization of particular historical trajectories and parochial texts (Grovogui 2001: 437). The modern state and colonization emerged together in the sixteenth century and together posed the fundamental questions of order and the legitimation of power that are still being addressed today. The adequacy of our understandings of these processes does not rest only in the veracity of our representations, for, as suggested, those representations can only ever be a part of the story. Adequacy, then, I would suggest, is also a matter of the responsibility of the communities in which such stories and knowledges circulate, and the political imperatives underpinning such considerations rest in the disruption of the continuity between the silence of subjects in history and theory and their subjection in the present (see Nandy 1987).

The social sciences, and sociology in particular, have constructed a particular 'scene of inquiry' that has, for the most part, occluded the colonial relations that were integral to the emergence of modern societies and the modern forms of explanation of those societies. From classifying to cataloguing, from surveillance of distant others to surveillance of our neighbours, from eradicating smallpox to eradicating measles, mumps and rubella, the discourses and practices cannot be isolated to any particular region, country, society, ethnicity, or geographical location. As has been demonstrated throughout this book, it is not simply a question of whatever Europe did also occurring elsewhere, nor were events in the colonies peripheral to those in Europe. It was often in the problems generated in the processes of interconnection and differentiation between places and peoples that particular solutions were imagined and implemented, transmitted and transformed, and transmitted again in renewed form.

The search for true origins, then, is a redundant task, all that is possible is the attribution of origin, and that is political. When it has suited authors – of whatever persuasion – origin rested in the invention of a thing. When it was 'proven' that someone else had invented it, then origin rested in the application of a thing (e.g., the invention of the printing press is attributed to the Chinese but claimed as European as a consequence of its replication). When it was 'proved' that someone else had also used it, then origin rested in the mass application of a thing (e.g., factory production of cotton). When it was 'proved' that someone else had also mass-produced it, then origin rested in the claim to have done it first. First and alone. This is as true of intellectual practices as material ones as the debates over the origins of modernity indicate. From the cosmopolitan endeavours of the French and Scottish Enlightenment thinkers to the evolutionary trajectory of modernization theory to its pluralization into multiple trajectories, the experience of Europe above all else has been privileged and this sense of privilege continues to inform our modernist, and postmodernist, sensibilities. All that is allowed in the alliterative form of modernity that is multiple modernities, for example, is the subsequent pluralization, adaptation, and domestication of processes that are regarded as originating in

Europe. No-one else is deemed to have anything to contribute to processes regarded as world-historical.

The dominant sociological approach(es) to modernity have argued for distinct developmental types of society and have suggested that the question of social development needs to be approached in terms of a comparative historical sociology which takes modernity as its point of reference. This comparative sociology treats different types of society as distinct and bounded and, as I have argued, proceeds by a method of ideal typical abstraction from wider interconnections and complex circumstances. This abstraction is designed to render certain interconnections 'visible' and capable of being submitted to systematic examination. What is neglected is the extent to which that systematic examination reinforces the 'invisibility' of other connections that might have been the object of investigation. What is generally rendered invisible in most considerations of modernity is the colonial relationship which has comprised a significant aspect of modernity from its inception and has been no less systematic than the interconnections that have otherwise been represented within dominant sociological approaches. While it is accepted that it is impossible to address 'everything', the selections made need to be justifiable on their own terms and the terms of the others who come to engage with them. Where the selections are deemed inadequate it is necessary not only to make other selections, but to understand why particular selections were initially made and how these can be enhanced and reconstructed through further engagement.

In presenting this argument, I have suggested that the sociological constructions of modernity – both in its conceptual structure and methodological underpinnings – are themselves framed by a particular historiography, one which is Eurocentric in character. If we can now understand dominant approaches as Eurocentric, it is, at least in part, because of new voices emerging in wider political arenas and in the academy itself. The demise of colonialism as an explicit political formation has given rise to understandings of postcoloniality and, perhaps ironically, an increased recognition of the role of colonialism in the formation of modernity. In this context, then, it is insufficient to regard postcolonialism as simply implying new ways of understanding modernity and its future(s). The contribution of postcolonialism to reconstructing modernity's past(s) also needs to be acknowledged. To do the latter, however, further requires a reconstruction of the forms of understanding – concepts, categories, and methods – within which particular events are rendered apparently insignificant. To this end, I have argued for a re-thinking of comparative historical sociology outside its dominant historiographic frame and within a new one of 'connected histories'. In this way, modernity is placed in a frame of interconnections, or networks, of peoples and places that transcend the boundaries established within the dominant approaches.

In this book, then, I have addressed the deeply embedded set of assumptions within sociological constructions of modernity where analytical categories and the 'facts' associated with them have been seen to be mutually constitutive. In challenging these assumptions, which have proved remarkably resilient over the period of sociological development, it has been necessary to engage in a detailed critique of the emergence and development of both the analytical categories and the 'facts' of modernity. The first part of the book, sought to make explicit the conceptual structure and methodological underpinnings of sociological ideas of modernity, arguing that this theory is virtually continuous with sociology itself, especially macro-sociological thinking. The second part of the book addressed the 'fact' of the European origins of modernity. In challenging dominant understandings of modernity and sociology, I put forward 'connected histories' as an alternative way of thinking about history and sociology.

In making this argument, two responses usually follow. First, an argument is made for the necessity of the categories being challenged. These are seen to be the categories of sociological reason and to challenge them, it is suggested, is unreasonable (or, to use Delanty's (2004, 2006) term, confused) and will lead to the problems of relativism associated with postmodernism. The second response is to argue that the Eurocentric assumptions built into analytical categories are held to have no substantive implications. It is suggested that this is simply a contingent aspect of the categories which have an independent justification in that they simply reflect the undeniable 'fact' of European modernity and its origins. Those who defend the dominant approach to comparative historical sociology, as I have shown in Chapter 3, come to accept that Eurocentrism is a problem that has sometimes distorted the way in which modernity has been conceived, but they see it as a contingent distortion on the part of particular writers or groups of writers, not as intrinsic to the methodology of comparative historical sociology itself. It is also argued that if 'Eurocentrism' is inappropriate as a methodological assumption, it cannot be denied as 'fact', that, put simply, the European origins of modernity cannot be denied.

In the second part of this book, then, I have challenged these 'facts' of modernity to show that they can be challenged and that, moreover, a different kind of historical approach – one oriented to interconnections – would provide a different understanding of modernity and the diversity of contributions to it. These include both the contributions of non-European 'others' and the contribution of European colonialism (the one innovation associated strongly with Europe that is systematically disregarded in favour of other 'European' innovations). I argued that it is precisely the force of a historiography of 'connected histories' to deny the 'facts' of European modernity in its challenge to Eurocentrism in method. Indeed, it would be strange if the reconstruction of method did not also reconstruct what had previously been seen.

While I suggest that 'connected histories' are superior to other sorts of history in bringing a wider range of phenomena and experiences into view, I am not claiming its appropriateness simply on those terms. Throughout this book, I have been referring to the politics of knowledge production and also to the historiographic impulse as deriving from present interests. This brings me close to one aspect of the Weberian approach to social science which I have otherwise criticized, namely, that history and social science depend on structures of value relevance that are subject to change. However, I have argued beyond the standard Weberian perspective to suggest that this change must be regarded as transforming the historical questions we deem to be interesting, but also the concepts through which we approach them. It is the argument of this book that our current global situation indicates that we are at a moment of change in structures of value relevance. A change inaugurated by different social movements and, in particular, decolonization and postcolonialism. These latter have inaugurated the possibility of understandings of modernity from other than European perspectives.

'Connected histories', then, is about an approach that re-thinks our current circumstances and the trajectories of change associated with them from multiple perspectives, rather than a dominant European one. This may, in part, be inaugurated by a heightened sense of globalization and its impact in the West, but, for the non-West, globalization has been a fact that they have endured for centuries. When the negative impact occurred primarily in the other direction – for example through processes of underdevelopment and de-industrialization, as argued in previous chapters – this was not understood in terms of globalization; in many cases it was not understood at all within the dominant conceptions of modernity and macro-sociological thinking (see Holmwood 2007a). If the interconnections of globalization are only just coming into the perspective of the West, then, that is not because they are novel, nor can a singular perspective be adequate to understand them.

Recently, Beck (2006) has argued that a cosmopolitan approach is necessary to engage critically with globalization and to go beyond the limitations of state-centred disciplinary approaches typical of sociology and political science. As should be evident from what I have argued so far, I regard this form of cosmopolitanism as equally limited as the state-centred approaches it criticizes precisely in the way that it sanctions the appropriateness of their concepts to the past, arguing that it is simply their application to the present, and the future, that is at issue. While I have also argued that sociological concepts are national state-centred – specifically Euro-national state-centred – this is not something that is only now becoming problematic as 'first modernity' has given way to a contemporary globalized world. Beck's argument for a cosmopolitan approach is part of a long line of social theory that takes Western perspectives as the truth of global processes. A cosmopolitan sociology that was open to different voices would, I suggest, be one that 'provincialized' European understandings (see Holmwood 2007a).

What I have argued throughout, then, is that understanding inter-connections in the present will require understanding them in the past *and* re-constructing our understandings *of* the past. The argument about power and knowledge is an argument about the structures of value relevance that inform history and how, when these structures change, history itself changes. The processes of decolonization and the emerging field of postcolonialism can be regarded as changing structures of value relevance. The issue is not that any new structure can become a totaliz-ing structure that renders history wholly intelligible in its terms until the next shift. There will always be issues of difference and dissension and valuable residues from older interpretations are necessary in developing new ones. While critical of some aspects of the postcolonial position, for example, what I take from it is the emphasis on the interconnectedness of histories, the recognition of colonialism as integral to the story of modernity and the formation of its institutions – that is, to understand-ing our contemporary world – and the critique of pre-determined hierarchies of knowledge. The question, however, is how to conceive of history as a dialogue in movement and I would argue that the answer to this is to conceive it as a process of learning. The only meaning of objectivity in history that makes sense is one that is consistent with a dialogue of learning and movement that builds knowledge through the address of problems.

Said (1975) has argued that a 'beginning' is the first step in the inten-tional production of meaning, where intention is defined as an intellectual appetite to do something in a specific way. The consciousness of begin-ning, he continues, projects the task in a particular way, that is, it provides 'the created inclusiveness within which the work develops' (1975: 12). This is neither to suggest inclusivity as totality, nor beginning as origin.

Said distinguishes the idea of 'created inclusiveness' by suggesting that the limits of the field of investigation already identify relationships and possibilities beyond those limits. This occurs, he suggests, through the use of examples (or empirical work) 'whose nonconforming, overflowing energy begins to carry them out of the field' (1975: 15). As Gadamer (1979), too, has argued, it is by recognizing the limits of our horizons that the possibility opens up for us to move beyond them. In other words, that is, in Gadamer's words: 'to have a horizon means not to be limited to what is nearest, but to be able to see beyond it' (1979: 269). Further, in making a distinction between origins and beginnings – where origins are seen as foundational and allowing no deviations, and beginnings are amenable to reconstruction and redeployment – Said (1975, 1978) points to the restructuring and animation of knowledge, not as something already achieved, but as a continual self-examination of methodology and practice.

The problem with the dominant sociological accounts is that they want something outside the dialogue which does not itself determine the substance of the dialogue. It has long since given up a standard positivistic account of agreement on substance, but instead wishes an 'objective', or 'analytical', agreement on concepts. Certain concepts, it argues, are necessary for intelligibility in sociology. What I have been looking at in this book is how these concepts, that sociologists argue to be necessary, are indeed bound up with the acceptance of a particular substance, moreover a substance that is contestable. I have argued that that substance is Eurocentric, but that in itself is no particular criticism. From the perspective of value relevance set out above, people can only enter dialogue from their particular perspectives. What is problematic is the representation of these perspectives as necessary for all and therefore to be the *condition* of dialogue rather than what is engaged with in dialogue. In addition, I have also shown that the historical record to which these concepts are applied is always richer and more varied than is generally allowed. It is richer and more varied precisely in relation to the experiences of others whose particularity is being denied (while the dominant particularity is effaced within a false universalism). In this sense, the re-interpretation of history is not just a different interpretation of the *same* facts, but the bringing into being of *new* facts; along with new facts, new voices, and with new voices, new possibilities for mutual learning and new beliefs and actions.

Notes

Introduction: Postcolonialism, Sociology, and the Politics of Knowledge Production

1. As will be discussed in Chapter 4, Europe is frequently understood as Christian and the historical presence of Jewish and Muslim populations within its borders is generally ignored.
2. In the sense that Marx's standpoint of the proletariat depends upon his perception of their potential agency as the solution to the problems of capitalism and not a statement about the understanding of those deemed to be proletariat.

1 Modernity, Colonialism, and the Postcolonial Critique

1. It must also be noted here that the solutions to colonialism as put forward by Nandy and Said on the one hand and Fanon on the other are radically opposed even if their diagnosis of the condition is similar. While Fanon (1968 [1961]) advocated a central role to violence in struggles for liberation, Nandy (1987) argues that this espousal of violence only bound one more closely to the culture of the oppressor rather than enabling any overcoming of it.
2. In the case of New Zealand/Aotorea, During (1998) suggests that scholars have demonstrated that white invasions were legitimately and productively resisted and in the process the colonizers and colonized, together, contributed to the creation of the contemporary society. The recovery of the colonial subject in history can be seen as analogous to the efforts of feminist historians, such as Joan Kelly (1986 [1984, 1976]), to restore women to history.
3. Burke's critique is admitted, albeit in attenuated form, in Eric Stokes' study, *The English Utilitarians and India*, where he argues that India played no central part in fashioning the qualities of English civilization and, in many ways, 'acted as a disturbing force, a magnetic power placed at the periphery tending to distort the natural development of Britain's character' (1959: xi). However, Stokes does also recognize that, as a disturbing force, India, in the nineteenth century, signified an expansive set of opportunities for an emerging middle class that saw its interests linked with the administration of empire (albeit an administration that then brought utilitarian principles into justification of empire undermining their purported emphasis on liberty). From a different perspective, Sankar Muthu (2003) examines the thought of late eighteenth-century intellectuals such as Diderot and Kant, whom, he suggests, were hostile to both the ideas of imperialism and the emerging political project of empire – a critique that was subsequently lost in the work of most nineteenth-century European thinkers.
4. For an alternative interpretation of the impact of the demise of empire see Holmwood (2000b) for an account of how the shift from a system of

Commonwealth 'preferences' to the EU is associated with a paradoxical 'Americanization' of social welfare arrangements in the United Kingdom and a fundamental shift in constitutional arrangements with the creation of national assemblies in Wales and Scotland.

5. For a discussion of the complex situations through which people come to understandings of nationalism and cosmopolitanism, situations which include those of colonialism and imperialism and their consequences, see Joan Cocks (2002).

6. One of the key components that was thought to mark out European historical consciousness from that of other cultures was its use and advocacy of linear time, for it was not believed that a people could be properly 'historical' if they maintained notions of cyclical time. The cyclical cosmology of the ancient Greeks, however, was not deemed to negate their claim to historical consciousness nor to a distinct identity; this claim was only made in the association of cyclical time with colonized societies (Thapar 1996: 43–4).

7. On the development of the modern idea of childhood see Philippe Ariès' (1965 [1960]) classic study, *Centuries of Childhood*.

8. Notwithstanding this argument, Guha's own premise for study – the *'historic failure of the nation to come into its own'* (Guha 1982: 7; emphasis added) – belies the linear narrative framework within which he himself works.

9. The academic focus on the peasantry in the 1980s in India is perhaps not surprising given the history of peasant rebellions that occurred in significant parts of the country in the late 1960s and 1970s.

10. In truth, Hartsock's version of a Marxist standpoint epistemology owes more to 'sociological' accounts of science after Kuhn (1962) with its emphasis upon social (and psychological) interests in the construction of knowledge.

11. Kaiwar has similarly contested those notions of history which understand themselves as being the 'biography of a people' and has argued for nationalist histories to be understood as crucibles within which global categories and narratives are forged and possibilities for memory and forgetting occur (2003: 51, footnote 2). Within geography, Taylor (2000) has similarly argued for the study of connections and has criticized the disciplines of sociology, politics, and economics of being (nation) 'state-centric'.

12. As Malkki (1997) argues, one of the strongest metaphors within our thinking on identity, for example, is that of roots which, together with our sedentarist assumptions about essential attachments to particular places, naturalizes difference in contexts that are plural, mixed, and hybrid.

2 European Modernity and the Sociological Imagination

1. I take it as understood that, except where explicitly stated, the histories of social thought discussed in this chapter make little or no reference to colonial encounters. Heilbron (1995), for example, is able to articulate his understanding of the rise of social theory without a single reference to the imperial activities of the French state during the period under consideration, despite claiming to combine social and intellectual history in his analysis of the birth of social theory.

2. Beate Jahn (1999), for example, has argued that European political thought was strongly influenced by the encounter with the Amerindians. It was in part as a consequence of this encounter, she argues, that 'the Golden Age which had previously been located in the past, in antiquity, gradually came to be placed in the future, the Christian *telos* of salvation replaced by a secular *telos* of human development' (1999: 428).

3. Slaves were regarded by Turgot as a kind of movable wealth similar to money; initially procured 'by violent means and later by way of Commerce and exchange' (1973 [1766]: 148). Although Meek, in his classic discussion of the stages theory, addresses the question of the 'savage' within this framework, he nowhere mentions the institution of slavery (again, except in the context of the ancient Greeks).

4. Buck-Morss (2000) suggests that more than 20 per cent of the French bourgeoisie was dependent upon the slave-connected commercial activity although other scholars, such as Sala-Molins (quoted in Buck-Morss), have suggested that the figure is closer to one third. On the North American fur trade, Eric Wolf writes that it began when European fishermen and sailors began to barter for fur with the local Algonkins (1997 [1982]: 160). While they were initially active participants in the growth of the trade, 'as European traders consolidated their economic and political position, the balanced relation between native trappers and Europeans gave way to imbalance' with the Amerindians gradually re-patterning their social relations and cultural habits around European demands and expectations leading ultimately to their dispossession (1997 [1982]: 194, 161).

5. Glausser states that Locke invested in the Royal African Company that traded along the West Coast of Africa providing slaves to planters in America (1990: 200–1).

6. As Hunting (1978) has noted, some readers of Montesquieu's *The Spirit of the Laws* have been baffled and misled by his use of irony, thinking that he was a supporter of slavery as opposed to being in favour of its abolition. Fletcher (1933), writing much earlier, has also noted that Montesquieu's ironical defence of slavery was misunderstood. Others have suggested, however, that his use of language on the question of colonial slavery was shrewdly ambiguous (see Davis 1971).

7. In his otherwise excellent and informative book on the social theory of the Scottish Enlightenment, Berry (1997) disappoints in his discussion of slavery where there is no mention of its contemporary practice nor the thinkers' responses to it save for this one comment.

8. The setting up of the state and civil society distinction further differentiated the pre-modern from the modern, with the modern being understood in terms of its claims to universalism and the development of impersonal relations, whether of market exchange relations or political obligation. The pre-modern, on the other hand, was bound up in worlds of personal and ascriptive relationships. This way of conceptualizing the gulf between the modern and the pre-modern also located the family, and kinship in general, outside of the public sphere, thereby rendering gender invisible to modern social analysis in a manner that is parallel to that of colonial relations. See Elshtain (1982) for a useful collection of essays on the ways in which political theorists have traditionally dealt with issues of kinship and the family, and contemporary challenges to such thinking.

9. This issue is currently a matter of debate concerning the recent impact of globalization on the social sciences. Taylor (2000) and Beck (2000), for example, regard the disciplines of economics, politics, and sociology as 'state-centric' disciplines. Chernilo (2006) has questioned this charge of 'methodological nationalism', arguing that the classic sociologists operated with a universalistic orientation. Although, neither Taylor nor Beck address issues of colonialism and postcolonialism in making their argument, it does seem straightforward that sociologists did equate 'society' or 'social systems' with 'national society'.

10. Hawthorn suggests that most thinkers of the eighteenth and nineteenth century believed that 'the ideal order was one without interior contradiction' (1976: 86). As such, he continues, '[i]t is clear why this abhorrence of inconsistency should have been so strong in France and Germany. Each in its different ways was incoherent, the one torn by wholly opposing ideologies, the other existing merely as an idea with no structural cohesion at all' (1976: 86).

11. The modern West, for Weber, is characterized by the rise of secular, instrumental rationality: by industrial capitalism, formalistic law, bureaucratic administration, and the ascetic ethic of vocation (Brubaker 1984: 30). This occurs concurrent with the growth of domination, depersonalization, and disenchantment resulting in the 'iron cage' of a modern world from which individuals cannot escape.

12. In the modernist vein, Habermas's *Theory of Communicative Action* has been seen by some commentators as offering a systematic understanding of societal modernization that is 'capable of explaining both the achievement *and* the pathologies of modernity' (d'Entreves 1996: 1; my emphasis).

13. In a recent article by Bryan Turner (2006) on 'Asia in European Sociology' what readily becomes apparent is that it is less a consideration of the impact of Asia within European sociology than a consideration of the take up of European sociologists in Asia.

14. For a strong sociological critique of this position see Holmwood, who argues that if 'current social developments and dilemmas of public life cannot be grasped in the categories of current social theories, it is more likely that the problem lies with the theories than that "reality" itself has become intrinsically ungraspable' (1996: 25). 'It is hard to resist the conclusion', he continues, 'that the perception of the "chaotic constellation" of modern social reality derives from the "chaotic" nature of contemporary social theory. If this is so, the challenge is to re-construct its explanatory categories, not to de-construct the explanatory undertaking' (1996: 25).

15. Trouillot argues that the premium of 'difference' can take on a doubly flattering form where praise of the 'other' is also praise for the self that 'accepts' difference and thereby perpetuates that very difference by reproducing the other's otherness as something to be accepted (2003: 72, 73). 'Every time a *francais de souche* (a white French citizen endowed with Frenchness since times immemorial) claims to have North African, black, or even Eastern European friends – and implicitly expects recognition for that deed – he also verifies his right to be both French – and therefore universal – yet open to diversity. This claim further locks the "friends" who become merely – at least for the moment – instances of Otherness and thus, by definition non-universal' (Trouillot 2003: 75).

3   From Modernization to Multiple Modernities: Eurocentrism *Redux*

1. Theorists of modernization, such as Rostow (1960) and Lerner (1964), perhaps unsurprisingly given their background in economics, tended to see the dispositions towards modernity as present in all societies, but blocked by certain institutional features. Sociologists tended to be much more influenced by the Weberian understanding that traditionalism in economic motivation was also an obstacle to be overcome.
2. Commenting on this study, Bernstein exclaims that it is hardly surprising that Anglo-American politics appears to approximate the model of a modern political system most closely as the model is derived from a study of Anglo-American politics (1971: 155, footnote 10).
3. Even theorists critical of the concept of modernity, such as Portes (1973), believed that if the psychosocial traits identified with modernity did possess some positive value for social and economic growth, then they needed to be given serious consideration.
4. This assumption is present in Marx – where he writes in the Preface to *Capital*, 'The country that is more developed only shows, to the less developed, the image of its own future' (Marx 1976 [1867]) – as well as in modernization theorists such as Parsons (1971) with his idea of the USA as the 'new lead society', and in Rostow (1960), Lerner (1958) and others.
5. In looking at colonial societies, Bendix suggests that it is necessary to 'take account of at least two traditions ... the native tradition and the tradition of a dual society created by the colonizing country' (1967: 323). In the context of 'European frontier settlements abroad', however, he did not believe that 'the native populations were ... strong enough to create the problem of a dual society' (1967: 323), thus failing to consider the effects of the colonized on the colonizer and seeing the occurrence of change as unidirectional (in contrast, see Wolf 1997 [1982]). While Bendix calls for theoretical considerations to be informed by empirical research, then, this is not necessarily borne out in even his own endeavours.
6. I have not dealt with 'world system theory' or Marxism directly in this part of the book, primarily because the former has not had a major influence over contemporary sociological constructions of modernity while the latter contains a similarly endogenous account of social change to that criticized in standard sociological accounts.
7. This is not to deny diversity among the core institutions of state, market, and bureaucracy – for example, Hall and Soskice (2001) refer to varieties of capitalism, distinguishing Anglo-American, German, and Japanese varieties among others – but to identify the way in which it is cultural difference that is believed to produce diversity within the institutional complex. The purpose of this chapter is to criticize the separation of the institutional complex and the cultural programme and the way in which this separation is then used to argue for a European origin of the institutional framework and the separate development of cultural traditions within which that framework can become inflected.
8. Arnason (2000) attributes to modernization theory the belief that communism is not truly modern, and himself argues for its distinctive modernity as one of modernity's multiples.

9. Anti-Eurocentrism itself, is regarded by Delanty (2006: 267), as having its origins in Europe. While, as we have seen in the previous chapter, European anti-modernism can be associated with the relativity of all values that Delanty claims is intrinsically anti-Eurocentric, two things need to be said. First, this involves the very association of anti-Eurocentrism with the embrace of tradition which I have argued to be problematic and merely the inverse of the modernist position. Second, it does not seem to be the position that Delanty himself advocates, which is a form of universalistic cosmopolitanism that seems to be decidedly Eurocentric. Indeed, his version of cosmopolitanism is both the standard European cosmopolitanism and hostile to particularity. For example, on global cosmopolitanism, Delanty writes that modernity 'is necessarily global in outlook; while it first emerged in western Europe, it is not western, American or European, but is an expression of cosmopolitanism' (2006: 274). Since I have suggested that this universalism is really European particularity projected as a universal it is difficult to see what a European anti-Eurocentrism consistent with cosmopolitanism could possibly be.

    Indeed, Delanty regards postcolonial theory as confused (2006: 267) but it is hard to resist the conclusion that the confusions are his own and derive from his unwillingness to concede that there is anything to be learnt from the perspective of those outside the mainstream of Eurocentric social theory.

10. As Harootunian has noted, in a different context, but applicable here nonetheless, 'France, Italy and England were countries where people went for study and research; Japan, Asia and Africa were simply fields that required first-hand observation, recording and, in some instances, intervention' (1999: 136). With this we are back at the problem highlighted in the Introduction and the first chapter where Europe is seen as the site of theoretical innovation and the rest of the world simply supplies the empirical data for those theories. Despite at least two decades of postcolonial and other scholarship, authors still feel able to write their theories in ignorance of the majority of the world and have the arrogance to posit for them a universality that is not applicable. In the case of theories of reflexive modernization it is peculiar, to say the least, to argue for the hegemonic position to be one that claims to understand itself (and others) where throughout the history of social thought, the hegemonic position has generally been the position that could not see beyond itself and was in need of criticism from elsewhere!

11. The idea of 'intersubjective agreement' replacing notions of 'objectivity' has been developed further by Rorty who also attempts to move beyond charges of ethnocentrism by advocating talking to representatives of other communities and trying to weave together their beliefs 'with beliefs which we already have' (1987: 43). While this goes some way to addressing the ethnocentric universalism of much social theory it also remains locked in ideas of 'us' and 'them' which this book ultimately contests. Further, the resolution of the problem appears to reside in incorporating 'other' knowledges into one's own knowledge schemes without an adequate appreciation that incorporation of that knowledge would necessitate a reconceptualization of the original schemes; and that this needs to occur within the context of analyzing the politics of knowledge production that has some schemes be dominant over others.

12. For a discussion of the restricted and problematic nature of ideal type analysis in the context of sociology and its relation to feminism, see Holmwood (2001).

13. The classical tradition in sociology can be seen to provide the basis for the comparative studies associated with modernization theory. The ideal-typical distinction that is set up between traditional societies and modern societies, for instance, finds resonances within the work of sociologists such as Durkheim, Tonnies, and Spencer among others who all set up a fundamental dualism in social organization which attributes to 'the "traditional' type of social organization a prominent emphasis on affectivity, consensus and informal controls and … to "modern" forms impersonality, interdependent specialization and formal controls' (Moore 1963: 522).

14. Theorists can recognize the violence of the transition to modernity at the same time as representing modernity itself in abstraction from that violence. Thus, John Scott refers to modernity simply as 'the great intellectual and social upheavals that destroyed the medieval European world' (1995: 1) and his ideal-typical representation of modernity is essentially peaceable. The one exception is perhaps Marx who views the violence of the dispossession from collective rights as an indication of the continued 'violence' of private property rights in capitalism, but his approach to capitalism is one which sees it in terms of endogenous processes where the mechanism of transformation is associated with the lead societies of capitalist modernity.

15. Suzanne Rudolph argues that ideal types are effective categories insofar as they 'capture enough of reality to make them credible even while they falsify reality in the service of the necessary hierarchies of domination' (2005: 6).

16. The example of the Haitian Revolution is illustrative here in that the clause abolishing slavery in the French Declaration of Human Rights was only included after a deputation from the colony of Saint Domingue went to France in 1794 and made the argument to the Constituent Assembly (see Dubois 2004; Fischer 2004; and Trouillot 1995 for more details).

17. I do not mean to imply acceptance of the wider claims made by Goldthorpe (1991) about the nature of differences between history and sociology, where the former must rely on 'given' facts, embedded in 'relics', while the latter can construct its facts through the administration of questionnaires and the like. Historical facts are no less artefacts of a research process than sociological facts, a reason that makes the questioning of those research processes of vital significance and makes unlikely any foundational agreement on principles.

4 Myths of European Cultural Integrity – The Renaissance

1. Burke (1964) argues that the realism of historians such as Machiavelli was seen as a 'conceptual realism' which was associated with the Renaissance's shift beyond simply recording events to incorporating a sense of perspective as well. This was understood as distinct from 'medieval realism', he suggests, which was seen to be naturalistic and purely descriptive.

2. While in the nineteenth century sociologists looked to the medieval period in order to provide a comparative offset to modernism and establish the comparative distinction between tradition and modernity (see Nisbet 1966: 15), later sociologists turned to the Renaissance as providing the cultural context for its subsequent emergence (Nisbet 1973; see also Stephen Toulmin 1990;

John Scott 1995). Garner (1990) has also suggested that the classic historian of the Renaissance, Jacob Burckhardt, should be understood as expounding 'sociological' themes precisely insofar as he is 'a theorist of modernity'.

3. The claim has occasionally been made that, because they were intent on restoring a lost condition, it is difficult to see the men of the Renaissance as anything other than conservative, for example, with regard to the Reformation, Elton makes the argument that: 'it is idle to credit the age with the beginning of modern times (in itself a sufficiently uncertain term) if only because its intellectual leaders looked determinedly back rather than forward' (1990: 21). However, it is important to highlight that the recovery of the wisdom of the ancients was not undertaken for its own sake, but in the context of wanting improvement in the present. The modern 'discoveries' of Copernicus and Columbus were believed to have enlarged the realm of the known world and, in doing so, to have surpassed the achievements of the ancients. This contributed, in large part, to their sense of difference from, and superiority over, the ancient world (see Pagden 1993).

4. The emergence of these secular modes of learning have often been used to argue for the Renaissance itself being seen as a secular movement with the humanist challenge to the Church's monopoly over education being seen as a prime example of this shift away from the importance and authority of religion. This, however, misses the fact that the Church, and Christianity more generally, continued to play an important role in both social and political affairs and that there was no necessary decline in religious sentiment in this period (see Ferguson 1953).

5. On the development of historical consciousness in this period and its relationship to later European historiographical trends, see Bouwsma (1965).

6. Rice and Grafton's claim that '[o]nly modern western civilization has produced a fully developed science ... so different and so much more successful than the sciences of the ancient Greeks, the medieval Arabs, the Indians, and the Chinese' (1994 [1970]: 18) is not uncommon within the mainstream literature on the subject.

7. Within the discipline of International Relations it has been suggested that, regardless of the different traditions to which theorists may belong, they all agree that 'the Westphalian treaties were a decisive turning point ... [formalizing] relations between modern sovereign states' (Teschke 2003: 2). Even the few scholars who do contest this particular thesis, however, do not call into question 'the development and dynamics of the European states-system' (Teschke 2003: 4), but rather, simply question the dominant interpretations of it.

8. The attempt to establish common ancestry through the classification of languages over time is one such example – Olender (1994), for example, discusses how the search for the 'original' language of Adam and Eve led to the 'purification' of European languages by, at various times, de-emphasizing Oriental, Semitic, and other influences. To make any sense, boundaries have to be drawn creating internal consistency and coherence even if these boundaries do not relate accurately to languages as they are used. Said further states that the emphasis on demonstrating that radical and ineradicable differences between languages 'set the real boundaries between human beings ... forced vision away from common, as well as plural, human realities' (1978: 233).

9. Rabil, in the introduction to his 'Renaissance Humanism' states that: 'On the basis of the most comprehensive study of its sources ever undertaken Kristeller effectively established the claim that humanism is part of a rhetorical tradition that has been a continuous aspect of western civilization since classical antiquity. Moreover, humanism has specific roots in the medieval culture from which it arose' (1988: xiii).

10. The key issue here, for Johns (1998), is the creation of confidence in the printed word for, as he suggests, such trust in not *inherent* in the texts themselves, but has to be generated in complex social contexts constituted by both printing and reading practices. Thus, the issue is less, as Eisenstein (1969) suggests, about the 'fixity of knowledge' than, as Johns argues, persuading sufficient people of the integrity of that knowledge.

11. Maya Jasanoff (2005) provides an excellent account of how these markets in commodities, and particularly in collectibles, were developed and extended from both 'sides' through imperial expansion in the following centuries.

12. Bartlett documents how 'Frank' came to refer to westerners as settlers or on aggressive missions away from home and writes that it 'is hence entirely appropriate that when the Portuguese and Spaniards arrived off the Chinese coasts in the sixteenth century, the local population called them *Fo-lang-ki*, a name adapted from the Arabic traders' *Faranga*. Even in eighteenth-century Canton the western barbarian carried the name of his marauding ancestors' (1993: 105). It could further be suggested that the English 'foreigner' came from the Hindi 'ferengi' meaning outsider.

5   Myths of the Modern Nation-State – The French Revolution

1. For discussions on the contested nature of interpretations of the French Revolution see Cavanaugh 1972; Furet 1981 [1978], 1990; Sprang 2003.

2. As Ford (1963) argues, de Tocqueville was a notable exception to this trend as he sought to understand the revolution in terms of the history of what had preceded it, that is, in terms of the *ancien regime*. See also Furet (1981 [1978], 1990).

3. As Pocock argues, in the context of constitutions constantly undergoing historical change, authority could no longer rest in principles of antiquity and so the case began to be made for 'sovereignty' to be seen as an 'absolute authority to which appeal might be made in fluctuating and lawless circumstances' (1985: 95). Further, while it could be argued that discussions about the nature and limits of political power go back as far as the emergence of notions of political power, these debates intensified in the sixteenth century with the schism in Christianity and the 'discovery' of the 'New World'.

4. The attempts to break away from claims of papal dominion have a longer history as the long wars between the Pope and the Holy Roman Emperor in the Middle Ages indicate (see Elliott 1968; Holmes 1975).

5. Again, it has to be recognized that the French Revolution was not the first instance of a challenge to the centrality of the monarch to political life – the English Civil War, for example, is an earlier instance within Europe and the

emergence of republics in India in a similar period offer non-European instances (Thapar 1966) – nor was it the first to suggest that political power resided in the people. What was significant about the French Revolution and the subsequent Napoleonic Wars was the dissemination of such ideas – and the example of their success in practice.

6. For a discussion of the ways in which the language of rights percolated into the colonies of what was then the French Caribbean and was transformed through the 'slave' revolutions in those islands – with that transformation having repercussions back in France as well as throughout the French Empire – see Dubois (2004). Sidbury (1997) also addresses the ways in which slaves in Virginia were inspired by events in Saint Domingue in their own struggles for emancipation and, in doing so, were instrumental in the further diffusion of the language of rights across the Americas.

7. 'Class' was established in the nineteenth century as one of the central categories of social analysis and was subsequently seen to be supplemented by categories such as 'gender' and 'the postcolonial'. What this fails to recognize, however, is that 'class' was an internal category complicit with the dominant debates of modernity whereas 'gender' and 'the postcolonial' were positions of critique from 'outside' the canonical understandings.

8. For a discussion of sovereignty from a perspective that acknowledges its multiple and related transformations within the modern period and focuses on developments and processes in parts of the world that are usually ignored, see Shilliam (2006).

9. Although, as Talmon notes, continental nationalism was not a mass phenomenon, at most it 'was a movement of numerical minorities, above all of the intelligentsia' (1967: 107).

10. Foucault sees the problem of government residing in a double movement 'of state centralization on the one hand and of dispersion and religious dissidence on the other' (1991: 88); a movement which, according to him, occurs throughout the West in the eighteenth century (1991: 102, 103). His stated intention was 'to show how governmentality was born out of, on the one hand, the archaic model of Christian pastoral, and, on the other, a diplomatic-military technique, perfected on a European scale with the Treaty of Westphalia' (1991: 104): colonialism does not even get a mention.

11. Many historians and theorists (e.g., Mann 1993; Lieberman 1999) direct attention to the emergence of ethnicity-based polities from previously cosmopolitan, or civilizational, entities as indicating a primary tension between the universal aspirations of the Church and the more particularistic ethnic ones. In doing so, however, they fail to recognize that even if 'proto-ethnic' or 'proto-national' tensions can occasionally be identified in the early modern period, the defining feature of such societies was still the tension 'between the high culture which was created and promulgated by the new elites and the local or regional values and solidarities which it overrode in the process' (Moore 1997: 597). Thus, calling into question the importance, and history, of 'ethnicities'.

12. One result of nineteenth-century political ideology, Rodríguez-Salgado argues, is that we are now less well equipped to understand forms of national identity that do not rest on exclusive ideas of patriotism and, further, that we are unable to integrate an understanding of early modern people, 'particularly

those living in composite monarchies', as being sensitive to the multiple layers of association and meaning which marked their lives (1998: 234).

13. This term is taken from Johannes Fabian's (1983) *Time and the Other* in which he discusses 'coevalness' in terms of it being anthropology's problem with Time in the context of understandings of 'self' and 'other' (1983: 37).

6   Myths of Industrial Capitalism – The Industrial Revolution

1. Although this is not to suggest that concern with the 'details' of the Industrial Revolution has at all diminished (see, for example, Hoppit 1990). Indeed, it is often contestations around the 'details' that lead to discussions, disputes, and transformations of the frameworks within which the details are located.

2. This is not to suggest that earlier critiques of industrialization did not exist. Cohen (1969) suggests that Bonald for example, writing in the early nineteenth century, prefigured later attacks on the industrial order with his searing critiques of industrialism in which he spoke of the 'sickness' of commerce and industry and decried the emergence of an industrial economy as one based on exploitation and human unhappiness.

3. This rehabilitation is argued for by Berg and Hudson (1992), for example, in opposition to what de Vries (1994) calls the 'Revolt of the Early Modernists', that is, the current gradualist orthodoxy which Berg and Hudson believe underplays the extent of the social and economic transformation apparent to theorists of the time. For recent arguments putting forward the view of the Industrial Revolution as a distinct, and discontinuous, period see also Hoppit (1990), and Greasley and Oxley (1994).

4. Marx, for example, writing in the mid-nineteenth century, linked industrialization to urbanization and proletarianization, and Tönnies (1955 [1887]), similarly, pursued a distinction between *Gemeinschaft*, an earlier, communal, family-based natural society, and *Gesellschaft*, the emerging individualized, contractual, mechanical modern society, of which the city was the archetype.

5. On the question of slavery and sugar production in the West Indies, Smith has the following to say (and this in the context of a discussion where Smith suggests that free labour is ultimately cheaper than slave labour): 'as there are no grounds for thinking that really free blacks will ever, of their own accord, undertake the drudgery of sugar planting, it would seem that compulsory or slave labour is not merely the cheapest that can be so employed, but that it is all but indispensable to the prosecution of the business' (1863 [1776]: 610). See Muthu (2003) for a discussion of the work of Diderot – a contemporary of Smith – but who starts from a position of opposition to the barbaric acts of Europeans towards non-Europeans.

6. This understanding, however, does not acknowledge the argument that the majority of British goods were not produced for internal consumption, but to export and that a lot of the goods bought from the colonies were also for re-export as opposed to domestic consumption (see Washbrook 1997; Frank 1998).

7. For a discussion of the various explanations given for England's primacy and the difficulties in ascertaining 'why' England was first, particularly in relation

to developments in France, see Crafts (1977) who suggests that asking the very question of why England was first is misconceived.

8. As O'Hearn (1994) writes in the context of a discussion of the relationship between the Irish and British cotton industries, the failure of the Irish cotton industry is generally attributed to internal shortcomings such as the lack of entrepreneurial spirit and the failure to modernize with little recognition of the way in which Irish cotton was peripheralized by Britain. Alongside this, Britain's success is also attributed to endogenous factors, an innovative spirit, the English-centred industrial revolution, and so forth. The importance of empire and relations of colonial domination are rarely considered. Not only is the impact of empire not considered in these ways, but the contribution made by immigrants from Ireland and elsewhere is not officially recognized, for example, in the construction of the transport network that is taken to be integral to the success of the Industrial Revolution in England.

9. Higman (2000) argues that above all other commodities, it was the production and trade of sugar that both created plantation economies and slave societies (with two-thirds of all people taken from Africa to the New World destined for the sugar colonies) as well as generating the greatest profits for those involved in this industry.

10. Although it has to be recognized, as Williams (1940) argues, that Negroes were not an uncommon sight in Britain in the first three-quarters of the eighteenth century, or at least not in London. Buck-Morss (2000) similarly makes the argument that African slaves were present in the Dutch Republic, Britain, and France.

11. This is made apparent if we shift the perspectival distance from which the events of modernity are seen from Paris to the Black Jacobins in Saint Domingue (Bhabha 1994: 244).

References

Abu-Lughod, Janet L. (1989) *Before European Hegemony: The World System A. D. 1250–1350* (Oxford: Oxford University Press).

Al-Azmeh, Aziz (1992) 'Barbarians in Arab Eyes' *Past and Present* 134, February, pp. 3–18.

Alexander, Jeffrey C. (1995) *Fin de Siècle Social Theory: Relativism, Reduction, and the Problem of Reason* (London: Verso).

Almond, Gabriel A. and James S. Coleman (eds) (1960) *The Politics of Developing Areas* (New Jersey: Princeton University Press).

Alvares, Claude (1991) *Decolonizing History: Technology and Culture in India, China and the West 1492 to the Present Day* (Goa: The Other India Press).

Amin, Samir (1972) 'Underdevelopment and Dependence in Black Africa – Origins and Contemporary Forms' *The Journal of Modern African Studies* 10/4, pp. 503–24.

Amin, Samir (1977) *Imperialism and Unequal Development* translated from the French (Hassocks: Harvester Press).

Amin, Samir (1989) *Eurocentrism* translated by Russell Moore (New York: Monthly Review Press).

Anderson, Benedict (1996) *Imagined Communities: Reflections on the Origin and Spread of Nationalism* (London: Verso).

Appadurai, Arjun (1981) 'The Past as a Scarce Resource' *Man* 16/2, pp. 201–19.

Appadurai, Arjun (1988) 'Putting Hierarchy in its Place' *Cultural Anthropology* 3/1, pp. 36–49.

Appiah, Kwame A. (1991) 'Is the Post- in Postmodernism the Post- in Postcolonial?' *Critical Inquiry* 17/2, pp. 336–57.

Apter, David E. (1965) *The Politics of Modernization* (Chicago: University of Chicago Press).

Ariès, Philippe (1965 [1960]) *Centuries of Childhood: A Social History of Family Life* (New York: Random House).

Arnason, Johann P. (2000) 'Communism and Modernity' *Daedalus: Multiple Modernities* 129/1, pp. 61–90.

Arnason, Johann P. (2003) 'Entangled Communisms: Imperial Revolutions in Russia and China' *European Journal of Social Theory* 6/3, pp. 307–25.

Arnold, David (1993) *Colonizing the Body: State, Medicine and Epidemic Disease in Nineteenth-Century India* (New Delhi: Oxford University Press).

Arnold, David (2000) *The New Cambridge History of India: III.5 Science, Technology and Medicine in Colonial India* (Cambridge: Cambridge University Press).

Assassi, Libby (forthcoming) *The Gendering of Global Finance* (Basingstoke: Palgrave Macmillan).

Badham, Richard (1984) 'The Sociology of Industrial and Post-Industrial Societies' *Current Sociology: The Journal of the International Sociological Association* 32/1, pp. 1–141.

Baehr, Peter (2002) 'Identifying the Unprecedented: Hannah Arendt, Totalitarianism, and the Critique of Sociology' *American Sociological Review* 67/December, pp. 804–31.

Baker, Keith M. (1989) 'Closing the French Revolution: Saint-Simon and Comte' in François Furet and Mona Ozouf (eds) *The French Revolution and the Creation of Modern Political Culture, Volume 3: The Transformation of Political Culture 1789–1848* (Oxford: Pergamon Press), pp. 323–39.

Barlow, Tani (1997) *Formations of Colonial Modernity in East Asia* (Durham: Duke University Press).

Bartelson, Jens (1995) *A Genealogy of Sovereignty* (Cambridge: Cambridge University Press).

Bartlett, Robert (1993) *The Making of Europe: Conquest, Colonization, and Cultural Change 950–1350* (London: The Penguin Press).

Bauman, Zygmunt (1987) *Legislators and Interpreters: On Modernity, Post-Modernity and Intellectuals* (Oxford: Polity Press).

Bayly, Christopher A. (1993) 'Knowing the Country: Empire and Information in India' *Modern Asian Studies Special Issue: How Social, Political and Cultural Information is Collected, Defined, Used and Analyzed* 27/1, pp. 2–43.

Beck, Ulrich (2000) *What is Globalization?* (Cambridge: Polity Press).

Beck, Ulrich (2006) *Cosmopolitan Vision* (Cambridge: Polity Press).

Bell, Daniel (1974) *The Coming of Post-Industrial Society: A Venture in Social Forecasting* (London: Heinemann).

Bell, Daniel (1976) *The Cultural Contradictions of Capitalism* (London: Heinemann).

Ben-David, Joseph (1965) 'The Scientific Role: The Conditions of its Establishment in Europe' *Minerva* 4, pp. 15–54.

Bendix, Reinhard (1967) 'Tradition and Modernity Reconsidered' *Comparative Studies in Society and History: An International Quarterly* IX, pp. 292–346.

Berg, Maxine and Pat Hudson (1992) 'Rehabilitating the Industrial Revolution' *The Economic History Review: New Series* 45/1, pp. 24–50.

Bernal, Martin (1987) *Black Athena: The Afroasiatic Roots of Classical Civilization Volume 1 The Fabrication of Ancient Greece 1785–1985* (London: Free Association Books).

Bernstein, Henry (1971) 'Modernization Theory and the Sociological Study of Development' *Journal of Development Studies* 7/2, pp. 141–60.

Berry, Christopher J. (1997) *Social Theory of the Scottish Enlightenment* (Edinburgh: Edinburgh University Press).

Best, Steven and Douglas Kellner (1991) *Postmodern Theory: Critical Interrogations* (London: Macmillan).

Bhabha, Homi K. (1992) 'Postcolonial Criticism' in Stephen Greenblatt and Giles B. Gunn (eds) *Redrawing the Boundaries: The Transformation of English and American Literary Studies* (New York: Modern Language Association of America), pp. 437–57.

Bhabha, Homi K. (1994) *The Location of Culture* (London: Routledge).

Biccum, April R. (2002) 'Interrupting the Discourse of Development: On a Collision Course with Postcolonial Theory' *Culture, Theory and Critique* 43/1, pp. 33–50.

Blackburn, Robin (1997) *The Making of New World Slavery: From the Baroque to the Modern 1492–1800* (London: Verso Books).

Blaut, James M. (1993) *The Colonizer's Model of the World: Geographical Diffusionism and Eurocentric History* (London: The Guildford Press).

Bluestone, Barry and Bennett Harrison (1982) *The Deindustrialization of America: Plant Closings, Community Abandonment, and the Dismantling of Basic Industry* (New York: Basic Books).

Blumenberg, Hans (1983) *The Legitimacy of the Modern Age* translated by R. M. Wallace (London: MIT Press).

Boas, Marie (1962) *The Scientific Renaissance 1450–1630* (London: Collins).

Bonnett, Alastair (2005) 'Occidentalism and Plural Modernities: Or How Fukuzawa and Tagore Invented the West' *Environment and Planning D: Society and Space* 23/4, pp. 505–25.

Bordo, Susan (1986) 'The Cartesian Masculinization of Thought' *Signs* 11/3, pp. 439–56.

Bouwsma, William J. (1965) 'Three Types of Historiography in Post-Renaissance Italy' *History and Theory* 4/3, pp. 303–14.

Bouwsma, William J. (1979) 'The Renaissance and the Drama of Western History' *The American Historical Review* 84/1, pp. 1–15.

Boxer, C. R. (1984) 'When the Twain First Met: European Conceptions and Misconceptions of Japan, Sixteenth-Eighteenth Centuries' *Modern Asian Studies: Special Issue: Edo Culture and Its Modern Legacy* 18/4, pp. 531–40.

Bradner, Leicester (1962 [1953]) 'From Petrarch to Shakespeare' in *The Renaissance: Six Essays* edited for the Metropolitan Museum of Modern Art, New York (New York: Harper Torchbooks), pp. 97–120.

Braudel, Fernand (1977) *Afterthoughts on Material Civilization and Capitalism* translated by Patricia M. Ranum (New York: The Johns Hopkins University Press).

Brenner, Robert (1976) 'Agrarian Class Structure and Economic Development in Pre-Industrial Europe' *Past and Present* 70, February, pp. 30–75.

Brenner, Robert (1977) 'The Origins of Capitalist Development: A Critique of Neo-Smithian Marxism' *New Left Review* 104, pp. 25–92.

Briggs, Asa (1960) *The Age of Improvement 1783–1867* (London: Longmans).

Broers, Michael (1989) 'Italy and the Modern State: The Experience of Napoleonic Rule' in François Furet and Mona Ozouf's (eds) *The French Revolution and the Creation of Modern Political Culture, Volume 3: The Transformation of Political Culture 1789–1848* (Oxford: Pergamon Press).

Broers, Michael (1996) *Europe Under Napoleon 1799–1815* (London: Arnold).

Brooke, Christopher (1969) *The Twelfth Century Renaissance* (London: Thames and Hudson).

Brubaker, Roger (1984) *The Limits of Rationality: An Essay on the Social and Moral Thought of Max Weber* (London: George Allen and Unwin).

Bryant, Joseph M. (1994) 'Evidence and Explanation in History and Sociology: Critical Reflection on Goldthorpe's Critique of Historical Sociology' *The British Journal of Sociology* 45/1, pp. 3–19.

Buck-Morss, Susan (2000) 'Hegel and Haiti' *Critical Inquiry* 26, Summer, pp. 821–65.

Burckhardt, Jacob (1990 [1860]) *The Civilization of the Renaissance in Italy* translated by S. G. C. Middlemore (London: Penguin Books).

Burger, Thomas (1987) *Max Weber's Theory of Concept Formation: History, Laws, and Ideal Types* (Durham: Duke University Press).

Burke, Peter (1964) *The Renaissance* (London: Longman).

Burke, Peter (1990) 'Introduction: Jacob Burckhardt and the Italian Renaissance' in Jacob Burckhardt (1990 [1860]) *The Civilization of the Renaissance in Italy* (London: Penguin Books), pp. 1–16.

Burke, Peter (1992) *History and Social Theory* (Cambridge: Polity Press).

Butterfield, Henry (1957) *The Origins of Modern Science 1300–1800* (London: G. Bell and Sons Ltd.).

Butzer, Karl W. (1992) 'From Columbus to Acosta: Science, Geography, and the New World' *Annals of the Association of American Geographers: The Americas Before and After 1492: Current Geographical Research* 82/3, pp. 543–65.

Bythell, Duncan (1993) 'Women in The Work Force' in Patrick K. O'Brien and Ronald Quinault (eds) *The Industrial Revolution and British Society* (Cambridge: Cambridge University Press).

Calhoun, Craig (1996) 'Whose Classics? Which Readings? Interpretation and Cultural Difference in the Canonization of Sociological Theory' in Stephen P. Turner (ed.) *Social Theory and Sociology: The Classics and Beyond* (Oxford: Blackwell Publishers), pp. 70–97.

Callinicos, Alex (1999) *Social Theory: A Historical Introduction* (Cambridge: Polity Press).

Cannadine, David (1984) 'The Present and the Past in the English Industrial Revolution 1880–1980' *Past and Present* 103, May, pp. 131–72.

Cannadine, David (2001) *Ornamentalism: How the British Saw Their Empire* (Oxford: Oxford University Press).

Carr, E. H. (1945) *Nationalism and After* (London: Macmillan).

Carrier, James G. (1995) 'Introduction' in James G. Carrier (ed.) *Occidentalism: Images of the West* (Oxford: Clarendon Press), pp. 1–32.

Carrithers, D. (1995) 'The Enlightenment Science of Society' in Christopher Fox, Roy Porter and Robert Wokler (eds) *Inventing Human Science: Eighteenth Century Domains* (Berkeley: University of California Press), pp. 232–70.

Cavanaugh, Gerald J. (1972) 'The Present State of French Revolutionary Historiography: Alfred Cobban and Beyond' *French Historical Studies* 7/4, pp. 587–606.

Césaire, Aimé (1972 [1955]) *Discourse on Colonialism* translated by Joan Pinkham (New York: Monthly Review Press).

Chakrabarty, Dipesh (1992) 'Postcoloniality and the Artifice of History Who Speaks for "Indian" Pasts?' *Representations: Special Issue: Imperial Fantasies and Postcolonial Histories* 37, Winter, pp. 1–26.

Chakrabarty, Dipesh (1994) 'The Difference – Deferral of a Colonial Modernity: Public Debates on Domesticity in British Bengal' in David Arnold and David Hardiman (eds) *Subaltern Studies, VIII: Essays in Honour of Ranajit Guha* (New Delhi: Oxford University Press).

Chakrabarty, Dipesh (2000) *Provincializing Europe: Postcolonial Thought and Historical Difference* (Princeton: Princeton University Press).

Chakrabarty, Dipesh (2002) *Habitations of Modernity: Essays in the Wake of Subaltern Studies* (Chicago: University of Chicago Press).

Chatterjee, Partha (1986) *Nationalist Thought and the Colonial World: A Derivative Discourse* (London: Zed Books).

Chatterjee, Partha (1994) 'Claims on the Past: The Genealogy of Modern Historiography in Bengal' in David Arnold and David Hardiman (eds) *Subaltern Studies, VIII: Essays in Honour of Ranajit Guha* (New Delhi: Oxford University Press), pp. 1–49.

Chatterjee, Partha (1996) 'Whose Imagined Community?' in Gopal Balakrishnan (ed.) *Mapping the Nation* (London: Verso), pp. 214–25.

Chernilo, Daniel (2006) 'Sociology's Methodological Nationalism: Myth and Reality' *European Journal of Social Theory* 9/1, pp. 5–22.

Cocks, Joan (2002) *Passion and Paradox: Intellectuals Confront the National Question* (Princeton: Princeton University Press).

Cohen, D. K. (1969) 'The Vicomte de Bonald's Critique of Industrialism' *The Journal of Modern History* 41/4, pp. 475–84.

Cohn, Bernard S. (1996) *Colonialism and its Forms of Knowledge: The British in India* (New Jersey: Princeton University Press).

Cohn, Bernard S. and N. B. Dirks (1988) 'Beyond the Fringe: The Nation-State, Colonialism, and The Technologies of Power' *Journal of Historical Sociology* 1/2, pp. 224–8.

Colley, Linda (1992) *Britons: Forging the Nation 1707–1837* (New Haven: Yale University Press).

Colley, Linda (2002) *Captives: Britain, Empire and the World 1600–1850* (New York: Pantheon Books).

Comaroff, Jean and John Comaroff (1993) 'Introduction' in Jean Comaroff and John Comaroff (eds) *Modernity and its Malcontents: Ritual and Power in Postcolonial Africa* (Chicago: University of Chicago Press), pp. xi–xiv.

Comte, Auguste (1903 [1844]) *A Discourse on the Positive Spirit* translated by Edward Spencer Beesly (London: William Reeves).

Cook, Harold J. (1993) 'The Cutting Edge of a Revolution? Medicine and Natural History near the Shores of the North Sea' in J. V. Field and Frank A. J. L. James (eds) *Renaissance and Revolution: Humanists, Scholars, Craftsmen and Natural Philosophers in Early Modern Europe* (Cambridge: Cambridge University Press), pp. 45–61.

Cooper, Frederick and Randall Packard (eds) (1997) *International Development and the Social Sciences: Essays on the History and Politics of Knowledge* (Berkeley: University of California Press).

Coser, Lewis A. (1971) *Masters of Sociological Thought: Ideas in Historical and Social Context* (New York: Harcourt Brace Jovanovich).

Crafts, N. F. R. (1977) 'Industrial Revolution in England and France: Some Thoughts on the Question, "Why was England First"' *The Economic History Review: New Series* 30/3, pp. 429–41.

Cranston, Maurice (1988) 'The Sovereignty of the Nation' in C. Lucas (ed.) *The French Revolution and the Creation of Modern Political Culture, Volume 2: The Political Culture of the French Revolution* (Oxford: Pergamon Press).

Crossley, Ceri (1993) *French Historians and Romanticism: Thierry, Guizot, the Saint-Simonians, Quinet, Michelet* (Routledge: London).

Daedalus (1998) 'Early Modernities' 127(3).

Daedalus (2000) 'Multiple Modernities' 129(1).

Das, Veena (1989) 'Discussion: Subaltern as Perspective' in Ranajit Guha (ed.) *Subaltern Studies VI: Writings on South Asian History and Society* (New Delhi: Oxford University Press), pp. 310–24.

Das Gupta, Ashin (1985) 'Indian Merchants and the Western Indian Ocean: The Early Seventeenth Century' *Modern Asian Studies: Special Issue: Papers Presented at the Conference on Indian Economic and Social History, Cambridge University, April 1984* 19/3, pp. 481–99.

Davis, David Brion (1971) 'New Sidelights on Antislavery Radicalism' *The William and Mary Quarterly* 28/4, pp. 585–94.

Deane, Phyllis and W. A. Cole (1962) *British Economic Growth 1688–1959: Trends and Structure* (Cambridge: Cambridge University Press).

Delanty, Gerard (1999) *Social Theory in a Changing World: Conceptions of Modernity* (Cambridge: Polity Press).

Delanty, Gerard (2004) 'Multiple Modernities and Globalization' *ProtoSociology* 20, pp. 162–182.

Delanty, Gerard (2006) 'Modernity and the Escape from Eurocentrism' in Gerard Delanty (ed.) *Handbook of Contemporary European Social Theory* (London: Routledge), pp. 266–78.

d'Entreves, M. P. (1996) 'Introduction' in M. P. d'Entreves and Seyla Benhabib (eds) *Habermas and the Unfinished Project of Modernity: Critical Essays on The Philosophical Discourse of Modernity* (Cambridge: Polity Press), pp. 1–37.

de Silva, Chandra Richard (1999) 'Indian Ocean but not African Sea: The Erasure of East African Commerce from History' *Journal of Black Studies: Special Issue: Political Strategies of Democracy and Health Issues and Concerns in Global Africa* 29/5, pp. 684–94.

de Vries, Jan (1994) 'The Industrial Revolution and the Industrious Revolution' *The Journal of Economic History: Papers Presented at the Fifty-Third Annual Meeting of the Economic History Association* 54/2, pp. 249–70.

Dirlik, Arif (2002) 'History Without a Centre? Reflections on Eurocentrism' in Eckhardt Fuchs and Benedikt Stuchtey (eds) *Across Cultural Borders: Historiography in Global Perspective* (New York: Rowman & Littlefield Publishers, Inc.).

Dirlik, Arif (2003) 'Global Modernity? Modernity in an Age of Global Capitalism' *European Journal of Social Theory* 6/3, pp. 275–92.

Doyle, William (1980) *Origins of the French Revolution* (Oxford: Oxford University Press).

Droz, Jacques (1967) *Europe Between the Revolutions 1815–1848* (Glasgow: Fontana).

Dubois, Laurent (2004) *A Colony of Citizens: Revolution and Slave Emancipation in the French Caribbean, 1787–1804* (Chapel Hill: The University of North Carolina Press).

During, Simon (1998) 'Postcolonialism and Globalization: A Dialectical Relation After All?' *Postcolonial Studies* 1/1, pp. 31–47.

Durkheim, Emile (1964 [1893]) *The Division of Labour in Society* translated by George Simpson (New York: The Free Press).

Durkheim, Emile (1992 [1937]) *Professional Ethics and Civic Morals* translated by Cornelia Brookfield (London: Routledge).

Eisenstadt, Shmuel N. (1965) 'Transformation of Social, Political, and Cultural Orders in Modernization' *American Sociological Review* 30/5, pp. 659–73.

Eisenstadt, Shmuel N. (ed.) (1968) *Comparative Perspectives on Social Change* (Boston: Little Brown and Company).

Eisenstadt, Shmuel N. (ed.) (1987) *Patterns of Modernity: Volume 1 The West* (London: Pinter).

Eisenstadt, Shmuel N. (1998) 'Comparative Studies and Sociological Theory: Autobiographical Notes' *The American Sociologist* 29/1, pp. 38–58.

Eisenstadt, Shmuel N. (2000) 'Multiple Modernities' *Daedalus: Multiple Modernities* 129/1, pp. 1–29.

Eisenstadt, Shmuel N. (2001) 'The Civilizational Dimension of Modernity: Modernity as a Distinct Civilization' *International Sociology* 16/3, pp. 320–40.

Eisenstadt, Shmuel N. and Wolfgang Schluchter (1998) 'Introduction: Paths to Early Modernities – A Comparative View' *Daedalus: Early Modernities* 127/3, pp. 1–18.

Eisenstein, Elizabeth L. (1968) 'Some Conjectures about the Impact of Printing on Western Society and Thought: A Preliminary Report' *Journal of Modern History* 40/1, March, pp. 1–56.

Eisenstein, Elizabeth L. (1969) 'The Advent of Printing and the Problem of the Renaissance' *Past and Present* 45, November, pp. 19–89.

Eisenstein, Elizabeth L. (1983) *The Printing Revolution in Early Modern Europe* (Cambridge: Cambridge University Press).

El-Bushra, El-Sayed (1992) 'Perspectives on the Contribution of Arabs and Muslims to Geography' *GeoJournal* 26/2, pp. 157–66.

Elias, Norbet (1978) *What is Sociology?* translated by S. Mennell and G. Morrisey (London: Hutchinson).

Elliott, J. H. (1968) *Europe Divided, 1559–1598* (Glasgow: Fontana/Collins).

Elshtain, Jean Bethke (1982) (ed.) *The Family in Political Thought* (Sussex: The Harvester Press).

Eltis, David and Stanley L. Engerman (2000) 'The Importance of Slavery and the Slave Trade to Industrializing Britain' *The Journal of Economic History* 60/1, pp. 123–44.

Elton, Geoffrey R. (1963) *Reformation Europe 1517–1559* (London: Collins).

Elton, Geoffrey R. (1990) 'The Age of the Reformation' in Geoffrey R. Elton (ed.) *The New Cambridge Modern History, Volume II: The Reformation 1520–1559* (Cambridge: Cambridge University Press, pp. 1–22).

Escobar, Arturo (1995) *Encountering Development: The Making and Unmaking of the Third World* (Princeton: Princeton University Press).

Fabian, Johannes (1983) *Time and the Other: How Anthropology Makes its Object* (New York: Columbia University Press).

Fabian, Johannes (1991) 'Dilemmas of Critical Anthropology' in *Time and the Work of Anthropology: Critical Essays, 1971–1991* (Amsterdam: Harwood Academic Publishers).

Fakhry, Majid (1965) 'Al-Farabi and the Reconciliation of Plato and Aristotle' *Journal of the History of Ideas* 26/4, pp. 469–78.

Fanon, Frantz (1967 [1952]) *Black Skin, White Masks* translated by Charles Lam Markmann (New York: Grove Press).

Fanon, Frantz (1968 [1961]) *The Wretched of the Earth* translated by Constance Farrington (New York: Grove Press).

Feldman, Arnold S. and Wilbert E. Moore (1962) 'Industrialization and Industrialism: Convergence and Differentiation' *Transactions of the Fifth World Congress of Sociology Volume II The Sociology of Development*, pp. 151–69.

Ferguson, Adam (1966 [1767]) *An Essay on the History of Civil Society* edited and with an introduction by Duncan Forbes (Edinburgh: Edinburgh University Press).

Ferguson, Wallace K. (1948) *The Renaissance in Historical Thought: Five Centuries of Interpretation* (Massachusetts: The Riverside Press).

Ferguson, Wallace K. (1953) 'The Church in a Changing World: A Contribution to the Interpretation of the Renaissance' *The American Historical Review* 59/1, pp. 1–18.

Fischer, Sibylle (2004) *Modernity Disavowed: Haiti and the Cultures of Slavery in the Age of Revolution* (London: Duke University Press).

Fisher, Michael H. (1993) 'The Office of Akhbar Nawis: The Transition from Mughal to British Forms' *Modern Asian Studies Special Issue: How Social, Political and Cultural Information is Collected, Defined, Used and Analyzed* 27/1, pp. 45–82.

Fletcher, F. T. H. (1933) 'Montesquieu's Influence on Anti-Slavery Opinion in England' *The Journal of Negro History* 18/4, pp. 414–25.

Flinn, M. W. (1966) *The Origins of the Industrial Revolution* (London: Longmans).

Fontana, Biancamaria (1985) 'The Shaping of Modern Liberty: Commerce and Civilization in the Writings of Benjamin Constant' *Annales Benjamin Constant* 5, pp. 2–15.

Ford, Franklin L. (1963) 'The Revolutionary-Napoleonic Era: How Much of a Watershed?' *The American Historical Review* 69/1, pp. 18–29.

Foucault, Michel (1991) 'Governmentality' in Graham Burchell, Colin Gordon and Peter Miller (eds) *The Foucault Effect: Studies in Governmentality* (Chicago: University of Chicago Press), pp. 87–104.

Foucault, Michel (2002 [1969]) *The Archaeology of Knowledge* translated by A. M. Sheridan-Smith (London: Routledge).

Fox, Christopher (1995) 'Introduction: How to Prepare a Noble Savage: The Spectacle of Human Science' in Christopher Fox, Roy Porter and Robert Wokler (eds) *Inventing Human Science: Eighteenth Century Domains* (Berkeley: University of California Press), pp. 1–30.

Frank, Andre Gunder (1975) *On Capitalist Underdevelopment* (Bombay: Oxford University Press).

Frank, Andre Gunder (1992) 'Fourteen Ninety-Two Once Again' *Political Geography* 11/4, pp. 386–93.

Frank, Andre Gunder (1998) *ReOrient: Global Economy in the Asian Age* (Berkeley: University of California Press).

Frothingham Jr, A. L. (1895) 'Notes on Byzantine Art and Culture in Italy and Especially in Rome' *The American Journal of Archaeology and of the History of the Fine Arts* 10/2, pp. 152–208.

Fukuyama, Francis (1992) *The End of History and the Last Man* (London: Hamish Hamilton).

Furet, François (1981 [1978]) *Interpreting the French Revolution* translated by Elborg Forster (Cambridge: Cambridge University Press).

Furet, François (1988 [1986]) *Marx and the French Revolution* translated by D. K. Furet (Chicago: University of Chicago Press).

Furet, François (1990) 'A Commentary' translated by Elborg Forster *French Historical Studies* 16/4, pp. 792–802.

Gadamer, Hans-Georg (1979) *Truth and Method* translated by W. Glen-Doeppel (London: Sheed and Ward).

Gaonkar, Dilip P. (2001a) (ed.) *Alternative Modernities* (Durham: Duke University Press).

Gaonkar, Dilip P. (2001b) 'On Alternative Modernities' in Dilip P. Gaonkar (ed.) *Alternative Modernities* (Durham: Duke University Press), pp. 1–23.

Garner, Roberta (1990) 'Jacob Burckhardt as a Theorist of Modernity: Reading the Civilization of the Renaissance in Italy' *Sociological Theory* 8/1, pp. 48–57.

Gates Jr, Henry Louis (1985) 'Editor's Introduction: Writing "Race" and the Difference it Makes' in *Critical Inquiry* 12/1, pp. 1–20.

Gay, Peter (1969) *The Enlightenment: An Interpretation. Vol. 2: The Science of Freedom* (London: W. W. Norton and Co.).

Geggus, David (1981) 'The British Government and the Saint Domingue Slave Revolt, 1791–1793' *The English Historical Review* 96/379, pp. 285–305.

Gershevitch, Ilya (1964) 'Zoroaster's Own Contribution' *Journal of Near Eastern Studies* 23/1, pp. 12–38.

Giddens, Anthony (1990) *The Consequences of Modernity* (Cambridge: Polity Press).

Gilmore, Myron P. (1952) *The World of Humanism 1453–1517* (New York: Harper and Row Publishers).

Gilmore, Myron P. (1960) 'Burckhardt as a Social Historian' in *Society and History in the Renaissance: A Report of a Conference Held at the Folger Library on April 23 and 24, 1960* (Washington: The Folger Shakespeare Library).

Gilroy, Paul (1993) *The Black Atlantic: Modernity and Double Consciousness* (Cambridge: Harvard University Press).

Glausser, Wayne (1990) 'Three Approaches to Locke and the Slave Trade' *Journal of the History of Ideas* 51/2, pp. 199–216.

Goldstone, Jack A. (1986) 'The Demographic Revolution in England: A Re-Examination' *Population Studies* 40/1, pp. 5–33.

Goldthorpe, John H. (1991) 'The Uses of History in Sociology: Reflections on Some Recent Tendencies' *British Journal of Sociology* 42/2, pp. 211–30.

Goody, Jack (2004) *Capitalism and Modernity: The Great Debate* (Cambridge: Polity Press).

Gombrich, Ernst H. (1995 [1950]) *The Story of Art* (London: Phaidon Press).

Gouldner, Alvin W. (1973) 'Romanticism and Classicism: Deep Structures in Social Science' in *For Sociology: Renewal and Critique in Sociology Today* (London: Allen Lane), pp. 323–66.

Gouwens, Kenneth (1998) 'Perceiving the Past: Renaissance Humanism After the "Cognitive Turn"' *The American Historical Review* 103/1, pp. 55–82.

Grafton, Anthony (1991) *Defender of the Text: The Traditions of Scholarship in an Age of Science, 1450–1800* (Massachusetts: Harvard University Press).

Greasley, David and Les Oxley (1994) 'Rehabilitation Sustained: The Industrial Revolution as a Macroeconomic Epoch' *The Economic History Review: New Series* 47/4, pp. 760–8.

Greasley, David and Les Oxley (1997) 'Endogenous Growth or "Big Bang": Two views of the First Industrial Revolution' *The Journal of Economic History* 57/4, pp. 935–49.

Green, William A. (1995) 'Periodizing World History' *History and Theory: Studies in the Philosophy of History, Theme Issue: World Historians and Their Critics* 34/2, pp. 99–111.

Greenblatt, Stephen (1980) *Renaissance Self-Fashioning: From More to Shakespeare* (Chicago: University of Chicago Press).

Greene, John C. (1981) *Science, Ideology, and World View: Essays in the History of Evolutionary Ideas* (Berkeley: University of California Press).

Grovogui, Siba N'Zatioula (1996) *Sovereigns, Quasi Sovereigns, and Africans: Race and Self-Determination in International Law* (Minneapolis: University of Minnesota Press).

Grovogui, Siba N'Zatioula (2001) 'Come to Africa: A Hermeneutics of Race in International Theory' in *Alternatives* 26/4, pp. 425–48.

Guha, Ranajit (1982) 'On Some Aspects of the Historiography of Colonial India' in Ranajit Guha (ed.) *Subaltern Studies I: Writings on South Asian History and Society* (Delhi: Oxford University Press), pp. 1–8.

Guha, Ranajit (1983) 'The Prose of Counter-Insurgency' in Ranajit Guha (ed.) *Subaltern Studies II: Writings on South Asian History and Society* (Delhi: Oxford University Press), pp. 1–42.

Guizot, François (1997 [1846]) *The History of Civilization in Europe* translated by W. Hazlitt (London: Penguin Books).

Gusfield, Joseph R. (1967) 'Tradition and Modernity: Misplaced Polarities in the Study of Social Change' *The American Journal of Sociology* 72/4, pp. 351–62.

Habermas, Jurgen (1996) 'Modernity: An Unfinished Project' in M. P. d'Entreves and Seyla Benhabib (eds) *Habermas and the Unfinished Project of Modernity: Critical Essays on The Philosophical Discourse of Modernity* (Cambridge: Polity Press), pp. 38–58.

Habib, Irfan (1980) 'The Technology and Economy of Mughal India' *The Indian Economic and Social History Review* XVII, pp. 1–34.

Hale, John R. (1971) *Renaissance Europe 1480–1520* (London: Collins).

Hale, John R. (1994) *The Civilization of Europe in the Renaissance* (New York: Atheneum).

Hall, Peter A. and David Soskice (eds) (2001) *Varieties of Capitalism: The Institutional Foundations of Comparative Advantage* (Oxford: Oxford University Press).

Hall, Stuart (1992) 'The West and the Rest: Discourse and Power' in Stuart Hall and Bram Gieben (eds) *Formations of Modernity* (Cambridge: Polity Press / Open University).

Hansen, Peo (2002) 'European Integration, European Identity and the Colonial Connection' *European Journal of Social Theory* 5/4, pp. 483–98.

Harding, Sandra (1986) *The Science Question in Feminism* (New York: Cornell University Press).

Harding, Sandra (1998) *Is Science Multicultural? Postcolonialisms, Feminisms, and Epistemologies* (Bloomington: Indiana University Press).

Harnetty, Peter (1991) '"Deindustrialization" Revisited: The Handloom Weavers of the Central Provinces of India, c. 1800–1947' *Modern Asian Studies* 25/3, pp. 455–510.

Harootunian, Harry D. (1999) 'Postcoloniality's Unconscious/Area Studies' Desire' *Postcolonial Studies* 2/2, pp. 127–47.

Harootunian, Harry (2000) *Overcome by Modernity: History, Culture, and Community in Interwar Japan* (Princeton: Princeton University Press).

Hartsock, Nancy C. M. (1984) 'The Feminist Standpoint: Developing the Ground for a Specifically Feminist Historical Materialism' in *Money, Sex and Power* (Boston: Northeastern University Press). Reprinted in Sandra Harding (ed.) *Feminism and Methodology: Social Science Issues* (Bloomington: Indiana University Press, 1987), pp. 157–80.

Hartwell, Ronald Max (1965) 'The Causes of the Industrial Revolution: An Essay in Methodology' *The Economic History Review: Essays in Economic History Presented to Professor M. M. Postan* 18/1, pp. 164–82.

Hartwell, Ronald Max (1971) *The Industrial Revolution and Economic Growth* (London: Methuen & Co Ltd.).

Haskins, Charles H. (1957) *The Renaissance of the Twelfth Century* (New York: Meridian).

Hawkesworth, Mary (1989) 'Knowers, Knowing, Known: Feminist Theory and Claims of Truth' *Signs: Journal of Women in Culture and Society* 14/3, pp. 533–57.

Hawthorn, Geoffrey (1976) *Enlightenment and Despair: A History of Sociology* (Cambridge: Cambridge University Press).

Hay, Denys (1957) *Europe: The Emergence of an Idea* (Edinburgh: Edinburgh University Press).

Headley, John M. (2000) 'Geography and Empire in the Late Renaissance: Botero's Assignment, Western Universalism, and the Civilizing Process' *Renaissance Quarterly* 53/4, pp. 1119–55.

Heilbron, Johan (1995) *The Rise of Social Theory* (Cambridge: Polity Press).

Heilbroner, Robert L. (1973) 'The Paradox of Progress: Decline and Decay in *The Wealth of Nations*' *Journal of the History of Ideas* 34/2, pp. 243–62.

Herder, Johann Gottfried von (1969) *J. G. Herder on Social and Political Culture* translated and edited by F. M. Barnard (Cambridge: Cambridge University Press).

Higman, B. W. (2000) 'The Sugar Revolution' *The Economic History Review: New Series* 53/2, pp. 213–36.

Hindess, Barry (1987) 'Rationality and the Characterization of Modern Society' in Sam Whimster and Scott Lash (eds) *Max Weber, Rationality and Modernity* (London: Allen and Unwin), pp. 137–53.

Hirschman, Albert O. (1977) *The Passions and the Interests: Political Arguments for Capitalism before Its Triumph* (New Jersey: Princeton University Press).

Hobsbawm, Eric J. (1977) *The Age of Revolution: Europe 1789–1848* (London: Abacus).

Hobsbawm, Eric J. (1994) *Nations and Nationalism Since 1780: Programme, Myth and Reality* (Cambridge: Cambridge University Press).

Holmes, George (1975) *Europe: Hierarchy and Revolt, 1320–1450* (Glasgow: Fontana/Collins).

Holmwood, John (1995) 'Feminism and Epistemology: What Kind of Successor Science?' *Sociology* 29/3, pp. 411–28.

Holmwood, John (1996) *Founding Sociology? Talcott Parsons and the Idea of General Theory* (Harlow: Longman Group Ltd.).

Holmwood, John (2000a) 'Sociology and its Audience(s): Changing Perceptions of Sociological Argument' in John Eldridge *et al.* (eds) *For Sociology: Legacies and Prospects* (Durham: Sociology Press), pp. 33–55.

Holmwood, John (2000b) 'Europe and the "Americanization" of British Social Policy' *European Societies* 2/4, pp. 453–82.

Holmwood, John (2001) 'Gender and Critical Realism: A Critique of Sayer' *Sociology* 35/4, pp. 947–65.

Holmwood, John (2007a) ' "Only Connect": The Challenge of Globalization for the Social Sciences' *Twenty-First Century Society: Journal of the Academy of the Social Sciences* 2/1, pp. 79–93.

Holmwood, John (2007b) 'Pragmatism and the Prospects of Sociological Theory' (forthcoming).

Holmwood, John and Alexander Stewart (1991) *Explanation and Social Theory* (London: Macmillan).

Holmwood, John and Maureen O'Malley (2003) 'Evolutionary and Functionalist Historical Sociology' in Gerard Delanty and Engin F. Isin (eds) *Handbook of Historical Sociology* (London: Sage Publications), pp. 39–57.

Hoppit, Julian (1990) 'Counting the Industrial Revolution' *The Economic History Review: New Series* 43/2, pp. 173–93.

Hourani, George F. (1976) 'Islamic and Non-Islamic Origins of Mu'tazilite Ethical Rationalism' *International Journal of Middle East Studies* 7/1, pp. 59–87.

Hume, David (1875 [1752]) *Essays, Moral, Political, and Literary* edited by T. H. Green and T. H. Grose (London: Longmans, Green & Co.).

Hunting, Claudine (1978) 'The *Philosophes* and Black Slavery: 1748–1765' *Journal of the History of Ideas* 39/3, pp. 405–18.

Iggers, Georg G. (1982) 'The Idea of Progress in Historiography and Social Thought Since the Enlightenment' in G. A. Almond, M. Chodorow and R. H. Pearce (eds) *Progress and its Discontents* (Berkeley: University of California Press), pp. 41–66.

Iggers, Georg G. (1997) *Historiography in the Twentieth Century: From Scientific Objectivity to the Postmodern Challenge* (Connecticut: Wesleyan University Press).

Inikori, Joseph E. (1987) 'Slavery and the Development of Industrial Capitalism in England' *Journal of Interdisciplinary History: Caribbean Slavery and British Capitalism* 17/4, pp. 771–93.

Inkeles, Alex (1969) 'Making Men Modern: On the Causes and Consequences of Individual Change in Six Developing Countries' *American Journal of Sociology* 75/2, pp. 208–25.

Jacques, T. Carlos (1997) 'From Savages and Barbarians to Primitives: Africa, Social Typologies, and History in Eighteenth-Century French Philosophy' *History and Theory* 36/2, pp. 190–215.

Jahn, Beate (1999) 'IR and the State of Nature: The Cultural Origins of a Ruling Ideology' *Review of International Studies* 25/3, pp. 411–34.

James, C. L. R. (1989 [1938]) *The Black Jacobins: Toussaint L'Ouverture and the San Domingo Revolution* second edition, revised (New York: Vintage Books).

James, William (1904) 'The Pragmatic Method' *Journal of Philosophy, Psychology and Scientific Methods* 1, pp. 673–87.

Jardine, Lisa (1996a) 'Penfriends and Patria: Erasmian Pedagogy and the Republic of Letters' *Erasmus of Rotterdam Society Yearbook* 16, pp. 1–18.

Jardine, Lisa (1996b) *Worldly Goods: A New History of the Renaissance* (London: Papermac).

Jardine, Lisa and Jerry Brotton (2000) *Global Interests: Renaissance Art between East and West* (London: Reaktion Books).

Jardine, Nicholas (2000 [1991]) *The Scenes of Inquiry: On the Reality of Questions in the Sciences* (Oxford: Clarendon Press).

Jasanoff, Maya (2005) *Edge of Empire: Conquest and Collecting in the East, 1750–1850* (London: Fourth Estate).

Jenkins, Keith (2003) *Refiguring History: New Thoughts on An Old Discipline* (London: Routledge).

Johns, Adrian (1998) *The Nature of the Book: Print and Knowledge in the Making* (Chicago: University of Chicago Press).

Joll, James (1980) 'Europe – An Historian's View' *History of European Ideas* 1/1, pp. 7–19.

Joseph, George G., Vasu Reddy and Mary Searle-Chatterjee (1990) 'Eurocentrism in the Social Sciences' *Race and Class* 31/4, pp. 1–26.

Joyce, Patrick (2002) 'Maps, Blood and the City: The Governance of the Social in Nineteenth-Century Britain' in Patrick Joyce (ed.) *The Social in Question: New Bearings in History and the Social Sciences* (London: Routledge), pp. 97–114.

Kaiwar, Vasant (2003) 'The Aryan Model of History and the Oriental Renaissance: The Politics of Identity in an Age of Revolutions, Colonialism, and Nationalism' in Vasant Kaiwar and Sucheta Mazumdar (eds) *Antinomies of Modernity: Essays on Race, Orient, Nation* (Durham: Duke University Press), pp. 13–61.

Kalberg, Stephen (1994) *Max Weber's Comparative-Historical Sociology* (Cambridge: Polity Press).

Kaplan, Martha (1995) 'Panoptican in Poona: An Essay on Foucault and Colonialism' *Cultural Anthropology* 10/1, pp. 85–98.

Kedourie, Elie (1994 [1960]) *Nationalism* fourth edition (Oxford: Blackwell).

Keita, Maghan (1994) 'Deconstructing the Classical Age: Africa and the Unity of the Mediterranean World' *The Journal of Negro History* 79/2, pp. 147–66.

Keita, Maghan (2002) 'Africa and the Construction of a Grand Narrative in World History' in Eckhardt Fuchs and Benedikt Stuchtey (eds) *Across Cultural Borders: Historiography in Global Perspective* (New York: Rowman & Littlefield Publishers, Inc.), pp. 289–93.

Kelley, Donald R. (1988) 'Humanism and History' in Albert Rabil (ed.) *Renaissance Humanism, Foundation, Forms and Legacy, Volume 3: Humanism and the Disciplines* (Philadelphia: University of Pennsylvania Press), pp. 236–70.

Kelley, Donald R. (1991) *Renaissance Humanism* (Boston: Twayne Publishers).

Kelly, Joan (1986 [1984]) *Women, History and Theory: The Essays of Joan Kelly* (Chicago: University of Chicago Press).

Kerr, Clark and John T. Dunlop, Frederick H. Harbison, Charles A. Myers (1960) *Industrialism and Industrial Man: the Problems of Labour and Management in Economic Growth* (Cambridge: Harvard University Press).

Kiernan, Victor G. (1980) 'Europe in the Colonial Mirror' *History of European Ideas* 1/1, pp. 39–61.

Koyré, Alexandre (1958) *From the Closed World to the Infinite Universe* (New York: Harper and Brothers Publishers).

Kraemer, Joel L. (1984) 'Humanism in the Renaissance of Islam: A Preliminary Study' *Journal of the American Oriental Society: Studies in Islam and the Ancient Near East Dedicated to Franz Rosenthal* 104/1, pp. 135–64.

Kristeller, Paul Oskar (1962) 'Studies on Renaissance Humanism During the Last Twenty Years' *Studies in the Renaissance* 29, pp. 7–30.

Kristeller, Paul Oskar (1974) *Medieval Aspects of Renaissance Learning* edited and translated by Edward P. Mahoney (Durham: Duke University Press).

Kuhn, Thomas S. (1962) *The Structure of Scientific Revolutions* (Chicago: Chicago University Press).

Kumar, Deepak (1995) *Science and the Raj 1857–1905* (New Delhi: Oxford University Press).

Kumar, Deepak (2003) 'Developing a History of Science and Technology in South Asia' *Economic and Political Weekly* June 7.

Kumar, Krishan (1978) *Prophecy and Progress: The Sociology of Industrial and Post-Industrial Society* (Middlesex: Penguin Books).

Landes, David S. (1969) *The Unbound Prometheus: Technological Change and Industrial Development in Western Europe from 1750 to the Present* (Cambridge: Cambridge University Press).

Landes, David S. (1999) *The Wealth and Poverty of Nations: Why Some Are So Rich and Some So Poor* (London: Abacus).

Latour, Bruno (1993) *We Have Never Been Modern* translated by Caroline Porter (Hertfordshire: Harvester Wheatsheaf).

Laures, Johannes (1952) 'Notes on the Death of Ninshitsu, Xavier's Bonze Friend' *Monumenta Nipponica* 8/1–2, pp. 407–11.

Law, Robin and Kristin Mann (1999) 'West Africa in the Atlantic Community: The Case of the Slave Coast' *The William and Mary Quarterly: Third Series: African and American Atlantic Worlds* 56/2, pp. 307–34.

Lee, Raymond L. M. (2006) 'Reinventing Modernity: Reflexive Modernization vs Liquid Modernity vs Multiple Modernities' *European Journal of Social Theory* 9/3, pp. 355–69.

Lehmann, Hartmut and Guenther Roth (eds) (1993) *Weber's Protestant Ethic: Origins, Evidence, Context* (Cambridge: Cambridge University Press).

Lemert, Charles (1995) *Sociology After the Crisis* (Oxford: Westview Press).

Lerner, Daniel (1958) *The Passing of Traditional Society: Modernizing the Middle East* (New York: The Free Press).

Levy Jr, Marion J. (1965) 'Patterns (Structures) of Modernization and Political Development' *The Annals of the American Academy of Political and Social Science* March, pp. 29–40.

Lewis, Archibald R. (1990) 'The Islamic World and the Latin West, 1350–1500' *Speculum* 65/4, pp. 833–44.

Lieberman, Victor (ed.) (1999 [1997]) *Beyond Binary Histories: Re-Imagining Eurasia to C. 1830* (Michigan: University of Michigan Press).

Locke, John (1764 [1689]) *Two Treatises of Government* edited by Thomas Hollis (London: A. Millar et al.).

Lukács, Georg (1999 [1968]) *History and Class Consciousness: Studies in Marxist Dialectics* translated by Rodney Livingstone (London: The Merlin Press Ltd.).

Lukes, Steven (1973) *Emile Durkheim: His Life and Work, A Historical and Critical Study* (Middlesex: Penguin Books).

Makdisi, George (1989) 'Scholasticism and Humanism in Classical Islam and the Christian West' *Journal of the American Oriental Society* 109/2, pp. 175–82.

Malkki, Liisa H. (1997) 'National Geographic: The Rooting of Peoples and the Territorialization of National Identity among Scholars and Refugees' in Akhil Gupta and James Ferguson (eds) *Culture, Power, Place: Explorations in Critical Anthropology* (Durham: Duke University Press), pp. 52–74.

Mann, Michael (1986) *The Sources of Social Power, Volume I: A History of Power from the Beginning to A.D. 1760* (Cambridge: Cambridge University Press).

Mann, Michael (1993) *The Sources of Social Power, Volume II: The Rise of Classes and Nation-States, 1760–1914* (Cambridge: Cambridge University Press).

Mann, Michael (1994) 'In Praise of Macro-Sociology: A Reply to Goldthorpe' *The British Journal of Sociology* 45/1, pp. 37–54.

Marshall, Gordon (1982) *In Search of the Spirit of Capitalism: An Essay on Max Weber's Protestant Ethic Thesis* (New York: Columbia University Press).

Marx, Karl (1976 [1867]) *Capital: A Critique of Political Economy Volume One* introduced by Ernest Mandel, translated by Ben Fowkes (Middlesex: Penguin Books).

Mazrui, Ali A. (1968) 'From Social Darwinism to Current Theories of Modernization: A Tradition of Analysis' *World Politics* 21/1, pp. 69–83.

McLennan, Gregor (2000) 'Sociology's Eurocentrism and the "Rise of the West" Revisited' *European Journal of Social Theory* 3/3, pp. 275–91.

McLennan, Gregor (2003) 'Sociology, Eurocentrism and Postcolonial Theory' *European Journal of Social Theory* 6/1, pp. 69–86.

McLennan, Gregor (2006) *Sociological Cultural Studies: Reflexivity and Positivity in the Human Sciences* (Basingstoke: Palgrave Macmillan).

Meek, Ronald (1976) *Social Science and the Ignoble Savage* (Cambridge: Cambridge University Press).

Mehta, Uday Singh (1999) *Liberalism and Empire: A Study in Nineteenth-Century British Liberal Thought* (Chicago: University of Chicago Press).

Memmi, Albert (1965 [1957]) *The Colonizer and the Colonized* (Boston: Beacon).

Michelet, Jules (1967 [1847]) *History of the French Revolution* edited by G. Wright (Chicago: University of Chicago Press).

Mignolo, Walter D. (1995) *The Darker Side of the Renaissance: Literacy, Territoriality, and Colonization* (Michigan: University of Michigan Press).

Mill, John Stuart (1865 [1861]) *Considerations on Representative Government* (London: Longman Green).

Mintz, Sidney W. (1986) *Sweetness and Power: The Place of Sugar in Modern History* (London: Penguin Books).

Mitchell, Timothy (1991) *Colonizing Egypt* (Berkeley: University of California Press).

Mitchell, Timothy (2000) 'The Stage of Modernity' in Timothy Mitchell (ed.) *Questions of Modernity* (Minneapolis: University of Minnesota Press), pp. 1–34.

Mohanty, Chandra Talpade (1991) 'Under Western Eyes: Feminist Scholarship and Colonial Discourses' in C. T. Mohanty, A. Russo and L. Torres (eds) *Third World Women and the Politics of Feminism* (Bloomington: Indiana University Press), pp. 51–80.

Montaigne, Michel de (1993 [1575]) *The Complete Essays* translated by M. A. Screech (London: Penguin Books).

Montesquieu, Baron de (1965 [1748]) *The Spirit of the Laws Volumes I & II* translated by Thomas Nugent (New York: Hafner Publishing Company).

Moore, Robert I. (1997) 'The Birth of Europe as a Eurasian Phenomenon' *Modern Asian Studies* 31/3, pp. 583–601.

Moore, Wilbert E. (1963) 'Introduction: Social Change and Comparative Studies' *International Social Science Journal* 14/4, pp. 519–27.

Morris, Meaghan (1990) 'Metamorphoses at Sydney Tower' *New Formations* 10, Summer, pp. 5–18.

Morris, Morris D. (1963) 'Towards a Reinterpretation of Nineteenth-Century Indian Economic History' *The Journal of Economic History* 23/4, pp. 606–18.

Moya, Paula M. L. (2000) 'Introduction: Reclaiming Identity' in Paula M. L. Moya and Michael R. Hames-Garcia (eds) *Reclaiming Identity: Realist Theory and the Predicament of Postmodernism* (Berkeley: University of California Press), pp. 1–28.

Muir, Edward (1979) 'Images of Power: Art and Pageantry in Renaissance Venice' *The American Historical Review* 84/1, pp. 16–52.

Muller, Jerry Z. (2002) *The Mind and the Market: Capitalism in Modern European Thought* (New York: Alfred A. Knopf).

Muthu, Sankar (2003) *Enlightenment Against Empire* (Princeton: Princeton University Press).

Nandy, Ashis (1983) *The Intimate Enemy: Loss and Recovery of Self under Colonialism* (New Delhi: Oxford University Press).

Nandy, Ashis (1987) *Traditions, Tyranny and Utopias: Essays in the Politics of Awareness* (New Delhi: Oxford University Press).

Nandy, Ashis (1994) *The Illegitimacy of Nationalism: Rabindranath Tagore and the Politics of Self* (New Delhi: Oxford University Press).

Nandy, Ashis (1995) 'History's Forgotten Doubles' *History and Theory: Studies in the Philosophy of History, Theme Issue: World Historians and Their Critics* 34/2, pp. 44–66.

Narayan, Uma (1998) 'Essence of Culture and a Sense of History: A Feminist Critique of Cultural Essentialism' *Hypatia* 13/2, pp. 86–106.

Nauert Jr, Charles G. (1995) *Humanism and the Culture of Renaissance Europe* (Cambridge: Cambridge University Press).

Nelson, Lynn Hankinson (1993) 'Epistemological Communities' in Linda Alcoff and Elizabeth Potter (eds) *Feminist Epistemologies* (London: Routledge).

Nettl, J. P. (1967) *Political Mobilization: A Sociological Analysis of Methods and Concepts* (London: Faber).

Nielsen, J. K. (1991) 'The Political Orientation of Talcott Parsons: The Second World War and Its Aftermath' in R. Robertson and Bryan Turner (eds) *Talcott Parsons: Theorist of Modernity* (London: Sage), pp. 217–33.

Nisbet, Robert A. (1966) *The Sociological Tradition* (New York: Basic Books Inc.).

Nisbet, Robert A. (1973) 'The Myth of the Renaissance' *Comparative Studies in Society and History* 15/4, pp. 473–92.

O'Brien, Patrick K. (1977) 'Agriculture and the Industrial Revolution' *The Economic History Review: New Series* 30/1, pp. 166–81.

O'Hearn, Denis (1994) 'Innovation and the World-System Hierarchy: British Subjugation of the Irish Cotton Industry, 1780–1830' *The American Journal of Sociology* 100/3, pp. 587–621.

Olender, Maurice (1994) 'Europe, or How to Escape Babel' *History and Theory: Studies in the Philosophy of History, Theme Issue: Proof and Persuasion in History* 33/4, pp. 5–25.

Outhwaite, William (1983) *Concept Formation in Social Science* (London: Routledge and Kegan Paul).

Outhwaite, William (1987) *New Philosophies of Social Science: Realism, Hermeneutics and Critical Theory* (London: Macmillan Press).

Outhwaite, William (2001) 'What is European Culture?' in Gyorgy Szell and Wiking Ehlert (eds) *New Democracies and Old Societies in Europe* (Frankfurt am Main: Peter Lang).

Pacheco, Diego (1974) 'Xavier and Tanegashima' *Monumenta Nipponica* 29/4, pp. 477–80.

Pagden, Anthony (1993) *European Encounters with the New World: From Renaissance to Romanticism* (New Haven: Yale University Press).

Pagden, Anthony (2002) 'Introduction' in Anthony Pagden (ed.) *The Idea of Europe From Antiquity to the European Union* (Cambridge: Cambridge University Press), pp. 1–32.

Pannikar, K. M. (1959) *Asia and Western Dominance: A Survey of the Vasco Da Gama Epoch of Asian History 1498–1945* (London: George Allen and Unwin Ltd.).

Panofsky, Erwin (1960) *Renaissance and Renascences in Western Art* (Copenhagen: Russak and Company Ltd.).

Panofsky, Erwin (1991) *Perspective as Symbolic Form* translated by Christopher S. Wood (New York: Zone Books).

Parry, J. H. (1963) *The Age of Reconnaissance: Discovery, Exploration, and Settlement, 1450–1650* (London: Weidenfeld and Nicolson Ltd.).

Parsons, Talcott (1937) *The Structure of Social Action: A Study in Social Theory with Special Reference to a Group of Recent European Writers* (New York: The Free Press of Glencoe).

Parsons, Talcott (1964) 'Evolutionary Universals in Society' *American Sociological Review* 29/3, pp. 339–57.

Parsons, Talcott (1966) *Societies: Evolutionary and Comparative Perspectives* (New Jersey: Prentice-Hall Inc.).

Parsons, Talcott (1971) *The System of Modern Societies* (New Jersey: Prentice-Hall Inc.).

Perlin, Frank (1983) 'Proto-Industrialization and Pre-Colonial South Asia' *Past and Present* 98, pp. 30–95.

Perlin, Frank (1994) *Unbroken Landscape: Commodity, Category, Sign and Identity; Their Production as Myth and Knowledge from 1500* (Hampshire: Variorum).

Persaud, Randolph B. and Rob B. J. Walker (2001) 'Apertura: Race in International Relations' *Alternatives* 26/4, pp. 373–76.

Petras, James and Henry Veltmeyer (2001) *Globalization Unmasked: Imperialism in the 21st Century* (New Delhi: Madhyam Books).

Pocock, John G. A. (1977) 'Gibbon's Decline and Fall and the World View of the Late Enlightenment' *Eighteenth-Century Studies* 10/3, pp. 287–303.

Pocock, John G. A. (1985) *Virtue, Commerce and History Essays on Political Thought and History, Chiefly in the Eighteenth Century* (Cambridge: Cambridge University Press).

Polanyi, Karl (2001 [1944]) *The Great Transformation: The Political and Economic Origins of Our Time* (Boston: Beacon Press).

Polanyi, Karl, C. M. Arensberg and H. W. Pearson (eds) (1957) *Trade and Market in the Early Empires: Economies in History and Theory* (New York: Glencoe Free Press).

Pollard, Sidney (1973) 'Industrialization and the European Economy' *The Economic History Review: New Series* 26/4, pp. 636–48.

Pollock, Sheldon, Homi K. Bhabha, Carol A. Breckenbridge and Dipesh Chakrabarty (2000) 'Cosmopolitanisms' *Public Culture* 12/3, pp. 577–89.

Pomeranz, Kenneth (2000) *The Great Divergence: China, Europe, and the Making of the Modern World Economy* (Princeton: Princeton University Press).

Portes, Alejandro (1973) 'Modernity and Development: A Critique' *Studies in Comparative International Development* 8/3, pp. 247–79.

Prakash, Gyan (1994) 'Subaltern Studies as Postcolonial Criticism' *The American Historical Review* 99/5, pp. 1475–90.

Prakash, Gyan (1997) 'Postcolonial Criticism and Indian Historiography' in Anne McClintock, Aamir Mufti and Ella Shohat (eds) *Dangerous Liaisons: Gender, Nation, and Postcolonial Perspectives* (London: University of Minnesota Press), pp. 491–500.

Prakash, Gyan (1999) *Another Reason: Science and the Imagination of Modern India* (New Jersey: Princeton University Press).

Prakash, Gyan (2002) 'The Colonial Genealogy of Society: Community and Political Modernity in India' in Patrick Joyce (ed.) *The Social in Question: New Bearings in History and the Social Sciences* (London: Routledge), pp. 81–96.

Rabil, Albert (ed.) (1988) *Renaissance Humanism, Foundation, Forms and Legacy, Volume 3: Humanism and the Disciplines* (Philadelphia: University of Pennsylvania Press).

Ralph, Philip Lee (1973) *The Renaissance in Perspective* (London: G. Bell and Sons, Ltd.).

Raychaudhuri, Tapan (2002 [1988]) *Europe Reconsidered: Perceptions of the West in Nineteenth-Century Bengal* second edition (New Delhi: Oxford University Press).

Rice, Eugene F. and Anthony Grafton (1994 [1970]) *The Foundations of Early Modern Europe 1460–1559* second edition (London: W. W. Norton and Company).

Richardson, David (1987) 'The Slave Trade, Sugar, and British Economic Growth, 1748–1776' *Journal of Interdisciplinary History: Caribbean Slavery and British Capitalism* 17/4, pp. 739–69.

Robertson, William (1818 [1777]) *The History of America Volume II* (Edinburgh: Peter Hill and Co.).

Rodríguez-Salgado, M. J. (1998) 'Christians, Civilized and Spanish: Multiple Identities in Sixteenth Century Spain' reprinted from *The Transactions of the Royal Historical Society 6th Series*, 8, pp. 233–51.

Rodríguez-Salgado, M. J. (2005) 'Europe of the Mind' (Part I), Radio 3 Sunday Feature, February 2005, repeated August 2005.

Rorty, Richard (1987) 'Science as Solidarity' in John S. Nelson, Allan Megill, and Donald N. McCloskey (eds) *The Rhetoric of the Human Sciences* (Madison: The University of Wisconsin Press), pp. 38–52.

Rostow, Walt W. (1960) *The Stages of Economic Growth: A Non-Communist Manifesto* (Cambridge: Cambridge University Press).

Roth, Guenther (1987) 'Rationalization in Max Weber's Developmental History' in Sam Whimster and Scott Lash (eds) *Max Weber, Rationality and Modernity* (London: Allen and Unwin), pp. 75–91.

Rousseau, Jean-Jacques (2004 [1762]) *The Social Contract, Or Principles of Political Right* translated by G. D. H. Cole (Montana: Kessinger Publishing).

Rudolph, Suzanne Hoeber (2005) 'The Imperialism of Categories: Situating Knowledge in a Globalizing World' *Perspectives on Politics* 3/1, pp. 5–14.

Runciman, W. Garry (1997) *A Treatise on Social Theory, Volume III: Applied Social Theory* (Cambridge: Cambridge University Press).

Rüsen, Jörn (1985) 'Jacob Burckhardt: Political Standpoint and Historical Insight on the Border of Post-Modernism' *History and Theory* 24/3, pp. 235–46.

Sabra, A. I. (1984) 'The Andalusian Revolt Against Ptolemaic Astronomy: Averroes and al-Bitruji' in E. Mendelsohn (ed.) *Transformation and Tradition in the Sciences: Essays in Honor of I. Bernard Cohen* (Cambridge: Cambridge University Press), pp. 133–54.

Said, Edward W. (1975) *Beginnings: Intention and Method* (New York: Basic Books Inc. Publishers).

Said, Edward W. (1978) *Orientalism: Western Conceptions of the Orient* (London: Routledge and Kegan Paul Ltd.).

Said, Edward W. (1986) 'Intellectuals in the Post-Colonial World' *Salmagundi* 70–71, Spring/Summer, pp. 44–64.

Said, Edward W. (1993) *Culture and Imperialism* (London: Chatto and Windus).

Said, Edward W. (1995 [1978]) *Orientalism: Western Conceptions of the Orient* with a new afterword (London: Penguin).

Sanford, Eva Mathews (1951) 'The Twelfth Century – Renaissance or Proto-Renaissance?' *Speculum* 26/4, pp. 635–42.

Scammell, G. V. (2000) 'After Da Gama: Europe and Asia since 1498' *Modern Asian Studies* 34/3, pp. 513–43.

Scott, John (1995) *Sociological Theory: Contemporary Debates* (Cheltenham: Edward Elgar).

Seidman, Steven (1997) *Difference Troubles: Queering Social Theory and Sexual Politics* (Cambridge: Cambridge University Press).

Seidman, Steven (1998) *Contested Knowledge: Social Theory in the Postmodern Era* (Oxford: Blackwell Publishers).

Sidbury, James (1997) 'Saint Domingue in Virginia: Ideology, Local Meanings, and Resistance to Slavery, 1790–1800' *The Journal of Southern History* 63/3, pp. 531–52.

Shilliam, Robbie (2006) 'What about Marcus Garvey? Race and the Transformation of Sovereignty Debate' *Review of International Studies* 32/3, pp. 379–400.

Silver, Allan (1990) 'Friendship in Commercial Society: Eighteenth-Century Social Theory and Modern Sociology' *American Journal of Sociology* 95/6, pp. 1474–1504.

Simmons, Colin (1985) '"De-Industrialization," Industrialization and the Indian Economy, c. 1850–1947' *Modern Asian Studies: Special Issue: Papers Presented at the Conference on Indian Economic and Social History, Cambridge University April 1984* 19/3, pp. 593–622.

Smart, Barry (1992) *Modern Conditions, Postmodern Controversies* (London: Routledge).

Smith, Adam (1863 [1776]) *An Inquiry into the Nature and Causes of the Wealth of Nations* with an introduction by J. R. M'Culloch (Edinburgh: Adam and Charles Black).

Smith, Adam (1982 [1759]) *The Theory of Moral Sentiments* edited by D. D. Raphael and A. L. Macfie (Indianapolis: Liberty Fund).

Smith, Anthony D. (1983 [1971]) *Theories of Nationalism* second edition (London: Duckworth).

Smith, Anthony D. (1986) *The Ethnic Origins of Nations* (Oxford: Blackwell).

Smith, Anthony D. (1996) 'Nationalism and the Historians' in Gopal Balakrishnan (ed.) *Mapping the Nation* (London: Verso), pp. 175–97.

Solow, Barbara L. (1987) 'Capitalism and Slavery in the Exceedingly Long Run' *Journal of Interdisciplinary History: Caribbean Slavery and British Capitalism* 17/4, pp. 711–37.

Spivak, Gayatri Chakravorty (1985a) 'The Rani of Sirmur: An Essay in Reading the Archives' *History and Theory – Studies in the Philosophy of History* XXIV, pp. 247–72.

Spivak, Gayatri Chakravorty (1985b) 'Subaltern Studies: Deconstructing Historiography' in Donna Landry and Gerald MacLean (eds) (1996) *Selected Works of Gayatri Chakravorty Spivak* (New York: Routledge), pp. 203–36.

Spivak, Gayatri Chakravorty (1988) 'Can the Subaltern Speak?' in Cary Nelson and Lawrence Grossberg (eds) *Marxism and the Interpretation of Culture* (Chicago: University of Illinois Press), pp. 271–316.

Spivak, Gayatri Chakravorty (1990) 'Post-structuralism, Marginality, Postcoloniality and Value' in Peter Collier and Helga Geyer-Ryan (eds) *Literary Theory Today* (Cambridge: Polity Press), pp. 219–44.

Sprang, Rebecca L. (2003) 'Paradigms and Paranoia: How Modern is the French Revolution?' *The American Historical Review* 108/1, pp. 119–48.

Stokes, Eric (1959) *The English Utilitarians and India* (Oxford: Oxford University Press).

Stoler, Ann Laura (1989) 'Rethinking Colonial Categories: European Communities and the Boundaries of Rule' *Comparative Studies in Society and History* 31/1, pp. 134–61.

Stråth, Bo (2002) 'A European Identity: To the Historical Limits of a Concept' *European Journal of Social Theory* 5/4, pp. 387–401.

Subrahmanyam, Sanjay (1988) 'Persians, Pilgrims and Portuguese: The Travails of Masulipatnam shipping in the Western Indian Ocean, 1590–1665' *Modern Asian Studies: Special Issue: Asian Studies in Honour of Professor Charles Boxer* 22/3, pp. 503–30.

Subrahmanyam, Sanjay (1990) 'Rural Industry and Commercial Agriculture in Late Seventeenth-Century South-Eastern India' *Past and Present* 126, pp. 76–114.

Subrahmanyam, Sanjay (1997) 'Connected Histories: Notes towards a Reconfiguration of Early Modern Eurasia' *Modern Asian Studies* 31/3, pp. 735–62.

Subrahmanyam, Sanjay (2005a) *Explorations in Connected Histories: Mughals and Franks* (Oxford: Oxford University Press).

Subrahmanyam, Sanjay (2005b) *Explorations in Connected Histories: From the Tagus to the Ganges* (Oxford: Oxford University Press).

Sullivan, Richard E. (1989) 'The Carolingian Age: Reflections on its Place in the History of the Middle Ages' *Speculum* 64/2, pp. 267–306.

Swingewood, Alan (1970) 'Origins of Sociology: The Case of the Scottish Enlightenment' *The British Journal of Sociology* 21, pp. 164–80.

Sylvester, Christine (1999) 'Development Studies and Postcolonial Studies: Disparate Tales of the "Third World"' *Third World Quarterly* 20/4, pp. 703–21.

Symonds, John Addington (1897) *Renaissance in Italy, Volume 1: The Age of the Despots* (London: Murray).

Talmon, J. L. (1967) *Romanticism and Revolt Europe 1815–1848* (New York: W. W. Norton and Company).

Taylor, Charles (1999) 'Nationalism and Modernity' in Ronald Beiner (ed.) *Theorizing Nationalism* (Albany: State University of New York Press), pp. 219–45.

Taylor, Charles (2001) 'Two Theories of Modernity' in Dilip P. Gaonkar (ed.) *Alternative Modernities* (Durham: Duke University Press), pp. 172–96.

Taylor, Peter J. (2000) 'Embedded Statism and the Social Sciences 2: Geographies and Meta-Geographies in Globalization' *Environment and Planning A* 32, pp. 1105–14.

Teschke, Benno (2003) *The Myth of 1648: Class, Geopolitics and the Making of Modern International Relations* (London: Verso).

Thapar, Romila (1966) *A History of India: Volume One* (Middlesex: Penguin Books Ltd.).

Thapar, Romila (1992) *Interpreting Early India* (New Delhi: Oxford University Press).

Thapar, Romila (1996) *Time as a Metaphor of History: Early India* (New Delhi: Oxford University Press).

Therborn, Goran (1995) *European Modernity and Beyond: The Trajectory of European Societies, 1945–2000* (London: Sage Publications).

Therborn, Goran (2003) 'Entangled Modernities' *European Journal of Social Theory* 6/3, pp. 293–305.

Tiryakian, Edward A. (1991) 'Modernization: Exhumetur in Pace (Rethinking Macrosociology in the 1990s)' *International Sociology* 6/2, pp. 165–80.

Tönnies, Ferdinand (1955 [1887]) Community and Association (Gemeinschaft und Gesellschaft) translated and supplemented by Charles P. Loomis (London: Routledge and Kegan Paul Ltd.).

Toulmin, Stephen E. (1990) *Cosmopolis: The Hidden Agenda of Modernity* (New York: Free Press).

Touraine, Alain (1971) *The Post-Industrial Society: Tomorrow's Social History – Classes, Conflicts and Culture in the Programmed Society* (London: Wildwood House).

Trinkaus, Charles (1970) *In Our Image and Likeness: Humanity and Divinity in Italian Humanist Thought Volume II* (London: Constable).

Trompf, G. W. (1973) 'The Concept of the Carolingian Renaissance' *Journal of the History of Ideas* 34/1, pp. 3–26.

Trouillot, Michel-Rolph (1991) 'Anthropology and the Savage Slot: The Poetics and Politics of Otherness' in Richard G. Fox (ed.) *Recapturing Anthropology: Working in the Present* (New Mexico: School of American Research Press), pp. 16–44.

Trouillot, Michel-Rolph (1995) *Silencing the Past: Power and the Production of History* (Boston: Beacon Press).

Trouillot, Michel-Rolph (2003) *Global Transformations: Anthropology and the Modern World* (New York: Palgrave Macmillan).

Turgot (1973 [1766]) 'Reflections on the Formation and the Distribution of Wealth' in Ronald Meek (ed.) *Turgot on Progress, Sociology and Economics* translated and edited by Ronald Meek (Cambridge: Cambridge University Press), pp. 119–82.

Turner, Bryan S. (1992) 'Preface to the Second Edition' in *Emile Durkheim Professional Ethics and Civic Morals* translated by Cornelia Brookfield (London: Routledge), pp. xiii–xlii.

Turner, Bryan S. (2006) 'Epilogue: Asia in European Sociology' in Gerard Delanty (ed.) *Handbook of Contemporary European Social Theory* (London: Routledge), pp. 266–78.

Van der Veer, Peter (1998) 'The Global History of "Modernity"' *Journal of the Economic and Social History of the Orient* 41/3, pp. 285–94.

Venn, Couze (2000) *Occidentalism: Modernity and Subjectivity* (London: Sage Publications).

Vermeule, Cornelius (1964) *European Art and the Classical Past* (Massachusetts: Harvard University Press).

Visvanathan, S. (1988) 'On the Annals of the Laboratory State' in Ashis Nandy (ed.) *Science, Hegemony and Violence A Requiem for Modernity* (New Delhi: Oxford University Press), pp. 257–88.

Viswanathan, Gauri (1989) *Masks of Conquest: Literary Study and British Rule in India* (New York: Columbia University Press).

Wagner, Peter (1994) *A Sociology of Modernity: Liberty and Discipline* (London: Routledge).

Wagner, Peter (2001a) *A History and Theory of the Social Sciences – Not All That is Solid Melts into Air* (London: Sage).

Wagner, Peter (2001b) *Theorizing Modernity: Inescapability and Attainability in Social Theory* (London: Sage).

Wallerstein, Immanuel (1974) *The Modern World-System I: Capitalist Agriculture and the Origins of the European World-Economy in the Sixteenth Century* (New York: Academic Press).

Wallerstein, Immanuel (1979) *The Capitalist World-Economy: Essays* (Cambridge: Cambridge University Press).

Wallerstein, Immanuel (1980) *The Modern World-System II: Mercantilism and the Consolidation of the European World-Economy, 1600–1750* (New York: Academic Press).

Wallerstein, Immanuel (1997) 'Eurocentrism and Its Avatars: The Dilemmas of Social Science' *New Left Review* 226, Nov–Dec, pp. 93–107.

Wang, Ning (1997) 'Orientalism versus Occidentalism?' *New Literary History* 28/1, pp. 57–67.

Washbrook, David A. (1988) 'Progress and Problems: South Asian Economic and Social History c.1720–1860' *Modern Asian Studies* 22/1, pp. 57–96.

Washbrook, David A. (1990) 'South Asia, the World System, and World Capitalism' *The Journal of Asian Studies* 49/3, pp. 479–508.

Washbrook, David A. (1997) 'From Comparative Sociology to Global History: Britain and India in the Pre-history of Modernity' *Journal of Economic and Social History of the Orient* 40/4, pp. 410–43.

Weber, Eugene (1976) *Peasants into Frenchmen: The Modernization of Rural France 1870–1914* (California: Stanford University Press).

Weber, Max (1949) *The Methodology of the Social Sciences* translated and edited by Edward A. Shils and Henry A. Finch (New York: The Free Press).

Whimster, Sam and Scott Lash (eds) (1987) *Max Weber, Rationality and Modernity* (London: Allen and Unwin).

White, Hayden (1978) *Tropics of Discourse: Essays in Cultural Criticism* (Baltimore: The Johns Hopkins University Press).

White, Hayden (1980) *Metahistory: The Historical Imagination in Nineteenth-Century Europe* (Baltimore: The Johns Hopkins University Press).

Williams, Eric (1940) 'The Golden Age of the Slave System in Britain' *The Journal of Negro History* 25/1, pp. 60–106.

Williams, Eric (1994 [1944]) *Capitalism and Slavery* (London: The University of North Carolina Press).

Wittrock, Bjorn (1998) 'Early Modernities: Varieties and Transitions' *Daedalus: Early Modernities* 127/3, pp. 19–40.

Wittrock, Bjorn (2000) 'Modernity: One, None, or Many? European Origins and Modernity as a Global Condition' *Daedalus: Multiple Modernities* 129/1, pp. 31–60.

Wokler, Robert (1987) 'Saint-Simon and the Passage from Political to Social Science' in Anthony Pagden (ed.) *The Languages of Political Theory in Early Modern* (Cambridge: Cambridge University Press), pp. 325–38.

Wokler, Robert (2002) 'Repatriating Modernity's Alleged Debts to the Enlightenment: French Revolutionary Social Science and the Genesis of the Nation State' in Patrick Joyce (ed.) *The Social in Question: New Bearings in History and the Social Sciences* (London: Routledge), pp. 61–80.

Wolf, Eric R. (1997 [1982]) *Europe and the People Without History* (Berkeley: University of California Press).

Wood, Ellen Meiksins (2002) *The Origin of Capitalism: A Longer View* (London: Verso).

Woolf, Stuart (1979) *A History of Italy 1700–1860: The Social Constraints of Political Change* (London: Methuen and Co. Ltd.).

Woolf, Stuart (1991) *Napoleon's Integration of Europe* (London: Routledge).

Woolf, Stuart (1992) 'The Construction of a European World-View in the Revolutionary-Napoleonic Years' *Past and Present: The Cultural and Political Construction of Europe* 137, pp. 72–101.

Yapp, M. E. (1992) 'Europe in the Turkish Mirror' *Past and Present: The Cultural and Political Construction of Europe* 137, November, pp. 134–55.

Yu, Pauline (2006) 'Comparative Literature in Question' *Daedalus* 135/2, pp. 38–53.

Index